The Marriage of Contraries

The Marriage of Contraries

Bernard Shaw's Middle Plays

J. L. Wisenthal

Harvard University Press
Cambridge, Massachusetts
1974

For My Wife

Acknowledgments

I want to express my gratitude to Mr. T. P. Roberts and Dr. Katharine Worth of the University of London, and to my colleague Dr. M. W. Steinberg at the University of British Columbia, for valuable suggestions in connection with this study.

Quotations from Shaw—previously published and unpublished —are used by permission of the Society of Authors, acting for the Shaw Estate. I am grateful to the British Drama League Library for permission to consult and use unpublished letters in their possession from Shaw to Gilbert Murray. For reasons of copyright, passages from these letters and certain others are paraphrased rather than quoted. For permission to quote a letter from Sir Almroth Wright to Shaw I thank Wright's grandson, Mr. Giles J. Romanes; and the two lines from Yeats's "The Choice" (from *Collected Poems,* copyright 1933, 1961) in Chapter V are quoted with the permission of Mr. M. B. Yeats and the Macmillan Companies of London, New York, and Canada.

This book has been published with the help of a grant from the Humanities Research Council of Canada, using funds provided by the Canada Council. I have also received financial assistance during the preparation of the book from the Canada Council itself and from the Committee on Research of the University of British Columbia.

Small parts of Chapters II and III appeared originally in a somewhat different form in journal articles: "The Cosmology of *Man and Superman,*" *Modern Drama,* XIV (Dec. 1971), 298–306, and "The Underside of Undershaft: A Wagnerian Motif in *Major Barbara,*" *Shaw Review,* XV (May 1972), 56–64.

Contents

The Marriage of Contraries

Note on References

Unless otherwise indicated, references to Shaw's writings are to the Standard Edition of the Works of Bernard Shaw (36 vols.; London: Constable, 1931–1950). For plays of more than one act the act number is given as well as the page number. For non-dramatic works a volume number is given, where relevant, as well as the page number.

A note on the location of Shaw's plays in the Constable Standard Edition will be found on p. 220.

I

Introduction

In the Preface to *Back to Methuselah,* Shaw discusses the limitation of Ibsen as an iconographer of a modern religion. "There is no trace in his plays," he observes, "of any faith in or knowledge of Creative Evolution as a modern scientific fact. True, the poetic aspiration is plain enough in his Emperor or Galilean; [1] but it is one of Ibsen's distinctions that nothing was valid for him but science; and he left that vision of the future which his Roman seer calls 'the third Empire' behind him as a Utopian dream when he settled down to his serious grapple with realities in those plays of modern life with which he overcame Europe" (p. lxxxiii). *Emperor and Galilean,* as this passage implies, held for Shaw an important place among Ibsen's works. In *The Quintessence of Ibsenism* he gives it more space than any other play of Ibsen's, and his comments on it have a distinct bearing on his own major plays, especially those of his middle period. For while Shaw began his dramatic career, in the *Plays Unpleasant,* with a "serious grapple with realities in . . . plays of modern life," he went on, it seems to me, particularly in the plays between *Man and Superman* and *Saint Joan,* to deal with aspects of that vision "which [Ibsen's] Roman seer calls 'the third Empire.'"

In *The Quintessence of Ibsenism,* Shaw treats the world-view of the seer Maximus at some length. He writes, for example, that "Maximus knows that there is no going back to 'the first empire' of pagan sensualism. 'The second empire,' Christian or self-abnegatory idealism, is already rotten at heart. 'The third empire' is what he looks for: the empire of Man asserting the eternal validity of his own will. He who can see that not on Olympus, not nailed to the cross, but in himself is God: he is the man to build Brand's bridge between the flesh and the spirit, establishing this third empire in which the spirit shall not be unknown, nor the flesh starved, nor the will tortured and baffled" (p. 54).[2] The main expression of the idea of the third empire in *Emperor and Galilean* is in Act III of the second part, *The Emperor Julian.* Julian, having failed so far in his effort to stamp out Christianity in the Roman Empire and replace it with Greek paganism, asks Maximus to foretell whether he or Christianity will ultimately triumph.

JULIAN. . . . Who shall conquer? The Emperor or the Galilean?

MAXIMUS. Both the Emperor and the Galilean shall succumb.

JULIAN. Succumb—? Both—?

MAXIMUS. Both. Whether in our times or in hundreds of years, I know not; but so it shall be when the right man comes.

JULIAN. And who is the right man?

MAXIMUS. He who shall swallow up both Emperor and Galilean.

JULIAN. You solve the riddle by a still darker riddle.

MAXIMUS. Hear me, brother and friend of truth! I say you shall both succumb—but not that you shall perish.

Does not the child succumb in the youth, and the youth in the man? Yet neither child nor youth perishes.

Oh, my best-loved pupil—have you forgotten our colloquies in Ephesus about the three empires?

JULIAN. Ah Maximus, years have passed since then. Speak!

MAXIMUS. You know I have never approved your policy as Emperor. You have tried to make the youth a child again. The empire of the flesh is swallowed up in the empire of the spirit. But the empire of the spirit is not final, any more than the youth is. You have tried to hinder the growth of the youth,—to hinder him from becoming a man. Oh fool, who have drawn your sword against that which is to be—against the third empire, in which the twin-natured shall reign!

JULIAN. And he—?

MAXIMUS. The Jews have a name for him. They call him Messiah, and they await him.

JULIAN [*slowly and thoughtfully*]. Messiah?—Neither Emperor nor Redeemer?

MAXIMUS. Both in one, and one in both.

JULIAN. Emperor-god;—god-emperor. Emperor in the
kingdom of the spirit,—and god in that of the flesh.
   MAXIMUS. *That* is the third empire, Julian!
   JULIAN. Yes, Maximus, that is the third empire.[3]

Shaw quotes almost all of this passage in *The Quintessence of Ibsenism,* and discusses the reason for Julian's failure to fulfil the role in which Maximus envisages him: "Maximus's idea is a synthesis of relations in which not only is Christ God in exactly the same sense as that in which Julian is God, but Julian is Christ as well.[4] The persistence of Julian's jealousy of the Galilean shews that he has not comprehended the synthesis at all, but only seized on that part of it which flatters his own egotism. And since this part is only valid as a constituent of the synthesis, and has no reality when isolated from it, it cannot by itself convince Julian" (p. 56). Julian cannot see that godhead is present in both himself and Christ, and his misinterpretation of the wisdom of Maximus leads him to defeat and destruction. Emperor and Galilean remain separate and opposed, and at the end of the play Christianity is triumphant. The third empire has not come.

   The division between the empire of the flesh and the empire of the spirit is one of the basic themes of Shaw's plays.[5] The middle plays are particularly concerned with the limitations of each when separated from the other. In the Hell Scene of *Man and Superman,* Don Juan, arguing that the Life Force needs a brain so that it will no longer waste and scatter itself, speaks of the defects of man as he is now: "Stupidity made sordid and cruel by the realities learnt from toil and poverty: Imagination resolved to starve sooner than face these realities, piling up illusions to hide them, and calling itself cleverness, genius! And each accusing the other of its own defect: Stupidity accusing Imagination of folly, and Imagination accusing Stupidity of ignorance: whereas, alas! Stupidity has all the knowledge, and Imagination all the intelligence" (III, 101). While this passage is probably too complicated to have much effect on the stage, it provides a significant statement of Shaw's view of life. Juan sees the human tragicomedy here in terms of a split between the world of solid realities on the one hand and the world of mind on the other. Each possesses what the other lacks: "Stupidity has all the knowledge, and Imagination all the intelligence." Man needs to evolve further, toward a state in which a synthesis is achieved between these opposing qualities, so that the solid practical man has intelligence and the imaginative, intelligent man has practical knowledge. This is Shaw's principal version of Ibsen's third empire.

II

Shaw's habit of seeing the world in terms of contraries that can find fulfillment only in union with each other is not difficult to illustrate. Take, for example, these excerpts from the music criticism which he wrote in the early 1890's:

I really cannot stand Brahms as a serious composer. It is nothing short of a European misfortune that such prodigious musical powers should have nothing better in the way of ideas to express than incoherent commonplace. However, that is what is always happening in music: the world is full of great musicians who are no composers, and great composers who are no musicians.

The great composer is he who, by the rarest of chances, is at once a great musician and a great poet—who has Brahms's wonderful ear without his commonplace mind, and Molière's insight and imagination without his musical sterility.

Rubinstein [whom Shaw regarded as a great pianist but a commonplace composer] . . . was a player of stupendous manual dexterity, with immense power, passion, and spontaneity. Had his intellect been as keen as his will was energetic he would have been unsurpassable.

On the whole I think I shall in future advise young pianoforte students to divide their apprenticeship between Madame Schumann and Sophie Menter, in order that they may lack neither the refinements of art nor "the joy of life." Those who stick to one school exclusively are apt to come out with slovenly habits of mind on the one hand, or ill-nourished hearts on the other.

The Philharmonic band . . . exactly lacks what the London Symphony band has, and has what the London Symphony band lacks. For my own part . . . I insist on the necessity of the combination of the qualities of both.

I will confess—nay, proclaim—that the combination of the professional steadiness and accuracy with the amateur freshness, excitement, and romance, produces a better result than an ordinary routine performance by professionals alone.[6]

Consider, too, the discussion of the English at the conclusion of *The Man of Destiny*, written in 1895. Napoleon divides humanity into three types of people: the low, the middle, and the high. "The low are beneath morality, the high above it. I am not afraid of either of them; for the low are unscrupulous without knowledge, so that they make an idol of me; whilst the high are unscrupulous without purpose, so that they go down before my will . . . It is the middle people who are dangerous: they have both knowledge and purpose" (p. 186). Here is one kind of potent combination: knowledge and purpose; and after Napoleon's long speech about English hypocrisy he tells the Lady that her behavior has been English, thus initiating this dialogue:

LADY. Nonsense! I am sure I am not a bit English. The English are a very stupid people.

NAPOLEON. Yes, too stupid sometimes to know when theyre beaten. But I grant that your brains are not English. You see, though your grandfather was an Englishman, your grandmother was—what? a Frenchwoman?

LADY. Oh no. An Irishwoman.

NAPOLEON [*quickly*] Irish! [*Thoughtfully*] Yes: I forgot the Irish. An English army led by an Irish general: that might be a match for a French army led by an Italian general. [*He pauses, and adds, half jestingly, half moodily*] At all events, *you* have beaten me; and what beats a man first will beat him last.

(p. 188)

The combination here is of English stupidity and Irish intelligence, which anticipates the passage from the Hell Scene of *Man and Superman* quoted above and the treatment of nationality that is the basis of *John Bull's Other Island*.

Moving forward over a third of a century from *The Man of Destiny*, one comes to a passage like this speech of Amanda's in *The Apple Cart:* "Poor darling Lizzie [Lysistrata, the Powermistress General]! She's a regular old true blue Diehard. If only I had her brains and education! or if she had my variety talent! What a queen she'd make! Like old Queen Elizabeth, eh?" (I, 236). And in the Interlude in this play, the king's mistress compares herself with his wife, saying, "Heaven is offering you a rose; and you cling to a cabbage." King Magnus replies by pointing out the importance of cabbages, and later he speculates that "some day perhaps Nature will graft the roses on the cabbages and make every woman as enchanting as you; and then what a glorious lark life will be!" (pp. 241, 246).

The metaphor of crossing used here is also found in a very different context in one of Shaw's dramatic reviews in *Our Theatres in the Nineties.* A frequent complaint in these volumes is that plays of the period lack contact with real life, and in one article Shaw comments specifically on the limitations of works of art that merely imitate previous works of art: "Art fecundated by itself gains a certain lapdog refinement, very acceptable to lovers of lapdogs. The Incas of Peru cultivated their royal race in this way, each Inca marrying his sister. The result was that an average Inca was worth about as much as an average fashionable drama bred carefully from the last pair of fashionable dramas, themselves bred in the same way, with perhaps a cross of novel. But vital art work comes always from a cross between art and life: art being of one sex only, and quite sterile by itself" (III, 236).[7]

The idea of cross-breeding was for Shaw not only a source of metaphors but a serious eugenic view. The notion that parents of different races produce the best offspring is found in several places in his works, particularly in those written during the later part of his life. In *The Simpleton of the Unexpected Isles* (1934) two Western couples and the Eastern couple Pra and Prola enter into a group marriage, which is, as one of the participants later explains, "a eugenic experiment. Its object was to try out the result of a biological blend of the flesh and spirit of the west with the flesh and spirit of the east." The result is four beautiful godlike children who "have the east in their brains and the west in their blood" and "the east in their blood and the west in their brains" (I, 43, 46). But in spite of their superiority they have no moral conscience, and the experiment is finally regarded as a failure. In *The Millionairess,* finished in

1935, East and West are united in the marriage between the Egyptian doctor and the European millionairess Epifania Ognisanti di Parerga.[8] Nothing is said in the play about their prospective children, but the Preface contains a discussion of Hitler which rejects his racial policies on the ground that a purebred German race is not a eugenically desirable goal. "Surely the average German can be improved," Shaw suggests. "I am told that children bred from Irish colleens and Chinese laundrymen are far superior to inbred Irish or Chinese." Nations "deteriorate without cross fertilization; and if Herr Hitler could put a stop to cross fertilization in Germany and produce a population of brainless Bismarcks Germany would be subjugated by crossfertilized aliens, possibly by cosmopolitan Jews" (pp. 120–121). The same argument is used in Chapter XXIX of *Everybody's Political What's What?* published in 1944 (pp. 248–250); and in an undated typescript in the British Museum, entitled "Further Meditations on Shaw's Geneva," he writes: "Teach Herr Hitler that the vigor of his nation and our [s] is due to the fact that we are nations of arrant mongrels, and that if we begin with inbreeding we should end with the brains of Borzoi dogs and a general prevalence of paralysis and haemophilia, and he will follow my advice and not only invite the Jews back to Germany but make it punishable incest for a Jew to marry anybody but an Aryan." [9]

Shaw also believed in the value of crossing people of different classes and temperaments. The idea of this kind of combination appears in his writing as early as 1882, in his fourth novel, *Cashel Byron's Profession.* The heroine, Lydia Carew, a cool, intelligent lady of property, decides to marry Cashel Byron, the prizefighter hero, after she discovers that her late father regretted his own cold-heartedness. She reflects: "If such a doubt as that haunted my father, it will haunt me, unless I settle what is to be my heart's business now and for ever. If it be possible for a child of mine to escape this curse, it must inherit its immunity from its father, and not from me—from the man of impulse who never thinks, and not from the rationalizing woman, who cannot help thinking. Be it so" (p. 204). Afterward, in defending her choice to her cousin, she says, "As to our personal suitability, I believe in the doctrine of heredity; and as my body is frail and my brain morbidly active, I think my impulse towards a man strong in body and untroubled in mind a trustworthy

one. You can understand that: it is a plain proposition in eugenics"
(p. 223). As it turns out, their sons are intellectual like their
mother, while their daughters take after their father; [10] but the intention of producing children who combine intelligence and physical strength is an interesting anticipation of significant elements in
Shaw's major works.

Moving once again from the early part of Shaw's career to the
late part, one finds at the end of *On the Rocks,* written in 1933, a
marriage planned between David Chavender, the slight, refined son
of the British prime minister, and Aloysia Brollikins, a vigorous pro-
letarian alderwoman from the Isle of Cats. Aloysia explains to her
prospective father-in-law that she was guided in her choice by "the
evolutionary appetite. The thing that wants to develop the race,"
and he warns her that the evolutionary appetite "doesnt care a rap
for domestic happiness. I have known the most remarkable children
come of the most dreadfully unsuitable and unhappy marriages." [11]
But he consents to the marriage, and his wife feels that it is a good
match because of the differences between Aloysia and David. "I daresay a match with you might be a very good thing for David," she
tells Aloysia. "You seem to have all the qualities in which he is deficient." And she says to her husband, "David is overbred: he is so
fine-drawn that he is good for nothing; and he is not strong enough
physically. Our breed needs to be crossed with the gutter or the soil
once in every three or four generations" (II, 266, 268, 270).[12]

Another kind of crossing in Shaw's plays is the association between characters of different types in partnerships. In *John Bull's
Other Island* the clever Irishman Doyle and the stupid but efficient
Englishman Broadbent combine to form a successful firm of civil engineers; and Shaw says in the Preface that "the combination was
probably much more effective than either of the partners would
have been alone" (p. 14). In *Major Barbara* the ruthless, Dionysiac
armaments manufacturer Andrew Undershaft has as his partner "a
gentle romantic Jew who cares for nothing but string quartets and
stalls at fashionable theatres" (III, 325–326); and of course at the
end of the play Adolphus Cusins, the cultivated, spectacled professor
of Greek enters into a partnership with Undershaft. A frivolous echo
of this union is to be found at the end of *Androcles and the Lion,*
where the gentle Greek tailor waltzes around the arena with the fe-

rocious lion. United they are able to control the emperor, and the play ends with the two of them leaving together: "Come, Tommy," says Androcles. "Whilst we stand together, no cage for you: no slavery for me" (II, 144). In *Pygmalion* the contrasting Higgins and Pickering act as partners in educating Eliza. She acquires her ladylike speech from the former, and her ladylike manners from the latter. In *Heartbreak House* Boss Mangan and Mazzini Dunn complement each other as business associates—an unholy alliance, like that between the burglars Aubrey and Sweetie in *Too Good To Be True:* "Sweetie," Aubrey says: "in our firm I am the brains: you are the hand" (I, 41). In the second play of *Back to Methuselah* the brothers Barnabas combine their special fields of knowledge to transform human life: Franklyn is a theologian, Conrad a biologist. This union has an ironic counterpart in the final play of the cycle when the artist Martellus and the scientist Pygmalion work together to produce not a higher form of being than themselves but a much lower one. In all of these combinations the assumption is that people with complementary abilities are more effective as partners than they would be by themselves [13]—except perhaps in the case of Undershaft and Lazarus, in which the latter is insignificant.

III

LADY CICELY. . . . Now, Howard, isnt that the exact truth, every word of it?

SIR HOWARD. It is the truth, Cicely, and nothing but the truth. But the English law requires a witness to tell the *whole* truth.

LADY CICELY. What nonsense! As if anybody ever knew the whole truth about anything!

(*Captain Brassbound's Conversion,* III, 274)

One of the most basic elements in Shaw's view of life is his rejection of absolutes, his distaste for finality. His perspective is evolutionary, and he thinks in terms of progress toward goals rather than their actual attainment. In an evolutionary world no stage is final, and in a neo-Lamarckian evolutionary world the human will is always aiming at something higher. "I dread success," Shaw wrote to Ellen Terry in 1896. "To have succeeded is to have finished one's business on earth, like the male spider, who is killed by the female the moment he has succeeded in his courtship. I like a state of continual *becoming,* with a goal in front and not behind." [14] This dis-like of finality also takes the form of a rejection of the concept of absolute truth. Any statement we make or belief we hold can be only partially true. "I learnt long ago," Shaw told his readers in one of his music reviews, "that though there are several places from which the tourist may enjoy a view of Primrose Hill, none of these can be called *the* view of Primrose Hill." [15]

The man who believes that his view of Primrose Hill is *the* view is both foolish and dangerous. One of the sections of the Preface to *Misalliance* is headed "The Sin of Athanasius": this is the sin of asserting, as the Athanasian creed does, not that one believes certain things, but "that certain things are so, and that anybody who doubts that they are so cannot be saved" (p. 47). In this section Shaw argues that adults should regard children as experiments made by the Life Force, and not pretend to know what is right for them. He proposes a law "that any person dictating a piece of conduct to a child or to anyone else as the will of God, or as absolutely right, should be dealt with as a blasphemer: as, indeed, guilty of the unpardonable sin against the Holy Ghost. If the penalty were death, it would rid us at once of that scourge of humanity, the amateur Pope" (pp. 45–46). Similarly, in the Preface to *The Doctor's Dilemma* Shaw condemns scientists whose point of view is this Athanasian one. "Science becomes dangerous," he writes, "only when it imagines that it has reached its goal." And he continues: "What is wrong with priests and popes is that instead of being apostles and saints, they are nothing but empirics who say 'I know' instead of 'I am learning,' and pray for credulity and inertia as wise men pray for scepticism and activity" (p. 76).

In his writings on education, Shaw stresses a corollary of this relativist view of truth. If no single position constitutes a complete, final statement of the truth, then it is always necessary to hear more than one point of view. Shaw, who as a young man was much influenced by John Stuart Mill, and who achieved eminence as a debater, believed that "it is in the conflict of opinion that we win knowledge and wisdom." [16] Therefore education ought to be "controversial": the student must hear partisans of opposing sides on religious, philosophical, and scientific questions "fighting it out in debate," instead of having one side imposed on him by a schoolmaster.[17]

Joey Percival in *Misalliance* has been educated in this way. He had three fathers: the "regulation natural chap," Bentley Summerhays explains, and also a philosopher who lived with the family and an Italian priest who was "always about." "The whole three of them took charge of Joey's conscience. He used to hear them arguing like mad about everything. You see, the philosopher was a freethinker, and always believed the latest thing. The priest didnt believe anything, because it was sure to get him into trouble with someone or another. And the natural father kept an open mind and believed whatever paid him best. Between the lot of them Joey got cultivated no end. He said if he could only have had three mothers as well, he'd have backed himself against Napoleon" (pp. 126–127). In *Sixteen Self Sketches* Shaw noted that this idea was drawn from his own upbringing. His natural father, an impecunious drinker, was supplemented by a "blasphemous Rabelaisian uncle" and by his mother's singing teacher, George John Vandeleur [18] Lee, "making three varieties for me to study. This widened my outlook very considerably" (pp. 14–15).[19]

"I did not know what my own house was like, because I had never been outside it," says Peter Keegan in *John Bull's Other Island,* explaining that he appreciated the wonders of Ireland only after he had seen different sorts of wonders in places like Rome and Oxford (II, 101). Similarly, Collins the greengrocer in *Getting Married* says that his wife has "never known any man but me; and she cant properly know me, because she dont know other men to compare me with" (p. 263). Kipling's line "And what should they know of England who only England know?" from "The English Flag," is (mis)quoted in the Preface to this play (p. 222), and paraphrased in the Preface to *Misalliance* as part of an argument that university students, in order to become cultivated, must know the everyday world outside the university: "What do they know of Plato that only Plato know?" (p. 37). The assumption in all of these cases is that in order to know anything one must know its contrary: one must know Rome in order to know Ireland; other, different men in order to know one's husband; ordinary life in order to know culture.

This is the assumption that lies behind Shaw's statement in the Preface to *The Shewing-Up of Blanco Posnet* that he would "not object to a law to compel everybody to read two newspapers, each violently opposed to the other in politics" (p. 418)—a suggestion which is expanded in the Preface to *Misalliance,* where he says that the ordinary man refuses to read a newspaper which dissents from his own political opinions: "The result is that his opinions are not worth considering. A churchman who never reads The Freethinker very soon has no more real religion than the atheist who never reads The Church Times. The attitude is the same in both cases: they want to hear nothing good of their enemies; consequently they remain enemies and suffer from bad blood all their lives; whereas men who know their opponents and understand their case, quite commonly respect and like them, and always learn something from them" (p. 27).

In order to know A you must know its contrary B, and A and B, it will be noticed in the examples which I have quoted, are extremes on either side. Shaw is not recommending, as Samuel Butler so often does, a comfortable *via media* which rejects both extremes, but an active, vital state of mind which *encompasses* both extremes. This approach to life is nicely expressed in E. M. Forster's *Howards End,* a novel which has much in common with the aspects of Shaw's thought being considered here. One passage is particularly worth quoting—a reflection of Margaret Schlegel's after she has decided to marry Mr. Wilcox: "The business man who assumes that this life is everything, and the mystic who asserts that it is nothing, fail, on this side and on that, to hit the truth. 'Yes, I see, dear; it's about halfway between,' Aunt Juley had hazarded in earlier years. No; truth, being alive, was not halfway between anything. It was only to be found by continuous excursions into either realm, and though proportion is the final secret, to espouse it at the outset is to insure sterility." [20]

This passage provides, I think, an important clue to the structure of Shaw's argumentative prose (to say nothing—for the present —of his plays). One does not find in Shaw's writings many careful, measured, moderate statements, and yet his views are seldom as extreme as the hyperbolical style and uncompromising tone of individual assertions might lead one to believe. Take, for example, the notorious review of Henry Irving's production of *Cymbeline* in 1896. The paragraph which has attracted most attention is the one in which Shaw declares that "with the single exception of Homer, there is no eminent writer, not even Sir Walter Scott, whom I can despise so entirely as I despise Shakespear when I measure my mind against his," and says, "There are moments when one asks despairingly why our stage should ever have been cursed with this 'immortal' pilferer of other men's stories and ideas, with his monstrous rhetorical fustian, his unbearable platitudes, his pretentious reduction of the subtlest problems of life to commonplaces against which a Polytechnic debating club would revolt, his incredible unsuggestiveness, his sententious combination of ready reflection with complete intellectual sterility, and his consequent incapacity for getting out of the depth of even the most ignorant audience, except when he solemnly says something so transcendently platitudinous that his more humble-minded hearers cannot bring themselves to believe that so great a man really meant to talk like their grandmothers." This sounds like a total dismissal of Shakespeare's plays as utterly worthless, and can be quoted to demonstrate that such was Shaw's whole view of Shakespeare. The next paragraph, however, begins: "But I am bound to add that I pity the man who cannot enjoy Shakespear. He has outlasted thousands of abler thinkers, and will outlast a thousand more. His gift of telling a story (provided some one else told it to him first); his enormous power over language, as conspicuous in his senseless and silly abuse of it as in his miracles of expression; his humor; his sense of idiosyncratic character; and his prodigious fund of that vital energy which is, it seems, the true differentiating property behind the faculties, good, bad, or indifferent, of the man of genius, enable him to entertain us so effectively that the imaginary scenes and people he has created become more real to us than our actual life—at least, until our knowledge and grip of actual life begins to deepen and glow beyond the common." [21] If we take both of these paragraphs together, we have what is admittedly an eccentric view of Shakespeare, but one which is not nearly as extreme as it first appears. Another writer who held Shaw's views on the subject might have begun by saying that while he recognizes Shakespeare's gift of telling a story, power over language, and so on, he cannot grant that Shakespeare's intellectual insight is equal to these other qualities. But such a moderate, balanced way of putting a case is not Shaw's: he hurls weights noisily onto one side of the scales, and then begins to even the balance by weighting the other side—although in this case the anti-Shakespearean side remains the heavier one. Shaw's view of Shakespeare, then, is expressed in terms of a clash of contrary assertions on the subject (and note that there are minor clashes of this kind *within* the second paragraph). Instead of beginning halfway between, he conducts excursions into either realm.

This dialectical method is a major factor in the strength of Shaw's prose. It enables him to achieve the simplicity of direct, bold assertion without sacrificing the complexity that his subjects and his views demand. And one is not permitted to know without effort just where the author stands—especially in the longer pieces of prose like the prefaces. He keeps presenting the other side of the question, following one striking assertion with another apparently contradictory one. Often (as in the *Cymbeline* review) an outrageous assertion is balanced by a much more conventional one, and when this happens on a large scale in a preface the reader is kept wondering whether Shaw is proposing a total reorganization of society or merely a few reforms of the institution under consideration. (See, for example, the prefaces to *The Doctor's Dilemma* and *Getting Married.*)

The Preface to *Misalliance,* while it is not one of Shaw's best pieces, provides the clearest examples of his rhetorical technique in his nondramatic prose of proceeding by contraries. Its discussion of how children ought to be brought up oscillates between extreme libertarian views on the one hand and on the other authoritarian views which seriously qualify them. Shaw does not begin by saying that children should be left free in some respects and coerced in others: he begins the discussion with the statement that the child is without rights and liberties and is thus in a condition of slavery to its parents; and he says that a child is an experiment—a fresh attempt to make humanity divine—which "you will vitiate . . . if you make the slightest attempt to abort it into some fancy figure of your own: for example, your notion of a good man or a womanly woman" (p. 7). This, along with other passages in the early part of the Preface, implies that adults should simply leave children to themselves. The child's basic right, Shaw says, is the right to live, and "this right to live includes, and in fact is, the right to be what the child likes and can, to do what it likes and can, to make what it likes and can, to think what it likes and can, to smash what it dislikes and can, and generally to behave in an altogether unaccountable manner within the limits imposed by the similar rights of its neighbors." Taken by itself, such a statement is almost completely anarchic in its implications. It is followed, however, by this: "And the rights of society over [the child] clearly extend to requiring it to qualify itself to live in society without wasting other people's time." This means, among other things, that a child "must know some law, were it only a simple set of commandments" and that it must acquire "religion enough to have some idea of why it is allowed its rights and why it must respect the rights of others" (pp. 32–33). Similarly, the libertarian assertion made early in the Preface that "there is no difference in principle between the rights of a child and those of an adult" is followed immediately by qualifications (p. 13), and later in the Preface we are told that "to treat a child wholly as an adult would be to mock and destroy it." Shaw continues here: "Infantile docility and juvenile dependence are, like death, a product of Natural Selection; and though there is no viler crime than to abuse them, yet there is no greater cruelty than to ignore them" (p. 58). This passage concentrates the two contraries into a single sentence; and this type of sentence, which says that though A is true (or false), so is its contrary B, is a common one in Shaw's writings.

Let us take one final example from the Preface to *Misalliance*. The section "English Physical Hardihood and Spiritual Cowardice" concludes with the declaration: "Whether the risks to which liberty exposes us are moral or physical, our right to liberty involves the right to run them. A man who is not free to risk his neck as an aviator or his soul as a heretic is not free at all; and the right to liberty begins, not at the age of 21 years but of 21 seconds." This sounds uncompromisingly libertarian, but the section which follows, "The Risks of Ignorance and Weakness," begins by saying that children "need protection from risks they are too young to understand, and attacks they can neither avoid nor resist"; then it goes on to say that adults too need protection from such risks, which it turns out include the possibility of making a foolish marriage, and it works around to the statement that "if a man is unbearably mischievous, he must be killed." And this leads, via a reference to the danger of persecution, to the next section, "The Common Sense of Toleration," where we find ourselves back in the libertarian realm, with Shaw insisting that society "must not persecute doctrines of any kind" (pp. 42–43).

IV

At the beginning of *Common Sense about the War* (1914), which consists of continuous excursions into anti-British and anti-German points of view, Shaw writes that the hysterical English reaction to the war made its early weeks a perilous time for him. For "I do not hold my tongue easily; and my inborn dramatic faculty and professional habit as a playwright prevent me from taking a one-sided view even when the most probable result of taking a many-sided one is prompt lynching." [22] The attitudes and rhetorical techniques of Shaw's that I have been discussing in this chapter are appropriate to the dramatist, and Shaw himself emphasizes the importance in his plays of the relativist attitude. Here, for example, is the passage in the Preface to *Plays Pleasant* in which he talks of the kind of conflict proper to the higher drama: "The obvious conflicts of unmistakeable good with unmistakeable evil can only supply the crude drama of villain and hero, in which some absolute point of view is taken, and the dissentients are treated by the dramatist as enemies to be piously glorified or indignantly vilified. In such cheap wares I do not deal. Even in my unpleasant propagandist plays I have allowed every person his or her own point of view [note the relativist implications of this phrase], and have, I hope, to the full extent of my understanding of him, been as sympathetic with Sir George Crofts as with any of the more genial and popular characters in the present volume" (pp. vi–vii). And in the Epistle Dedicatory to *Man and Superman* he speaks more directly about the idea of allowing every person his or her point of view: he writes to A. B. Walkley that in the Revolutionist's Handbook he "will find the politics of the sex question as I conceive Don Juan's descendant to understand them. Not that I disclaim the fullest responsibility for his opinions and for those of all my characters, pleasant and unpleasant. They are all right from their several points of view; and their points of view are, for the dramatic moment, mine also. This may puzzle the people who believe that there is such a thing as an absolutely right point of view, usually their own. It may seem to them that nobody who doubts this can be in a state of grace. However that may be, it is certainly true that nobody who agrees with them can possibly be a dramatist, or indeed anything else that turns upon a knowledge of mankind. Hence it has been pointed out that Shakespear had no conscience. Neither have I, in that sense" (p. xxvi).

When Shaw says that all his characters are right from their several points of view, he means that each character is presented as he sees himself, from the standpoint of his own criteria of judgment: each character acts according to values in which he genuinely believes and which are made in the play to seem at least plausible. Reviewing the published version of Pinero's *The Second Mrs. Tanqueray* in 1895, he discusses the weakness inherent in the play's presentation of its central character: "The moment the point is reached at which the comparatively common gift of 'an eye for character' has to be supplemented by the higher dramatic gift of sympathy with character—of the power of seeing the world from the point of view of others instead of merely describing or judging them from one's own point of view in terms of the conventional systems of morals, Mr Pinero breaks down." And in another of his *Saturday Review* articles he writes that a particular actor is the best Osric he has ever seen, because "he plays Osric from Osric's own point of view, which is, that Osric is a gallant and distinguished courtier, and not, as usual, from Hamlet's, which is that Osric is 'a waterfly.' " [23] What Shaw tries to achieve in most of his plays is the inclusion of a wide variety of points of view—that is, types of values—in conflict, instead of taking the point of view of one character and judging the behavior of the others in relation to it. Each character tries to live up to his own values, and usually defends them forcefully: this means that the audience must judge the character's point of view more than his motives, which tend to be both pure and simple.

It is obvious, though, that not all characters in Shaw's plays have an equal claim to our admiration. As I have just said, we are put in the position of having to judge a character's point of view more than his motives—more than his *character*. But a particular point of view, within the context of other points of view in the same play, may strike one as most inadequate. Sir George Crofts in *Mrs Warren's Profession* is right from his own point of view in the sense that his actions are based on values in which he himself believes, and which he defends with considerable force and effectiveness in the scene with Vivie in Act III. Nor are his values rejected out of hand; although Vivie is disgusted by what he says she offers no arguments in opposition to it. But when we consider Sir George Crofts's view that there is no harm in acting corruptly when others do in relation to Mrs. Warren's view that it is better to be a prostitute than to starve, or Vivie's view that it is best to be independent of corruption if one can (which means being independent of all other people), then we find that while each character's view is limited, his is less acceptable than theirs.[24]

There are many cases, too, in Shaw's plays, where characters cannot really be said to be presented from their own point of view at all. Octavius in *Man and Superman,* for example, is seen not from his point of view but from that of Tanner; he is an obviously foolish man, and his amoristic values are given no plausibility whatever. He presents no problem to our judgment, in the way that Sir George Crofts does, because he is judged within the play by Tanner.

Most of Shaw's characters, however, are presented from their own point of view, and the major conflicts in his best plays are often between characters whose respective values are of equal validity. At the center of plays like *Man and Superman, John Bull's Other Island,* and *Major Barbara* are oppositions between characters who are complementary; each character's values are *partially* valid, and what is missing in one character is found in those opposing him. These plays—and others of this same type—will be discussed in the following chapters. Let us for the present look briefly at an earlier play which anticipates some of the distinctive features of the works of Shaw's middle period.

The passage that I quoted earlier from the Preface to *Plays Pleasant* is part of Shaw's account of his intentions in *Candida;* he is explaining why he did not "dramatize the prosaic conflict of Christian Socialism with vulgar Unsocialism" (p. vi). This would have involved writing the play with the Christian Socialist vicar Morell's values as its basis, and presenting Morell as the hero and (say) Burgess as an antagonist with whose position we could have no sympathy. Shaw avoids conflicts of this kind, in which he would be compelled to commit himself (and thus the play) to one side; this is, I think, the principal reason why he never in his plays has a Socialist, *qua* Socialist, as a major character. In *Candida,* the conflict is not between Morell as a Socialist and Burgess as a capitalist; it is between Morell as a solid bourgeois husband and Eugene Marchbanks as a youthful poet. Shaw thought it crucial that in production Marchbanks should not be made the hero from whose point of view Morell is judged. Marchbanks thinks Morell a pompous fool, but we must be made to see him as he sees himself, as an impressive, dedicated, reliable man. When Arnold Daly was producing *Candida* in New York, Shaw wrote to him that the actor who was playing Morell opposite his Eugene must not allow himself to seem merely ridiculous: "It is important that Morell should be made very sympathetic . . . In my plays an actor is often as [?so] puzzled by the fact that his most earnest efforts bring him laughs—which he doesnt understand—that after the first performance he begins to play for the laughs; and then goodbye to the piece. So you must look after your Morell's & see that they do not resign themselves to being mere butts for you. Eugene scoring off a conceited fool is an ungenerous & cheap spectacle; but the apparently weak Eugene mysteriously coming in on top of a really good and able man who is doing his best according to his lights, and is really deep enough to feel, if not to understand, that there is some higher force than his own in the 'little snivelling cowardly whelp,' is quite another matter." [25] In the final moments of the play, Marchbanks finds his role in life, and goes into the night to fulfill it; he is revealed to have, unexpectedly, more maturity than Morell (he speaks at the end *"with the ring of a man's voice,"* while Morell embraces his wife Candida *"with boyish ingenuousness"*), more strength (he is strong enough to do without Candida), and even more religion, in Shaw's sense ("I no longer desire happiness: life is nobler than that," he says) (III, 140).[26] But while the two characters are in conflict in Acts I and II, we feel that although Marchbanks' clear-sightedness is preferable to Morell's self-delusion, nevertheless the vicar's public-spiritedness is preferable to the poet's desire for an eternity of personal bliss with Candida; and so, until the last minutes of the play, a balance is kept between them.

And even at the end of the play Marchbanks' triumph is not final and clear-cut. The conflict in a drama, Shaw wrote in the section of the Preface to *Plays Pleasant* I have been considering, may end in reconciliation or destruction; "or, as in life itself, there may be no end" (p. vi). Shaw's distaste for finality is reflected in the fact that in most of his plays there is no end: that is, the issues and conflicts of the play are not finally resolved; there is always the question of what will happen *after* the fall of the curtain.[27] Just before the curtain falls on *Candida,* Marchbanks flies out into the night to fulfill his destiny; this destiny is presumably as a poet, but it is not made at all specific. Morell is left embracing Candida; he has discovered that he is a boy rather than a man, but whether this disillusionment will lead to collapse or growth is an open question. Similarly, we do not know what will become of the disillusioned Captain Brassbound at the end of *Captain Brassbound's Conversion;* and in *Man and Superman* the Hell Scene ends with Ana's recognition that her "work is not yet done," while at the end of the whole play Tanner and Ann have their work—of producing children—in front of them: marriage is much more a beginning than a fulfillment. Barbara and Cusins plan to marry at the end of *Major Barbara,* but their marriage is insignificant next to the public roles they have proposed for themselves, as savior of souls and transformer of society, respectively. Here the question of what will take place after the play's conclusion forces itself on us with particular urgency, and the play does not enable us to feel certain about what will happen at the foundry after Barbara and Cusins have joined it. The conclusion of *Heartbreak House* is the most enigmatic of all. After the bomber has left, Hesione says, "I hope theyll come again tomorrow night," to which Ellie replies, "Oh, I hope so" (III, 142); the question of whether or not they will come, and the fate of Heartbreak House, England, and mankind are all in doubt. While *Heartbreak House* ends with the reference to "tomorrow night" (compare the final speech of *Major Barbara,* with its reference to "tomorrow morning," III, 340), Shaw's next play—or cycle of plays—ends with the word "beyond." Lilith's speech at the conclusion of *Back to Methuselah* has as its last sentence: "It is enough that there is a beyond"

(*As Far as Thought Can Reach,* p. 254). This work, like so many of Shaw's, ends not with a final, neat resolution but with a look forward toward a possibly better future.

V

My central concern in the study of Shaw's middle plays that follows is with a pattern implicit in what I have been discussing in this introductory chapter. As Shaw believed that no position is perfectly or completely true, so characters in his plays are limited in their point of view and qualities. These limitations, as I have noted, can be complementary; and this is particularly the case in the plays between *Man and Superman* and *Pygmalion*—and in *Heartbreak House, Back to Methuselah,* and *Saint Joan* one finds significant variations on this pattern. I have used as a basis for discussing all these plays the idea that valuable qualities are dissociated, and that their union is desirable. Such a marriage of contraries [28] is achieved at the end of *Man and Superman* and *Major Barbara,* while in other plays limited, complementary qualities remain separate. In approaching the plays in this way, I want to explore relationships between them, so that one play can be made to illuminate another. It is this consideration that governs the order in which the plays are discussed, which is not strictly chronological.

The designation "middle plays" is of course arbitrary: one finds continuity between Shaw's plays of all periods. I think my grouping, though, beginning with *Man and Superman* and ending with *Saint Joan,* an obvious one which would prove generally acceptable. Charles A. Carpenter ends his study of the "early plays" [29] with *Captain Brassbound's Conversion,* and Shaw's next full-length play, *Man and Superman,* was written in a new century. The six-year gap between *Saint Joan* and its successor would indicate this play as an appropriate terminal point. But my main reason for selecting the plays I do in this study is that they form a group which can profitably be discussed together, a group in which large patterns are discernible that link the plays to one another and bring out important motifs within individual plays. I believe, too, that this group represents Shaw at his best.

II

Man and Superman

The first problem that confronts the student of *Man and Superman* is one of definition. Just what constitutes *Man and Superman?* Should the title be taken (as it often is) to refer only to the three-act comedy consisting of Acts I, II, and IV, or should the Hell Scene in Act III be considered an integral part of the play? And what status is the Revolutionist's Handbook to have?

The play is constructed so that the third act can be omitted in performance, leaving a self-contained comedy which is short enough to comply with ordinary theatrical requirements, and which is a delightful entertainment. But with the inclusion of Act III *Man and Superman* becomes a different, a much more interesting and (to my mind) satisfying play. A very satisfactory way to approach *Man and Superman,* too, is not as a stage production at all, but as a book; for the Comedy, the Hell Scene, and the Revolutionist's Handbook are all closely related to one another, and the play has some of Shaw's longest "stage directions," of which a theater audience is unaware. One might bear in mind that it was as a book that *Man and Superman* first reached its public, and that none of it was seen on the stage (apart from a copyright performance) for almost two years after the book's publication in 1903.[1]

When *Man and Superman* is approached in this way, its scope and variety—two of its most appealing qualities—become fully apparent. Shaw wrote in 1921 that he had "put all [his] intellectual goods in the shop window under the sign of Man and Superman," [2] and H. L. Mencken, writing in 1905, stresses this aspect of the work in his exuberant manner:

Measured with rule, plumb-line or hay-scales, "Man and Superman" is easily Shaw's *magnum opus.* In bulk it is brobdi[n]gnagian; in scope it is stupendous; in purpose it is one with the Odyssey. Like a full-rigged ship before a spanking breeze, it cleaves deep into the waves, sending ripples far to port and starboard, and its giant canvases rise half way to the clouds, with resplendent jibs, skysails, staysails and studdingsails standing out like quills upon the fretful porcupine. It has a preface as long as a campaign speech; an interlude in three scenes, with music and red fire; and a complete digest of the German philosophers as an appendix. With all its rings and satellites it fills a tome of 281 closely-printed pages. Its epigrams, quips, jests, and quirks are multitudinous; it preaches treason to all the schools; its hero has one speech of 350 words. No one but a circus press agent could rise to an adequate description of its innumerable marvels. It is a three-ring circus, with Ibsen doing running high jumps; Schopenhauer playing the calliope and Nietzsche selling peanuts in the reserved seats.[3]

Probably the first recorded response to *Man and Superman* is that of Beatrice Webb, who in January 1903, several months before its publication, spent "three delightful evenings , . . listening to G.B.S. reading his new work." This entry in her diary goes on: "To me it seems a great work; quite the biggest thing he has done. He has found his *form:* a play which is not a play; but only a combination of essay, treatise, interlude, lyric—all the different forms illustrating the same central idea, as a sonata manifests a scheme of melody and harmony." [4] The central idea which all of the different forms illustrate is what Tanner in one of his Maxims for Revolutionists calls Vital Economy. "Political Economy and Social Economy are amusing intellectual games," this particular maxim reads; "but Vital Economy is the Philosopher's Stone" (p. 225). Vital Economy concerns itself with the need to evolve a higher type of man. Each of the three main parts of *Man and Superman* deals with this theme on a different level. The Comedy (Acts I, II, and IV) deals with the sexual aspect of the question: its world is the physical, tangible one of the present—the world of flesh and blood. The principal agent of evolutionary progress in this part of the book is Ann Whitefield, who is very much a flesh-and-blood creature. The Hell Scene in Act III, "the centre of the intellectual whirlpool," [5] is concerned with the philosophical aspects of the question: it discusses the ideas underlying the other parts of the book. Here the present, the world, which dominates the Comedy, is merely one part of a much larger picture—of which the future is a more significant part. Now the Tanner-surrogate, the philosopher Don Juan, is the principal agent of evolutionary progress. The Revolutionist's Handbook deals with the political and social level; with, in Shaw's words, "the politics of the sex question" (Epistle Dedicatory, p. xxvi). The two main questions it asks are, why, from a political standpoint, is a higher form of man necessary; and what political and social measures are needed in order to bring him into being?

Man and Superman, as a book, is unified in several ways. All of its parts, as already noted, are concerned with a common theme. Much of the talk about sex in the Hell Scene and Revolutionist's Handbook is illustrated in the Comedy. Structurally, the Hell Scene and Revolutionist's Handbook are integrated with the Comedy by the device of making the former Tanner's dream and the latter his manifesto. The Handbook is referred to in all three acts of the Comedy, and the Hell Scene is referred to indirectly in Act IV, when Tanner speaks of the Life Force, and when Octavius repeats the Statue's romantic compliment (and Ann feels she has heard it in a former existence). And the transition from the Hell Scene back to the real world of the present is neat, and important thematically: the final words of the Hell Scene are Ana's cry, "A father! a father for the Superman!" (III, 131), and the first event on the return to the real world is Ann's capture of Tanner. The two parts of the play—the Comedy and the Hell Scene—are also unified by the parallels between Jack Tanner and Don Juan, Ann Whitefield and Doña Ana, Roebuck Ramsden and the Statue, and Mendoza and the Devil.[6] These pairs of characters are similar not only in appearance (they would be played by the same actors), but in terms of symbolic function. The symbolic nature of characters in the Comedy is fully apparent only when the Comedy is taken together with the Hell Scene. The distinctions in the Hell Scene between hell, heaven, and earth underlie the whole of *Man and Superman* and unite it.

II

One of the major comic devices in *Man and Superman* is the use of paradoxical reversals of the expected. Two such reversals are in-

troduced by Shaw within the first few pages of the Epistle Dedicatory. His Don Juan is to be, in one sense, the opposite of the traditional Don Juan: not an aggressive lover, but a fugitive from
women and love.[7] Octavius, not Tanner, is the persistent wooer.
Also, woman is to be the pursuer in the Comedy, the opposite of her
conventional role as the passive object of man's pursuit. Both of
these reversals are dramatized and discussed in Act I. In Acts I and
II we find two more reversals of customary roles: the daughter who
tyrannizes over her mother and the servant who dominates his master. In Act III, in the Hell Scene, the roles of Don Juan and the
Devil are reversed, in that Juan is the diabolonian (in the Shavian
sense—the rebel), while the Devil is more like the traditional
Don Juan figure. But the most interesting and complex reversal in
Man and Superman is the one which underlies the whole of the
Hell Scene: the reversal of the traditional ideas of what heaven and
hell are like. Thus hell becomes the place of pleasure and ease, and
heaven the place where happiness (as Shaw defines it) is absent.
Shaw is saying here, in effect, "What you conventional people think
of as heaven is really hell, and what you would consider hell is
really heaven."

Heaven and hell are metaphors for opposing sets of values governing the way in which life is lived on earth. The frontier between
hell and heaven, the Statue tells Don Juan, is "only the difference
between two ways of looking at things," and earlier in the Hell
Scene the Devil explains to Doña Ana that the "great gulf fixed"
between heaven and hell is "the difference between the angelic and
the diabolic temperament" (III, 129, 97). This difference is what
the Hell Scene is principally about.

The diabolic temperament belongs to those who make no contribution toward human progress. Indeed, the basis of the diabolic position is the view that human progress is impossible; it is fundamentally this question which divides the Devil and Juan in their debate
in the Hell Scene. The Statue, in his first significant speech in the
Hell Scene, indicates the consequences of diabolic pessimism. If
there is nothing to hope for in the future, he explains, then one
might as well live for the pleasures of the moment: "Written over
the gate here are the words 'Leave every hope behind, ye who enter.'
Only think what a relief that is! For what is hope? A form of moral
responsibility. Here there is no hope, and consequently no duty, no

work, nothing to be gained by praying, nothing to be lost by doing what you like. Hell, in short, is a place where you have nothing to do but amuse yourself" (III, 93). Here we see the relevance of the Devil's denial of the possibility of human progress. Just what kind of enjoyment occupies eternity in hell is indicated in the Devil's speeches, with their repeated references to joy, love, happiness, beauty, warmth of heart, sincere unforced affection, and so on. Hell is the home of the sentimental pleasure-seeker, who refuses to face the world of solid fact and real problems. The sentimentalist's unwillingness to accept the real world is reflected in the Hell Scene by the immateriality of hell. Even the pleasures of hell are not actual physical pleasures but the worship of incorporeal abstractions— "sheer imaginative debauchery," Juan calls it (III, 91). Hell offers the escape from the real that sentimentalists on earth long for; here romantic ideals are not mocked by physical reality. Conventions are unchallenged. "Here," says Don Juan, "you escape this tyranny of the flesh; for here you are not an animal at all: you are a ghost, an appearance, an illusion, a convention, deathless, ageless: in a word, bodiless. There are no social questions here, no political questions, no religious questions, best of all, perhaps, no sanitary questions. Here you call your appearance beauty, your emotions love, your sentiments heroism, your aspirations virtue, just as you did on earth; but here there are no hard facts to contradict you, no ironic contrast of your needs with your pretensions, no human comedy, nothing but a perpetual romance, a universal melodrama" (III, 99–100). Those of diabolic temperament would consider this a highly desirable state: Shaw's hell is the sentimentalist's heaven.

For one of angelic temperament, on the other hand, it is truly a hell, a place of torment. Don Juan finds the pleasures of hell unspeakably boring, unsatisfying, and distasteful. This is because his temperament is angelic: he desires something higher and nobler than what hell offers. Unlike the truly damned, he does believe in the possibility of progress in the real world, and can find personal fulfillment only in working for human improvement. "I tell you that as long as I can conceive something better than myself I cannot be easy unless I am striving to bring it into existence or clearing the way for it. That is the law of my life. That is the working within me of Life's incessant aspiration to higher organization, wider, deeper, intenser self-consciousness, and clearer self-understanding. It was the supremacy of this purpose that reduced love for me to the mere pleasure of a moment, art for me to the mere schooling of my faculties, religion for me to a mere excuse for laziness, since it had set up a God who looked at the world and saw that it was good, against the instinct in me that looked through my eyes at the world and saw that it could be improved. I tell you that in the pursuit of my own pleasure, my own health, my own fortune, I have never known happiness" (III, 123–124). This, one of the seminal passages in Shaw's work, is parallel to the lines from the Epistle Dedicatory which are often quoted as his personal credo: "This is the true joy in life, the being used for a purpose recognized by yourself as a mighty one; the being thoroughly worn out before you are thrown on the scrap heap; the being a force of Nature instead of a feverish selfish little clod of ailments and grievances complaining that the world will not devote itself to making you happy" (p. xxxi). Both of these passages are about the distinction between the angelic and diabolic temperaments; and the debate in the Hell Scene is between these two different views of life. Just what happens in heaven is not made clear in the Hell Scene; most of the talk about heaven comes from Juan, who has not been there. One can take it, however, that it is a place where he would be at home, as the Devil and the Statue are at home in hell; it is a place where angelic natures work to raise the level of human life.

One character in the Hell Scene advances a point of view that differs from both the Devil's and Don Juan's. This is Doña Ana, who begins by sounding like a natural candidate for hell, but who at times talks in a different way during the debate between the Devil and Juan. When Juan speaks of his phase of woman-worship while he was on earth, Ana's response is, "Well, was it her fault that you attributed all these perfections to her?" (III, 111). And shortly after this, in her longest speech in the Hell Scene, she says to the three men: "I daresay you all want to marry lovely incarnations of music and painting and poetry. Well, you cant have them, because they dont exist. If flesh and blood is not good enough for you you must go without: thats all. Women have to put up with flesh-and-blood husbands—and little enough of that too, sometimes; and you will have to put up with flesh-and-blood wives" (III, 113). This, like

Ana's remark that "most marriages are perfectly comfortable" (III, 116), is the point of view of prosaic common sense. While the Devil and the Statue are spokesmen for the diabolic, and Juan is the spokesman for the angelic, Ana, although she says little, is in the main the spokesman for the earthly, for the real, tangible world of flesh and blood. This real world the Devil will not face, and while Juan accepts its importance, his is the life of the mind.

These three points of view in the Hell Scene are related to Shaw's discussion in *The Quintessence of Ibsenism* of the three different types of people who would be found in a hypothetical community: Idealists, Realists, and Philistines. "Let us imagine," Shaw writes in the second section of *The Quintessence,* entitled "Ideals and Idealists," "a community of a thousand persons, organized for the perpetuation of the species on the basis of the British family as we know it at present." A substantial minority of these would find the institution of marriage and the family unsatisfactory for them, but instead of admitting this and demanding something better they persuade themselves that the present arrangements are perfect. These are the Idealists, who "try to graft pleasure on necessity by desperately pretending that the institution forced upon them is a congenial one, making it a point of public decency to assume always that men spontaneously love their kindred better than their chance acquaintances, and that the woman once desired is always desired: also that the family is woman's proper sphere, and that no really womanly woman ever forms an attachment, or even knows what it means, until she is requested to do so by a man" (p. 26). The Idealists "try to persuade themselves that, whatever their own particular domestic arrangements may be, the family is a beautiful and holy natural institution" (p. 27). This attitude corresponds in significant ways to the diabolic point of view in the Hell Scene in that it assumes the reality of sentimental illusions and conventions, an assumption which in Shaw's world implies a conservative opposition to reform of established institutions. Idealists, like the diabolic people in the Hell Scene, are those who think, but think wrongly.

The Philistines, on the other hand, do not think. The Philistines, who constitute the majority of the community, find the institution of marriage satisfactory for them, without concerning themselves with the theory of it. They "comfortably accept marriage as a matter of course, never dreaming of calling it an 'institution,' much less a holy and beautiful one" (p. 27). They are less highly evolved than the Idealists, but also less dangerous. The correspondence between the Philistine's point of view and the down-to-earth attitude of Doña Ana in the speeches quoted above is clear enough. The Realist, who is one man in a thousand, is the most highly evolved person of all. Like the Idealist, he is dissatisfied with present arrangements, but unlike him, he is highly conscious of his dissatisfaction and therefore demands a change—the alteration or destruction of established institutions. He is the prophetic character, the man who publicly proclaims the inadequacy of existing arrangements, who will not accept society as it is. The most unequivocal example of the Realist in Shaw's works is Don Juan in the Hell Scene of *Man and Superman.*

Shaw's terms can be confusing, as he himself was aware, because in ordinary usage his Realist would be called an idealist, and his Philistine would be called a realist. One must bear in mind that the Realist is not "realistic" about the world around him; he is not worldly-wise. This is the characteristic of the Philistine, the man who is perfectly at home in this world. And the Realist does believe in ideals—but as objects of aspiration, goals of effort, while the Idealist forces himself to accept what *is* as ideal, as absolutely right.

Whatever the value of these terms in *The Quintessence* in relation to Ibsen's plays or to real life, they can often provide useful labels when one is discussing Shaw's works. This is not to say that characters who can conveniently be called Idealists, Philistines, and Realists will always conform exactly to what Shaw says about the types in this early work. The Idealists in the plays, in particular, are seldom repressed and seldom dangerous, as they are in the second chapter of *The Quintessence.* But if by Idealists we mean the people who worship abstractions and who regard conventional institutions and values as beautiful, natural, holy, and absolutely binding, then the term is both a useful and legitimate one to denote a general type of character who is found in many different forms in Shaw's plays. The same is true of the other terms if by Philistines we mean solid, practical, commonsensible people whose kingdom is of this world and by Realists men and women of vision who see the inadequacies of the world around them and want to bring a better world into existence.[8]

III

The distinctions between hell, heaven, and earth, or Idealist, Realist, and Philistine, underlie the conflicts in the Comedy part of *Man and Superman.* The main diabolic characters in the Comedy are Octavius, Mendoza, and Ramsden. Octavius' counterpart in hell is of course his Mozartian original, Don Ottavio, who does not appear in the Hell Scene, but who is mentioned by the Statue and Juan in terms which make it clear that he is an inhabitant of hell. The counterpart of Octavius could be nowhere but in hell, for Octavius is the chief representative in the Comedy of the diabolic spirit. He is an amorist, a sentimental worshipper of love. "Ah," he says to Tanner, "if we [men] were only good enough for Love! There is nothing like Love: there is nothing else but Love: without it the world would be a dream of sordid horror" (II, 52–53)— a speech which makes one think of Juan's plea to Ana in the Hell Scene "not to begin talking about love. Here they talk of nothing else but love: its beauty, its holiness, its spirituality, its devil knows what!" (III, 91).

Octavius is, in some ways, like the poet Marchbanks in *Candida;* he shares all of Marchbanks' weaknesses but none of his greatness. Marchbanks' idolizing love for Candida, which he grows out of by the end of the play, is like Octavius' love for Ann (who, like Candida, is unsentimental and somewhat cruelly flirtatious)—but Octavius never grows out of his love for Ann, and he never will. Octavius, on being rejected by Ann, does not go "out . . . into the night" to begin a new, more truthful and useful life, but becomes the sentimental, self-pitying suitor, who in fact enjoys his desolation. Octavius' love has a hellish unreality about it, in that it leads to nothing; as Ann points out to him, it would not survive a knowledge of her real flesh-and-blood everyday self, so he must become a "sentimental old bachelor" for her sake (IV, 151). Mendoza, similarly, spends his life as a sentimental rejected lover, writing doggerel in the Sierra Nevada to his Louisa—devoting himself to love in the abstract in a way of which his counterpart in the Hell Scene, the Devil, would presumably approve. The other main representative of hell in the Comedy, Roebuck Ramsden, is rather different: he incarnates the conventional more than the sentimental aspects of the diabolic temperament. On the issue of Violet's pregnancy in the first act, which puts all the characters to the test, he, like Octavius, places moral abstractions above practical, human considerations.

TANNER. . . . The need of the present hour is a happy mother and a healthy baby. Bend your energies on that; and you will see your way clearly enough.
Octavius, much perplexed, goes out.
RAMSDEN [*facing Tanner impressively*] And Morality, sir? What is to become of that?
TANNER. Meaning a weeping Magdalen and an innocent child branded with her shame. Not in our circle, thank you. Morality can go to its father the devil.

(pp. 29–30)

It is appropriate that Ramsden's counterpart, the Statue, announces in the Hell Scene his decision to leave heaven and to live permanently in the Devil's realm, for hell, as Don Juan says, "is the home of honor, duty, justice, and the rest of the seven deadly virtues," and the Devil's friends are "not moral: they are only conventional" (III, 87, 124). The Statue's conventional nature would make hell attractive to him; he explains to Juan that while on earth he tried to kill him to vindicate Ana's honor because "that is how things were arranged on earth. I was not a social reformer; and I always did what it was customary for a gentleman to do" (III, 123). He felt obliged to protect Ana from the outrages of Juan, as Ramsden in the Comedy feels obliged to protect Ann from Tanner.

The one angelic character in the Comedy is Tanner, who, like his counterpart Don Juan, wants to bring a better world into being and finds the sentimental gratifications sought by Octavius and Mendoza inadequate as a basis for life. In Act I, Tanner tells Octavius that he had set his heart on saving him from Ann:

OCTAVIUS. Oh, Jack, you talk of saving me from my highest happiness.
TANNER. Yes, a lifetime of happiness. If it were only the first half hour's happiness, Tavy, I would buy it for you with my last penny. But a lifetime of happiness! No man alive could bear it: it would be hell on earth.

(pp. 12–13)

In an exchange like this, Tanner is able to make Octavius look foolish, just as he is able to make the other diabolic characters look foolish all through the first two acts—his victories over Ramsden are among the best moments in all of Shaw's plays. But one's final impression of Tanner is that he himself is somewhat foolish. This impression is largely derived from his encounters with the third group of characters in the Comedy, the earthly people, the Philistines.

In the Epistle Dedicatory, Shaw writes that the two chief concerns of prosaic people are money, which means nourishment, and marriage, which means children (p. xvi)—the two most necessary conditions for man's physical survival.[9] In the Comedy, the desire for money is represented by Violet and the desire for marriage by Ann. Both of these earthly, Philistine characters are unscrupulous, highly efficient, and utterly unromantic in their attainment of very practical, worldly goals. The desire for money is the cause of Violet's every action in the Comedy. Her wish to be married is not based on any respect for marriage as an institution or any feeling of duty, but on the knowledge that she can acquire greater wealth by marrying. Nor is her marriage based on romantic love. The secrecy about her marriage, we learn in Act II, has nothing romantic about it; it is necessary so that Hector will not be disinherited by his title-loving millionaire father.

> HECTOR. . . . Here's my silly old dad, who is the biggest awffice furniture man in the world, would shew me the door for marrying the most perfect lady in England merely because she has no handle to her name. Of course it's just absurd. But I tell you, Violet, I dont like deceiving him. I feel as if I was stealing his money. Why wont you let me own up?
> VIOLET. We cant afford it. You can be as romantic as you please about love, Hector; but you mustnt be romantic about money.
>
> (p. 64)

Violet's practical, sensible behavior in her quest for money is seen at its best in Act IV, in her efficient handling of Mr. Malone, whom she wins over with a cool, businesslike efficiency that the millionaire businessman cannot cope with.

Ann's pursuit of marriage is no less determined and unscrupulous than Violet's pursuit of money. She is like her counterpart Doña

Ana in that her realm is that of flesh and blood and her attitude toward marriage is solid and practical rather than diabolically romantic. Ann's object in life is to find the right husband to father her children. Whereas Octavius' goal in sexual pursuit is romantic happiness, Ann's motivation derives from Schopenhauer's view that sexual attraction has its basis in an instinctive desire to produce the best possible children.

Her attraction to Tanner is entirely unsentimental; she is not romantic but predatory: Tanner, at various points in the Comedy, likens Woman in general and Ann in particular to the cat, the boa constrictor, the lioness, the tiger, the spider, the bee,[10] and the elephant. The best expression of Ann's nature, however, is to be found not in any of Tanner's speeches, but in her own final dialogue with Octavius, when she rejects him. Her desire to shock and hurt him causes her to be entirely candid about herself. In reply to Octavius' incredulous question, "Ann: would you marry an unwilling man?" she says, "Theres no such thing as a willing man when you really go for him" (IV, 152). And a few lines later comes the following exchange:

OCTAVIUS. It's quite simple. I love you; and I want you to be happy. You dont love me; so I cant make you happy myself; but I can help another man to do it.
ANN. Yes: it seems quite simple. But I doubt if we ever know why we do things. The only really simple thing is to go straight for what you want and grab it.

(p. 153)

This speech emphasizes Ann's predatory nature, and also the fact that her motives are not conscious and reasoned, but instinctive. She is an unconscious agent of evolutionary progress. She cannot explain why she wants Tanner: she just knows in a primitive way that she does want him. This lack of self-consciousness distinguishes her sharply from the highly self-conscious Tanner, and makes her relevant to much of the discussion in the Hell Scene and the Revolutionist's Handbook.

Like Violet, Ann can sound conventional, but she merely uses conventions for her own purposes. Thus we have the comic irony of almost all of her speeches: she professes to be surrendering her own will, while in fact she is cunningly asserting it. This is what she does, for example, in her final scene with Octavius.

> OCTAVIUS. . . . I love you. You know I love you.
> ANN. Whats the good, Tavy? You know that my mother is deter-mined that I shall marry Jack.
> OCTAVIUS [*amazed*] Jack!
> ANN. It seems absurd, doesnt it?
> OCTAVIUS [*with growing resentment*] Do you mean to say that Jack has been playing with me all this time? That he has been urging me not to marry you because he intends to marry you himself?
> ANN [*alarmed*] No, no: you mustnt lead him to believe that I said that. I dont for a moment think that Jack knows his own mind. But it's clear from my father's will that he wished me to marry Jack. And my mother is set on it.
> OCTAVIUS. But you are not bound to sacrifice yourself always to the wishes of your parents.
> ANN. My father loved me. My mother loves me. Surely their wishes are a better guide than my own selfishness.
>
> (IV, 150–151)

Ann merely thinks this sort of talk a good way to get rid of Octav-ius; like Violet she has the Philistine's knack of handling people, of manipulating them for her own advantage. Another superb use of this device by Ann is in Act I, when everyone is considering what to do about Violet. Here is Ann's maneuver to be left alone with her intended prey:

> ANN [*rising and coming to Ramsden*] Granny: hadnt you better go up to the drawing room and tell them what we intend to do?
> RAMSDEN [*looking pointedly at Tanner*] I hardly like to leave you alone with this gentleman. Will you not come with me?
> ANN. Miss Ramsden would not like to speak about it before me, Granny. I ought not to be present.
> RAMSDEN. You are right: I should have thought of that. You are a good girl, Annie.
>
> (p. 30)

Ann is worldly-wise, and within the Comedy's realm of this world she is able to dominate Tanner completely.[11] Tanner's weapon is thought, which takes the form of talk. This has power over the Idealist, to whom thought means something, but to a Philistine like Ann thought is a realm of which she knows nothing and for which she cares nothing. Tanner's thought, to her, is just talk, just form. He is not important to her as a thinker, but as a potential husband and father. The Life Force may impel her toward him because he is intelligent, but that does not mean that she cares about the specific activities of his intelligence. The advantage Ann's limitation gives her is delightfully illustrated in all three acts of the Comedy. In Act I Tanner delivers his spirited speech on the need for men to assert their own wills, and not to be enslaved by women. Ann's reply, which entirely ignores the content of what he has said, is far more effective than the retort which an Idealist like Ramsden would have attempted.

ANN [*placidly*] I am so glad you understand politics, Jack: it will be most useful to you if you go into parliament [*he collapses like a pricked bladder*]. But I am sorry you thought my influence a bad one.
TANNER. I dont say it was a bad one. But bad or good, I didnt choose to be cut to your measure. And I wont be cut to it.
ANN. Nobody wants you to, Jack. I assure you—really on my word—I dont mind your queer opinions one little bit. You know we have all been brought up to have advanced opinions. Why do you persist in thinking me so narrow minded?
TANNER. Thats the danger of it. I know you dont mind, because youve found out that it doesnt matter. The boa constrictor doesnt mind the opinions of a stag one little bit when once she has got her coils round it.

(p. 38)

In Act II Ann replies in a similar vein to Tanner's denunciation of parental tyranny:

ANN [*watching him with quiet curiosity*] I suppose you will go in seriously for politics some day, Jack.
TANNER [*heavily let down*] Eh? What? Wh—? [*Collecting his scattered wits*] What has that got to do with what I have been saying?
ANN. You talk so well.

TANNER. Talk! Talk! It means nothing to you but talk.

(pp. 57–58)

And finally, there is the famous conclusion to the play.

TANNER . . . I solemnly say that I am not a happy man. Ann *looks* happy; but she is only triumphant, successful, victorious. That is not happiness, but the price for which the strong sell their happiness. What we have both done this afternoon is to renounce happiness, renounce freedom, renounce tranquillity, above all, renounce the romantic possibilities of an unknown future, for the cares of a household and a family. I beg that no man may seize the occasion to get half drunk and utter imbecile speeches and coarse pleasantries at my expense. We propose to furnish our own house according to our own taste; and I hereby give notice that the seven or eight travelling clocks, the four or five dressing cases, the carvers and fish slices, the copies of Patmore's Angel In The House in extra Morocco, and the other articles you are preparing to heap upon us, will be instantly sold, and the proceeds devoted to circulating free copies of the Revolutionist's Handbook. The wedding will take place three days after our return to England, by special licence, at the office of the district superintendent registrar, in the presence of my solicitor and his clerk, who, like his clients, will be in ordinary walking dress—

VIOLET [*with intense conviction*] You *are* a brute, Jack.

ANN [*looking at him with fond pride and caressing his arm*] Never mind her, dear. Go on talking.

TANNER. Talking!

Universal laughter.

(IV, 165–166)

It is noticeable that the climax in Act IV, when Tanner is finally conquered, is carefully prepared for all through the Comedy. Each act of the Comedy ends with Tanner's discomfiture by a Philistine, someone more of the world than he. At the end of Act I Violet deflates him by telling him angrily, after he has congratulated her on conceiving a child while single, that she is in fact married. At the end of Act II Straker, the competent driver and mechanic, another of the play's earthly, Philistine characters, astounds Tanner and puts him to flight by announcing to him that Ann is "arter summun else

. . . You" (p. 67). Then the whole play ends with the conquest of Tanner by Ann, and in particular with the "Go on talking" scene, quoted above, in which Ann comfortably asserts her possessive power over him. And as the play advances Ann comes to dominate Tanner more and more. In the first two acts he tries to teach her, in his spirited speeches about the need for men to be free of women and daughters of mothers. By the fourth act he no longer does so; in fact she is now the teacher and he the pupil. She teaches him what she is competent to teach; she teaches about this world and the behavior of flesh-and-blood men and women (as opposed to Man and Woman in the abstract, which is Tanner's own province). The scene is the one in which Ann tells Tanner about men like Octavius.

TANNER. Why dont you marry Tavy? He is willing. Can you not be satisfied unless your prey struggles?

ANN [*turning to him as if to let him into a secret*] Tavy will never marry. Havnt you noticed that that sort of man never marries?

TANNER. What! a man who idolizes women! who sees nothing in nature but romantic scenery for love duets! Tavy, the chivalrous, the faithful, the tenderhearted and true! Tavy never marry! Why, he was born to be swept up by the first pair of blue eyes he meets in the street.

ANN. Yes, I know. All the same, Jack, men like that always live in comfortable bachelor lodgings with broken hearts, and are adored by their landladies, and never get married. Men like you always get married.

TANNER [*smiting his brow*] How frightfully, horribly true! It has been staring me in the face all my life; and I never saw it before.

(IV, 161) [12]

The conflict between Ann and Tanner is between opposing qualities, each of which has its importance. Using the Vitalist language of *Man and Superman,* one would say that Ann and Tanner represent two different ways of serving the Life Force. Each contributes in his own way toward the improvement of the human species. Tanner represents the intellectual way: the contribution of the philosopher; Ann represents the instinctive way: the contribution of the mother. Tanner has something of "the great man who incarnates the philosophic consciousness of Life," while Ann is "the woman who incarnates its fecundity" (Epistle Dedicatory, p. xx). Each of the two characters has what the other lacks. This is brought out in their discussion of Octavius in Act I.

> ANN. Do you think I have designs on Tavy?
> TANNER. I know you have.
> ANN [*earnestly*] Take care, Jack. You may make Tavy very unhappy if you mislead him about me.
> TANNER. Never fear: he will not escape you.
> ANN. I wonder are you really a clever man!
> TANNER. Why this sudden misgiving on the subject?
> ANN. You seem to understand all the things I dont understand; but you are a perfect baby in the things I do understand.
>
> (p. 39)

It is this complementary relationship which makes their marriage of such symbolic importance: it is through the union of their qualities that progress lies.

At the end of the play Tanner has found his proper role. "We do the world's will, not our own," he says to Ann in the scene in Act IV in which he surrenders himself to the urgings of the Life Force. "I have a frightful feeling that I shall let myself be married because it is the world's will that you should have a husband" (p. 160).[13] Tanner can contribute more to evolutionary progress by helping to produce intelligent children than he can as a philosopher and propagandist. The events of the Comedy reveal that the philosopher by himself is at present useless. Tanner neither converts nor even slightly influences anyone. Ramsden, on whom Tanner produces the greatest effect, is too hostile to him to give his views serious consideration. Ramsden has not read his book, and there is no evidence that anyone else in the Comedy has either. Tanner's victories are merely verbal: they are debating-society victories. To all the others in the Comedy he is just a man of words, a fine (or infamous) talker. This Shaw felt to be the public's response to himself, and in Tanner's confrontation with Ann one can see a comic presentation of Shaw's own confrontation with society. Take, for example, one of

Ann's replies to Tanner in Act I: "Thats like the things you say on purpose to shock people: those who know you pay no attention to them" (p. 21). In the portrait of Tanner we find, as in the presentation of Morell in *Candida,* a reflection of Shaw's fear that words in themselves accomplish nothing.[14] Therefore Tanner can be useful only by submitting his will to Ann's, by placing himself at the service of Ann and the instinctive level of activity which she represents. Tanner is much more highly developed than Ann, but as in Hardy's novels, a higher evolutionary level does not necessarily mean that a man is useful in his present environment.

The venue of the Comedy is the earth, the solid world in which practical concerns like marriage and money are basic, and in the Comedy the earthly Philistines—in particular, the two worldly women—are the characters who are always victorious. The main diabolic Idealists, on the other hand—Octavius and Ramsden—are always made to look foolish. The role of Tanner, the angelic Realist, is ambivalent. He is victorious over the Idealists; he is able time after time to expose their illusions in a trenchant and impressive manner. But in his conflicts with the Philistines he is always the loser; in these conflicts it is *he* who is made to look foolish, by Violet and more significantly by Ann. Tanner's ability to destroy illusions is of no use to him here, for the Philistines have no illusions. Tanner is the prophetic character who is not of this world and therefore has little sense of mundane realities; he is at home only in the world of spirit, of ideas. Tanner shares with the Philistines a contempt for sentiment and illusion, but he also shares with the Idealists a remoteness from the real world. This remoteness makes him nobler than the Philistines, but it also makes him absurd in situations calling for a grasp of the actual. As Shaw says in *The Quintessence* about Don Quixote,[15] he "acts as if he were a perfect knight in a world of giants and distressed damsels instead of a country gentleman in a land of innkeepers and farm wenches" (p. 48).[16] *Mutatis mutandis,* this would nicely describe Tanner's behavior toward Violet in Act I of *Man and Superman.*

The dichotomy in Tanner's character is the main source of comedy in *Man and Superman.* The play's comic situations mostly arise from the fact that his knowledge is universal rather than particular, theoretical rather than practical. He is always right (in the context of the book) in principle, but absurdly wrong in his application of the principle to human situations—until the final act, at any rate.

He knows, for example, all about the nature of sexual pursuit, about the predatory woman, the role of man as victim—he knows all of this in theory, but in practice he is completely unaware of Ann's designs on him. The extent of his ignorance of human beings is seen in his belief that the sexually unattractive Octavius is "the destined prey." He also overestimates Octavius, and again puts him in his own place, in proclaiming the sacred purpose of the artist. He knows in theory about the role of the artist, but in practice he thinks that Octavius is one. The Comedy makes it clear that Octavius is only a pseudo-artist of the type found in Shaw's novels, whereas Tanner, as a philosopher, would clearly be included in his own definition of the artist: "a profounder philosophy" is one of the goals for which the artist will sacrifice his wife and family (I, 23–24).

Tanner also knows all about the value of free love, in theory, but in practice thinks Violet one of its practitioners. He again "acts as if he were a perfect knight in a world of . . . distressed damsels" in Act II, when he tells Ann about the evils of parental tyranny ("Oh, I protest against this vile abjection of youth to age! . . . I tell you, the first duty of manhood and womanhood is a Declaration of Independence," p. 57). He is right again in theory, but in practice ignores the fact that Ann tyrannizes over her mother, rather than vice versa.

IV

In the Hell Scene, where the real world no longer exists, Tanner's qualities of thought and intelligence are of value; here theoretical knowledge is more important than the practical ability to deal with one's material environment, for here there is no material environment. In the Hell Scene the major conflict is not between Realist and Philistines, as in the Comedy, but between Realist and Idealists; the conflict is in the realm of ideas. Not that Don Juan easily defeats his diabolic opponent: major debates in Shaw's best plays are never one-sided, as a thirty-five page discussion between Tanner and

Ramsden, Octavius or Mendoza would inevitably be. While the Idealists in the Comedy provide no serious threat to Tanner, their attitude now assumes a more formidable aspect in the person of the Devil. Through the mouth of the Devil, Shaw presents the Idealist's case with sufficient cogency to make the debate with Juan an almost even match. For the Devil is by no means an entirely contemptible figure. He is like his counterpart Mendoza, who is impressive at times (as the brigands' leader) and ridiculous at others (as the maudlin rejected suitor). The kind of mixture we find in the Devil is noted by Juan himself in his final speech to him: "Though there is much to be learnt from a cynical devil, I really cannot stand a sentimental one" (III, 129). The Devil's "cynicism" is better described as pessimism—it is the absence of hope for improvement which the Statue cited as the basis of the diabolic philosophy. This pessimism Shaw recognizes as diabolic, but it was undoubtedly part of his own temperament, which is one reason why the Devil's speeches about the wretchedness of man and his achievements have such force, and why the debate in the Hell Scene is a genuine debate. As in all of Shaw's major debates and conflicts, it is not a question of Shaw versus anti-Shaw, but of one aspect of his temperament in opposition to another. The same is true of the Comedy, where Shaw's love of intellectual and verbal revolutionary activity collides with his respect for the forces of this world.

Juan does not have easy answers for the Devil's powerful arguments. It is particularly noticeable that he does not disagree at all with the Devil's condemnation of man's social achievements so far. That is, he tacitly accepts a good portion of the Devil's case. What he does not accept is the Devil's view that progress is impossible. That Shaw himself was sympathetic to both Juan and the Devil is suggested not only in Juan's acceptance of much of what the Devil says, but in the fact that Tanner's Revolutionist's Handbook is a mixture of the Devil's pessimism and Juan's optimism. Chapters VII to IX contain the Devil's argument about man's *in*capacity for progress, while in Chapter X we find Juan's argument about man's capacity for progress: "Where there is a will, there is a way," says the first sentence of this chapter (p. 204).

There are other specific pessimistic arguments of the Devil's which Juan is not able to answer satisfactorily—particularly toward the end of the debate. Here is the passage in which the Devil uses a weapon he has hitherto held in reserve:

> THE DEVIL. Don Juan: shall I be frank with you?
> DON JUAN. Were you not so before?
> THE DEVIL. As far as I went, yes. But I will now go further, and confess to you that men get tired of everything, of heaven no less than of hell; and that all history is nothing but a record of the oscillations of the world between these two extremes. An epoch is but a swing of the pendulum; and each generation thinks the world is progressing because it is always moving. But when you are as old as I am; when you have a thousand times wearied of heaven, like myself and the Commander, and a thousand times wearied of hell, as you are wearied now, you will no longer imagine that every swing from heaven to hell is an emancipation, every swing from hell to heaven an evolution. Where you now see reform, progress, fulfilment of upward tendency, continual ascent by Man on the stepping stones of his dead selves to higher things, you will see nothing but an infinite comedy of illusion.
>
> (III, 126)

Juan's reply to this is spirited and self-confident, but not entirely convincing. As with the question of man's achievements, he accepts the major part of the Devil's argument. Here he does not deny that history is cyclical rather than rectilinear—a very damaging admission for him to make, one would think. He then tries to graft this cyclical view onto his own theory of progress. The result is, as I say, not entirely convincing, for what he presents is the theory that development is both cyclical and purposeful: "Granted," he says, that the Life Force "has hit on the device of the clockmaker's pendulum, and uses the earth for its bob; that the history of each oscillation, which seems so novel to us the actors, is but the history of the last oscillation repeated; nay more, that in the unthinkable infinitude of time the sun throws off the earth and catches it again a thousand times as a circus rider throws up a ball, and that our agelong epochs are but the moments between the toss and the catch, has the colossal mechanism no purpose?" (III, 127).[17] Juan may mean that while human history is cyclical, biological evolution is purposeful and progressive, but he does not say this.

The Devil's final major speech is a contemptuous—and trenchant—dismissal of reformers, on the ground that they are vulgar and credulous and therefore deceived by illusory panaceas —religious, scientific, and political. Juan's end as a reformer, he predicts, "will be despair and decrepitude, broken nerve and shattered hopes, vain regrets for that worst and silliest of wastes and sacrifices, the waste and sacrifice of the power of enjoyment: in a word, the punishment of the fool who pursues the better before he has secured the good." (III, 128). Juan's reply to this is particularly interesting. It is his final argument and really his main reason for leaving hell for heaven. It is by no means a refutation of what the Devil has just said, and amounts to an existentialist argument in favor of world (or universe) betterment. "But at least I shall not be bored," he says. "The service of the Life Force has that advantage, at all events. So fare you well, Señor Satan" (III, 128).

One other element in the Hell Scene adds to the stature of the diabolic, and hence makes the debate more evenly balanced. This is the revelation, by the Statue and the Devil, that hell has a substantial numerical majority over heaven.

THE STATUE. . . . So few go to heaven, and so many come here, that the blest, once called a heavenly host, are a continually dwindling minority. The saints, the fathers, the elect of long ago are the cranks, the faddists, the outsiders of today.

THE DEVIL. It is true. From the beginning of my career I knew that I should win in the long run by sheer weight of public opinion, in spite of the long campaign of misrepresentation and calumny against me. At bottom the universe is a constitutional one; and with such a majority as mine I cannot be kept permanently out of office.

(III, 98–99)

One is perhaps reminded here of Tanner's minority position in the Comedy, and of Shaw's own feeling that he himself was fighting the world single-handedly.

Although a reasonable balance is maintained between the two sides in the debate, there can be no doubt that Juan is the victor, and that we are meant to be very much on his side. For Juan proclaims the "new religion" that Shaw said is at the center of *Man and Superman*. This is Creative Evolution, the religion whose god is the Life Force.

The basic assumption of this religion is that the universe (which means here the sum of organic life) is purposeful, its purpose being the evolution of higher and higher forms of life. This purpose gives the hope which is the basis of the angelic point of view. The Life Force is the collective will of organisms to improve: Juan and Shaw believe that this kind of willing is natural to all organisms. Thus an organism which does will to improve is fulfilling its own natural purpose and at the same time the universal purpose of the collective will of which it is a part. The Life Force must rely on the individual wills which constitute it; therefore its upward tendency can be fulfilled only if individuals do the world's will (Shaw's version of God's will). It is possible for individuals to choose not to serve the Life Force; these are the followers of the Devil, who are false to their real purpose in life. This is another way of putting the basic conflict in the Hell Scene. Juan, at the end of the speech in which he proclaims his law of life, tells the Devil that it is the absence of the instinct for progress that "makes you that strange monster called a Devil." Furthermore: "It is the success with which you have diverted the attention of men from their real purpose, which in one degree or another is the same as mine, to yours, that has earned you the name of The Tempter. It is the fact that they are doing your will, or rather drifting with your want of will, instead of doing their own, that makes them the uncomfortable, false, restless, artificial, petulant, wretched creatures they are" (III, 124).

There are two important implications of this religion with respect to the role of the individual, both of which profoundly affect Shaw's work as a dramatist. First, there is the Protestant emphasis on individual responsibility: the view that the individual is responsible not only for his own welfare, but for the welfare of the whole race. Second, Shaw's religion eliminates any inevitable conflict between self-assertion and public usefulness; by asserting his own will (which is naturally progressive in tendency) the individual is making himself the servant of the universal will. The individual will is not isolated and selfish but part of a larger purpose. The assumption here is that the selfish person—the Idealist—is not fulfilling the natural urgings of his will, that he is behaving in an unnatural way. This view that self-assertion and world betterment are not only compatible but necessary to each other is one of the major attitudes underlying Shaw's plays. It enables him to create characters who are egotists in the Romantic tradition, and to ascribe to them the Utilitarian virtue of public usefulness (Caesar and Undershaft are conspicuous examples of this).

The Life Force can operate in two ways; that is, there are two different kinds of progressive striving: the instinctive and the intellectual. In both cases the will asserts itself, but the instinctive will asserts itself blindly, with undirected power, while the intellectual will asserts itself in an open-eyed, clear-sighted, conscious manner. In the Comedy these two kinds of willing are symbolized by Ann and Tanner, respectively, and the emphasis is on the value of Ann's instinctive power. In the Hell Scene, on the other hand, the emphasis is on the need for more intellect. Juan implies that the necessary balance between body and brain, instinct and intellect, matter and spirit, does not exist. Instinctive willing is of value, but without intellect to give it direction, the progress that it can make is limited. This is in precise counterpoint to the Comedy, where intellect is of value, but can make no progress without the instinctive force of Ann to give it power.

Juan says that the Life Force has progressed hitherto by means of instinctive willing; it has worked, that is to say, through Anns, through Philistines. It has therefore not progressed very far—man at present is not much of an achievement, Juan and Shaw feel.

DON JUAN. . . . So far, the result of Life's continual effort not only to maintain itself, but to achieve higher and higher organization and completer self-consciousness, is only, at best, a doubtful campaign between its forces and those of Death and Degeneration. The battles in this campaign are mere blunders, mostly won, like actual military battles, in spite of the commanders.

THE STATUE. That is a dig at me. No matter: go on, go on.

DON JUAN. It is a dig at a much higher power than you, Commander. Still, you must have noticed in your profession that even a stupid general can win battles when the enemy's general is a little stupider.

THE STATUE [*very seriously*] Most true, Juan, most true. Some donkeys have amazing luck.

DON JUAN. Well, the Life Force is stupid; but it is not so stupid as the forces of Death and Degeneration. Besides, these are in its pay all the time. And so Life wins, after a fashion. What mere copiousness of fecundity can supply and mere greed preserve, we possess.

(III, 107–108)

That this instinctive willing can be connected with the Philistines of the Comedy is demonstrated in the last sentence I have quoted: "What mere copiousness of fecundity can supply and mere greed preserve, we possess." Our degree of evolutionary success is that which results from the quest for marriage and money—represented in the Comedy by Ann and Violet, respectively. The connection is also made in a passage in the Epistle Dedicatory. Shaw is speaking, as Juan does in the Hell Scene, of the limitations of Philistinism.

What is wrong with the prosaic Englishman is what is wrong with the prosaic men of all countries: stupidity. The vitality which places nourishment and children first, heaven and hell a somewhat remote second, and the health of society as an organic whole nowhere, may muddle successfully through the comparatively tribal stages of gregariousness; but in nineteenth century nations and twentieth century commonwealths the resolve of every man to be rich at all costs, and of every woman to be married at all costs [in the Comedy both these resolves are represented by women], must, without a highly scientific social organization, produce a ruinous development of poverty, celibacy, prostitution, infant mortality, adult degeneracy, and everything that wise men most dread. In short, there is no future for men, however brimming with crude vitality, who are neither intelligent nor politically educated enough to be Socialists . . . If I appreciate the vital qualities of the Englishman as I appreciate the vital qualities of the bee, I do not guarantee the Englishman against being, like the bee (or the Canaanite) smoked out and unloaded of his honey by beings inferior to himself in simple acquisitiveness, combativeness, and fecundity, but superior to him in imagination and cunning.

(pp. xvi–xvii)

This is the same point that Juan makes in the Hell Scene, except that Shaw's context here is social and political rather than evolutionary. Note that the bee, which is used by Tanner in Act II as an illustration of woman's (that is, Ann's) role in the duel of sex, is used here as an example of "crude vitality." And the sentence that contains this phrase perfectly describes Ann: she is one of those who, "however brimming with crude vitality . . . are neither intelligent nor politically educated enough to be Socialists."

The main point that Shaw and Juan are making is this: we have reached the stage in social and evolutionary development when "crude vitality" is no longer adequate. We must develop greater powers of intelligence or face dire consequences. Intelligence must control instinct, the Realist must control the Philistine, Tanners must control Anns. The development which must take place on an evolutionary scale is parallel to that which took place within Tanner himself as he grew up and the moral passion came to dominate and direct the lower passions. Tanner explains this to Ann in Act I: "All the other passions were in me before; but they were idle and aimless—mere childish greedinesses and cruelties, curiosities and fancies, habits and superstitions, grotesque and ridiculous to the mature intelligence . . . [The moral passion] dignified them, gave them conscience and meaning, found them a mob of appetites and organized them into an army of purposes and principles" (p. 35). The human race must grow up, as Tanner did, so that man can direct his affairs (both social and evolutionary) in a conscious and intelligent manner.

In the Hell Scene—as opposed to the Comedy—the philosopher is the type of man who contributes most to evolutionary (and by implication social and political) progress. The evolutionary need itself is for greater intelligence, and it is men of intelligence like Juan who are of value at present, who help life in its upward struggle by trying to discover its nature so that evolution can be consciously directed toward intelligently willed ends.[18]

But although Juan, the philosopher, is the central figure in the Hell Scene, the scene ends not with him but with Ana. Her stirring affirmation is of the greatest importance to the whole of *Man and Superman.* She has found her role. Here again the Hell Scene and the Comedy are complementary. In the Comedy the emphasis is on the need for intellect to acquire instinctive power: here Tanner finds his role as a father, which he learns through Ann. In the Hell Scene the emphasis is on the need for instinct to acquire controlling, directing intellect: here Ana finds her role as a mother, which she learns through Juan.

Shaw writes in the Epistle Dedicatory to *Man and Superman* that the character of Ann Whitefield was conceived by him as he watched a performance of *Everyman* (a title which is echoed by Shaw's): "I said to myself Why not Everywoman?" (p. xxviii). Doña Ana, it seems to me, relates in a more direct way to *Everyman*. One can see the Hell Scene as a kind of morality play, in which the question is whether Ana, who as a Philistine represents ordinary, worldly humanity, will go to hell or to heaven. This is not determined by her past deeds as in the Christian *Everyman,* but by her present choice: the Hell Scene takes the principle of free choice to its utmost limit—beyond death, in fact. Ana chooses heaven: that is, the ordinary human being chooses the life of world betterment rather than that of self-indulgence, just as Ann has chosen Tanner rather than Octavius in the Comedy—Ann's marriage has as its purpose children, not sentimental pleasure. But Ana is not a philosopher, and serving the Life Force does not mean the same for her as it means for Juan. "I can find my own way to heaven, Ana; not yours," Juan tells her (III, 129). (Compare the Statue's reply to Juan's request for directions to the frontier between hell and heaven: "Any road will take you across it if you really want to get there," III, 129.) Ana's way to heaven is the Philistine's way, through the flesh, through matter. Just as Ann in the play is quite distinct from Octavius on the one hand and Tanner on the other, so Ana in the Hell Scene is quite distinct from both the Devil and Juan. As a Philistine, she will imitate neither of them; she has her own role to fulfill. Shaw himself explains this in a note which he wrote for the program for the first production of the Hell Scene, at the Court Theatre in 1907:

Doña Ana, being a woman, is incapable both of the devil's utter damnation and of Don Juan's complete supersensuality. As the mother of many children she has shared in the divine travail, and with care and labor and suffering renewed the harvest of eternal life . . . . She cannot, like the male devil, use love as mere sentiment and pleasure; nor can she, like the male saint, put love aside when it has once done its work as a developing and enlightening experience. Love is neither her pleasure nor her study: it is her business. So she, in the end, neither goes with Don Juan to heaven nor with the devil and her father to the palace of pleasure, but declares that her work is not yet finished. For though by her death she is done with the bearing of men to mortal fathers, she may yet, as Woman Immortal, bear the Superman to the Eternal Father.[19]

By "Woman Immortal" and "the Eternal Father" Shaw means simply woman and man, just as by the phrase "eternal life" he means simply life (to which he wishes to attach religious significance). Ana's work is what is begun in Act IV of the play. The Philistine's home is the earth, and the Philistine's work can be done only on earth. The implication of the last part of Act III is that Ana— the symbolic woman—returns to earth as Ann Whitefield to work toward the creation of the Superman by marrying Tanner: this is her way to heaven. This is partly borne out by the suggestion that Ann is a reincarnation of Ana when she tells Octavius that his compliment (which was the Statue's) gives her "that strange sudden sense of an echo from a former existence" (IV, 151).[20] And a close look at the final part of Act III makes the matter even clearer. The following two passages are within two pages of each other:

ANA. . . . Tell me: where can I find the Superman?
THE DEVIL. He is not yet created, Señora.
THE STATUE. And never will be, probably . . .
ANA. Not yet created! Then my work is not yet done. [*Crossing herself devoutly*] I believe in the Life to Come. [*Crying to the Universe*] A father! a father for the Superman! [21]
She vanishes into the void.

(III, 131)

ANN. It's Jack!
TANNER. Caught!
HECTOR. Why, certainly it is. I said it was you, Tanner. We've just been stopped by a puncture: the road is full of nails.
VIOLET. What are you doing here with all these men?
ANN. Why did you leave us without a word of warning?
HECTOR. I wawnt that bunch of roses, Miss Whitefield. [*To Tanner*] When we found you were gone, Miss Whitefield bet me a bunch of roses my car would not overtake yours before you reached Monte Carlo.

TANNER. But this is not the road to Monte Carlo.
HECTOR. No matter. Miss Whitefield tracked you at every stop-
ping place: she is a regular Sherlock Holmes.
TANNER. The Life Force! I am lost.

(III, 133)

If by *Man and Superman* one means the Comedy alone, then the
play appears to be about the defeat of Tanner by Ann. If, however,
all four acts are taken together as a whole, the picture changes: Act
IV assumes a quite different complexion when it is preceded by the
Hell Scene. What seems to be Tanner's defeat now appears as a first
step toward an eventual victory for what he represents.

Marriages in Shaw's plays are usually not ends but beginnings.
This is true in *Man and Superman* in the sense that the purpose of
the marriage of Tanner and Ann is not their own pleasure but the
production of children. (Shaw is in agreement with the Roman
Catholic Church here; and a marriage devoted to sexual pleasure
rather than procreation would be, in the context of *Man and Superman,* the work of the Devil.) We are reminded that breeding is the
proper purpose of marriage not only in the Hell Scene but also in
the Comedy itself. In particular, there is the climactic moment when
the Life Force, via Ann, has overcome Tanner:

TANNER. You would sell freedom and honor and self for happiness?
ANN. It will not be all happiness for me. Perhaps death.
TANNER [*groaning*] Oh, that clutch holds and hurts. What have
you grasped in me? Is there a father's heart as well as a mother's?

(IV, 163)

Tanner realizes here that marriage is not just a matter of hellish
happiness, but of heavenly world betterment through procreation.[22]

With so much emphasis in *Man and Superman* on the production
of children, it is reasonable to speculate on what sort of children
might be born to Ann and Tanner. According to the Revolutionist's
Handbook, the union of people with different temperaments is apt
to produce desirable offspring: "There is no evidence that the best
citizens are the offspring of congenial marriages, or that a conflict of

temperament is not a highly important part of what breeders call crossing. On the contrary, it is quite sufficiently probable that good results may be obtained from parents who would be extremely unsuitable companions and partners, to make it certain that the experiment of mating them will sooner or later be tried purposely almost as often as it is now tried accidentally . . . In conjugation two complementary persons may supply one another's deficiencies." [23] The example Tanner gives here of a eugenically beneficial union is parallel to his own: between "the son of a robust, cheerful, eupeptic British country squire" and "a clever, imaginative, intellectual, highly civilized Jewess" (p. 175)—beween, that is, Philistine vitality and intellectual acuteness.

The union of Ann and Tanner is hopeful because it will presumably produce offspring who will combine their opposing qualities; who will combine, that is to say, Tanner's intellect with Ann's instinctive practical force. Their immediate children would not, one assumes, be a perfect synthesis of these qualities; evolution is a slow business, working over many generations. But the marriage of Tanner and Ann is a symbolic step toward the union of the qualities that they represent—a step toward the creation of a type of person who will have not only a fine intellect but the power to give that intellect useful expression in the world. Such is the man of the third empire "who shall swallow up both Emperor and Galilean"; and in quoting this phrase of Maximus' in *The Quintessence of Ibsenism* Shaw adds a footnote (dated 1912), "Or, as we should now say, the Superman" (p. 55). Shaw's Superman would be a synthesis of matter and mind, a synthesis which would transcend the limitations of each part. The Superman would have the worldly power that attaches to matter, without the limitation of matter: its stupidity. And he would have the intellectual strength that attaches to spirit, without the limitation of spirit: ineffectuality. [24]

Tanner's marriage, then, is a defeat for him only in the short run: he will be a husband and father rather than a creative thinker (*Man and Superman* assumes that one cannot be both). But while as a creative thinker he has had no effect on society, as a father he may; in the descendants of Tanner and Ann her power could be the instrument of his intelligence. The highly developed man must lower himself to unite with the primitive and earthly so that progress can be made beyond this level.[25]

V

The theme of *Man and Superman* is the question of biological (and by implication social) progress. The particular area in which progress is discussed is the institution which is directly concerned with both biological and social considerations: marriage. The most obvious link between the Comedy, the Hell Scene, and the Revolutionist's Handbook is that they all deal with sex and marriage. This is the main issue that Tanner orates about in the Comedy; it is one of Juan's major concerns in the Hell Scene; and it is the principal subject of the Revolutionist's Handbook.

The central doctrine about sex and marriage which one finds in *Man and Superman* is that we must learn to take sex seriously, to see it as a means of breeding a better kind of man. This means doing away with the present institution of marriage, for, as one of the Maxims for Revolutionists declares, "Marriage, or any other form of promiscuous amoristic monogamy, is fatal to large States because it puts its ban on the deliberate breeding of man as a political animal" (p. 215). Marriage is based on the illusory assumption that impersonal sexual attraction and personal sentimental attraction are the same. What *Man and Superman* tells us is that we must make sex a heavenly rather than a hellish affair: we must make it the servant of thought and purpose as opposed to personal, sentimental gratification. In the book sex is an affair of the earth, so that one could say that *Man and Superman* urges us to raise earth to heaven instead of dragging it down to hell. It is this apotheosis of sex that Juan predicts: "The great central purpose of breeding the race: ay, breeding it to heights now deemed superhuman: that purpose which is now hidden in a mephitic cloud of love and romance and prudery and fastidiousness, will break through into clear sunlight as a purpose no longer to be confused with the gratification of personal fancies, the impossible realization of boys' and girls' dreams of bliss, or the need of older people for companionship or money" (III, 119). Apart from "the need of older people for companionship or money," all of the barriers to eugenic progress which Juan cites here are aspects of the diabolic-Idealistic temperament.

Relations between the sexes must be based on the recognition that sex is impersonal. (Anything that Shaw considers important he sees as impersonal.) A similar treatment of sexual attraction as something impersonal is found in *You Never Can Tell* (1895–96), where Valentine and Gloria are thrown together by a force they cannot control, even though they do not particularly like each other and are not particularly well suited to each other. In the Comedy in *Man and Superman,* this is true of the relationship between Ann and Tanner. Tanner in particular discovers that the Life Force throws him into Ann's arms, regardless of his personal wishes. In the Hell Scene, it is true of Juan's sexual relationships during his lifetime. "Do you not understand," he tells the others, "that when I stood face to face with Woman, every fibre in my clear critical brain warned me to spare her and save myself." But in spite of this intellectual disinclination, the attraction was irresistible: "Whilst I was in the act of framing my excuse to the lady, Life seized me and threw me into her arms as a sailor throws a scrap of fish into the mouth of a seabird" (III, 114).

The Revolutionist's Handbook uses this idea that sex is impersonal as the basis of an attack on the institution of marriage. We should divide marriage, the Handbook says, into its two separate functions: the sexual and the personal. Thus one would have two different types of relationship between the sexes: sexual relationships, between eugenically compatible people, and personal, domestic relationships, between personally compatible people. All children would be produced by the first kind of relationship (and would presumably be brought up by the State, an idea which Shaw suggests elsewhere). This is what is referred to in Chapter II of the Handbook as "the dissolution of the present necessary association of marriage with conjugation" (p. 177).[26] The argument assumes that people who are sexually attracted to each other are likely to be eugenically compatible: this is an application of Shaw's view that in following our own wills we are serving the Life Force and helping the race to advance. What we must do (for a start, at any rate) is to prevent diabolic behavior from obstructing the instinctive workings of the Life Force.

We must liberate sex so that it can fulfill its natural heavenly function as a servant of the Life Force.

The Revolutionist's Handbook suggests a few other immediate reforms. The most important of these is the abolition of property, on the ground that the class distinctions which property creates are, like marriage, barriers to the mating of eugenically suitable partners. "There should be no possibility of such an obstacle to natural selection as the objection of a countess to a navvy or of a duke to a charwoman" (p. 174).[27] Another suggestion which the Handbook makes with characteristically deceptive casualness is to reject "from the list of eligible parents all persons who are uninteresting, unpromising, or blemished without any set-off" (p. 174). Yet another is that society should reward a woman who produces sound offspring "by careful selection of a father, and nourishment of herself" (p. 204).

The main suggestion made in the Handbook, however, is that *for the present* we should allow the Life Force to work in its instinctive way; about the most we can do is to remove the barriers which Idealists set up: "What is really important in Man is the part of him that we do not *yet* understand. Of much of it we are not even conscious, just as we are not normally conscious of keeping up our circulation by our heart-pump, though if we neglect it we die. We are therefore driven to the conclusion that when we have carried selection as far as we can by rejecting from the list of eligible parents all persons who are uninteresting, unpromising, or blemished without any set-off, we shall still have to trust to the guidance of fancy (*alias* Voice of Nature), both in the breeders and the parents, for that superiority in the unconscious self which will be the true characteristic of the Superman" (p. 174). The first italics here are mine: the "yet" seems to me most important. At present, we must rely on instinct, on Ann's way of serving the Life Force, because our knowledge and understanding are limited. But it is this knowledge and understanding which the philosopher seeks. Thus the philosopher, in making us more aware of the part of man which we do not yet understand, will enable us to *direct* our eugenic progress toward the Superman. We must begin by relying on Ann's kind of willing, but we will progress to Tanner's. This idea is also found at the beginning of Chapter X of the Handbook, the chapter entitled "The Method":

As to the method, what can be said *as yet* except that where there is a will, there is a way? If there be no will, we are lost. That is a possibility for our crazy little empire, if not for the universe; and as such possibilities are not to be entertained without despair, we must, whilst we survive, proceed on the assumption that we have still energy enough to not only will to live, but to will to live better. That may mean that we must establish a State Department of Evolution, with a seat in the Cabinet for its chief, and a revenue to defray the cost of direct State experiments, and provide inducements to private persons to achieve successful results. It may mean a private society or a chartered company for the improvement of human live stock. But *for the present* it is far more likely to mean a blatant repudiation of such proposals as indecent and immoral, with, nevertheless, a general secret pushing of the human will in the repudiated direction; so that all sorts of institutions and public authorities will under some pretext or other feel their way furtively towards the Superman.

(p. 204)

My italics here again emphasize the temporary nature of the reliance that we must place on instinctive willing before we can proceed consciously and intelligently, which we will be able to do as instinctive willing produces people who are more intelligent and conscious. It is the beginning of this stage of progress that is dramatized in the Comedy.

Another principal concern of the Revolutionist's Handbook is the political need for a higher level of intelligence in human beings. The Handbook says that our present level of intelligence is sufficient to govern small, simple nations but not large, complex empires, and that we must therefore evolve a more intelligent form of man in order for civilization to be possible in the future. *Man and Superman*'s reply to the Devil's pessimism about progress is that there is hope, if human nature can be changed. But the Handbook is more a warning than a comfort; it emphasizes that unless the needed change occurs, society is doomed. Until man acquires more intellect, "his early successes in building commercial civilizations (and such civilizations, Good Heavens!) are but preliminaries to the inevitable later stage, now threatening us, in which the passions which built the civilization become fatal instead of productive, just as the same qualities which make the lion king in the forest ensure his destruction when he enters a city. Nothing can save society then except the clear head and the wide purpose: war and competition, potent instruments of selection and evolution in one epoch, become ruinous instruments of degeneration in the next" (p. 192). The passions which built our present commercial civilization are those of the Philistine, of Ann. (Note the reference to lions.) In this sense Ann is, as Emil Strauss suggests, a symbol of the world as it is, of capitalist society.[28] A society of Anns is no longer adequate; man must become more like Tanner, in order to shape his social and political development with conscious ends in mind. This increase in the intelligence of *homo sapiens* can be achieved only through evolutionary means. The first step would be the evolution of men with both brains and practical power who could direct the biological progress of mankind. Hence the central position in *Man and Superman* of the marriage of Tanner and Ann, a union of forces which are only of limited value when separated, but which when combined could raise the human race to a higher level.

III

Major Barbara

Since Shaw's Preface to *Major Barbara* is presented as an explanation of the play, one might begin a discussion of the play by looking at it. The opening section of the Preface is entitled "First Aid to Critics," and the next begins by saying that Shaw is driven "to help [his] critics out with Major Barbara by telling them what to say about it" (p. 209). In accepting Shaw's help, however, critics might bear in mind his own critical dictum that "the existence of a discoverable and perfectly definite thesis in a poet's work by no means depends on the completeness of his own intellectual consciousness of it." [1] And what Shaw says about the play in the Preface does not, in any case, necessarily represent his whole view of it. His explanations of everything are deliberately one-sided: he brings to his public's attention the aspects of a question which he wishes them to consider.

The aspect of *Major Barbara* which Shaw wished his readers to consider, or which he himself saw as the essence of the play, is the economic one. The second section of the Preface is entitled "The Gospel of St Andrew Undershaft," and this gospel has to do with money and poverty—according to the Preface. After his statement that he will tell critics what to say about the play, Shaw begins to do so: "In the millionaire Undershaft I have represented a man who has become intellectually and spiritually as well as practically conscious of the irresistible natural truth which we all abhor and repudiate: to wit, that the greatest of our evils, and the worst of our crimes is poverty, and that our first duty, to which every other consideration should be sacrificed, is not to be poor" (p. 209). In the play itself Undershaft's gospel is twofold. His religion, he tells Cus-

ins in Act II, is "that there are two things necessary to Salvation
. . . money and gunpowder" (p. 283). In the Preface the second article of Undershaft's faith is not really dealt with at all; the manufacture of weapons is referred to only in an economic context, as the
profession which was his alternative to poverty: "Undershaft, the
hero of Major Barbara, is simply a man who, having grasped the
fact that poverty is a crime, knows that when society offered him
the alternative of poverty or a lucrative trade in death and destruction, it offered him, not a choice between opulent villainy and hum-
ble virtue, but between energetic enterprise and cowardly infamy"
(p. 212). This argument is identical with Shaw's analysis of Mrs.
Warren's profession (see Preface to *Mrs Warren's Profession,* pp.
165–166), and Undershaft's gospel, as presented by Shaw in the
Preface to *Major Barbara,* is no different from Mrs. Warren's in es-
sentials.

In many ways *Major Barbara* is similar to *Mrs Warren's Profession.* According to Archibald Henderson, Shaw told him that "perhaps a more suitable title for this play [*Major Barbara*] . . . would
have been *Andrew Undershaft's Profession,"* if it had not been for
the fact that he had already used the formula twice before, in *Mrs
Warren's Profession* and *Cashel Byron's Profession* (the novel that
he wrote in 1882).[2] Both *Major Barbara* and *Mrs Warren's Profession* proclaim Shaw's instrumentalist, relativist morality: one must
act, not from any absolute moral principles, but according to the
practical demands of a particular set of circumstances. Both Undershaft and Mrs. Warren make the more moral choice—that is, the
more practical, useful one—while Mrs. Warren's half-sisters and
Peter Shirley illustrate the error of basing one's actions on the dic-
tates of conventional "morality." Given a badly organized society
which forces one to choose between "moral virtue" and material
well-being, it is more moral to be "wicked" than to be good. In both
plays a high-minded daughter learns unpleasant truths about the
real world through a parent whose profession represents its most
shocking features; and each daughter must decide whether to accept
or reject her parent. Although Barbara and Vivie make opposite
choices, they both base their choice on the desire not to be useless,
and they both reject the life of the leisured middle-class lady.[3]

Also, *Major Barbara,* like *Mrs Warren's Profession,* is much con-

cerned in a direct way with money. In the masterly opening scene
Lady Britomart has summoned Stephen to discuss the family's
money problem with him; his sisters' impending marriages, she tells
him, require her to find a way of increasing the family's income. It is
this necessity that sets in motion the events of the play: Undershaft,
the provider of money, is brought into contact with his family after
a separation of many years. In this first scene Stephen is disillusioned
about the source of his wealth in a way reminiscent of Vivie's disillusionment by Crofts (and of Trench's discovery in Act II of *Widowers' Houses*).

> LADY BRITOMART. I must get the money somehow.
> STEPHEN. We cannot take money from him. I had rather go and
> live in some cheap place like Bedford Square or even Hampstead
> than take a farthing of his money.
> LADY BRITOMART. But after all, Stephen, our present income
> comes from Andrew.
> STEPHEN [*shocked*] I never knew that.
>   (I, 251)

This nicely anticipates, in a minor and comic way, Barbara's shatter-
ing discovery in Act II that because she is a member of the Salvation Army her money "comes from Andrew" and his like. Similarly,
Lady Britomart's statement to Stephen that "it is not a question of
taking money from him or not: it is simply a question of how
much" (I, 251) anticipates the Salvation Army's behavior in Act II
in rejecting Bill Walker's pound while accepting Undershaft's five
thousand. The question in both cases is not a moral one, but a practical, economic one. As Frank Gardner says to Praed, in a remark
which sums up so much of *Mrs Warren's Profession*, "It's not the
moral aspect of the case: it's the money aspect" (IV, 238). It would
be true to say that in *Major Barbara* the first act is in part concerned with the economic problems of the rich, the second with the
economic problems of the poor, and that in both cases the money
comes from Undershaft. The settings of all three acts draw one's attention to the importance of money. The Salvation Army shelter in
Act II is a symbol of the fruits of poverty, while the aristocratic opu-
lence of Wilton Crescent and the bourgeois amenity of Perivale St.
Andrews reveal the advantages of money. Undershaft himself points

to the contrast between the cannon works and the shelter: "I see no darkness here, no dreadfulness. In your Salvation shelter I saw poverty, misery, cold and hunger" (III, 328). Undershaft is here justifying the superiority of his kind of salvation over that of the Salvation Army, and in the speeches of his that follow he proclaims the importance of money and the sinfulness of poverty.

But is the need for money the central concern of *Major Barbara?* In order to answer this, one must ask how important it is that Undershaft's way of making money is the manufacture of weapons. Given what Shaw says in the Preface about the play, Undershaft's profession could be anything lucrative and unsavory: he could be a slum landlord like Sartorius, a brothel owner like Crofts, or a distiller like Bodger. But if he had been one of these, the play would have been profoundly different. There is a crucial distinction between Undershaft's profession and the others: weapons can be a direct instrument of social change, which slum dwellings, brothels, and whisky are obviously not. Undershaft defends gunpowder in a way in which the other immoralists could not defend their wares. He does not simply say (as Mrs. Warren does) that it is better to engage in disreputable activities than to starve: he goes much further than Mrs. Warren in that he offers a positive defense of his weapons as the necessary means of reforming society. The climactic debate at the end of the play is more concerned with gunpowder itself as an instrument of change than it is with its manufacture as a source of money. The debate ends with Undershaft's challenge to Cusins, "Dare you make war on war?" (III, 334), and Cusins is more central than Barbara in Act III as a whole. But Cusins is mentioned only once in the Preface, and then only as the "Euripidean republican" who is perfectly understood by Undershaft (p. 216). The Preface is prefatory mostly to Act II and hardly at all to Act III, for it is in Act III that the second article of Undershaft's faith is dealt with. The conflict in Act III is not about money, except in the indirect sense that Barbara is offered well-fed men to save (and note that although they are well-fed, they still need saving: money is a means, not an end). Undershaft talks about the choice that he made as a young man not to be poor, but no party to the debate is in fact poor; neither Barbara nor Cusins joins the cannon works in order to acquire money. The play would have been more consistent with the

Preface (and of course a much less interesting play) if Peter Shirley's decision to join the cannon works, rather than Cusins', had formed the basis of the final act. But as the play stands, the Preface provides a very misleading introduction to it.

II

Major Barbara is not so much about money as about power. It can best be seen as an exploration of the nature of power: the possession of control or command over others. The word itself occurs twenty-eight times in the last fourteen pages of the play, and all through the play examples are to be found of different kinds of power, of which money is only one. We have seen, for example, that the power of money is made manifest in the scene between Lady Britomart and Stephen. But so is Lady Britomart's power over Stephen: the power of an authoritarian, domineering mother over an uncertain, immature son. In the course of the play she loses her power over Stephen, who is the only person she has really dominated: clearly an authoritarian personality by itself is of little use. Undershaft, who is less authoritarian and domineering than his wife, has more power; and Cusins, who is far less authoritarian than either of them, has in a sense more significant power than anyone else in the play, as we shall see later.

The Bill Walker episode in Act II dramatizes various kinds of power. Bill's own kind of power is brute force, which is a crude and inadequate version of Undershaft's weapons. The parallel with Undershaft, in fact, extends further: both Bill Walker and Undershaft are trying to win a young woman back from the Salvation Army (and Undershaft has fallen in love with Barbara, "with a father's love," II, 286); both have determination and a touch of brutality; and both offer money to the Salvation Army. A stage direction at the end of Act II describes Bill as *"unashamed,"* which is Undershaft's motto. I think that one of the functions of the Bill Walker episode is to demonstrate these parallels between Bill Walker and Undershaft: parallels which suggest both Bill's potential strength and Undershaft's limitations.

Also related to the major strands of the play is Bill's near-conversion. It is brought about largely by Barbara, but not entirely by her. He is subdued as well by the threat of superior physical force in the person of Todger Fairmile, the wrestler; he speaks with *"undissembled misgiving"* when he learns that it is Todger Fairmile who has taken his girl-friend from him, and his belligerence disappears. As Bill says on the point of conversion, "Aw cawnt stend aht agen music awl wrastlers and awtful tangued women" (II, 293). This almost successful combination of Barbara's religious power and the brute force of Todger Fairmile prefigures the union of Barbara and Undershaft at the climax of the play.

Barbara's power over Bill is itself a mixture of various kinds. The first factor to subdue him has nothing to do with her personal qualities: he is much taken aback when Peter Shirley tells him that "the major here is the Earl o Stevenage's granddaughter" (II, 273); and his awe of the aristocracy is clearly one of the reasons why Barbara is able to deal with him while Jenny Hill is not. Another factor is Barbara's ladylike self-possession and calm superiority in handling Bill, as opposed to Jenny Hill's lack of self-control. That these qualities of Barbara's can be attributed to her aristocratic background is implied by what Lady Britomart says in Act I: "It is only in the middle classes, Stephen, that people get into a state of dumb helpless horror when they find that there are wicked people in the world. In our class, we have to decide what is to be done with wicked people; and nothing should disturb our self-possession" (p. 248). In this, as in her power to command her subordinates in the Salvation Army, Barbara is her mother's daughter.[4]

But the principal element in her near-success with Bill is what she has inherited from her father: her religious nature. She derives personal forcefulness and the ability to sway others from her feeling that she is working not for her own happiness but for a larger purpose. She feels herself to be an agent of the Life Force, which she calls God. Her religion, though, is not based (at any point in the play) on the two articles of her father's creed, money and gunpowder. Nor is it the traditional Christianity of the Salvation Army. As Cusins tells Undershaft, "Barbara is quite original in her religion" (II, 286). Barbara's religion, which is revealed mainly in her wooing of Bill Walker's soul, has to do with making men of people.

BARBARA [*softly: wooing his soul*] It's not me thats getting at you, Bill.

BILL. Oo else is it?

BARBARA. Somebody that doesnt intend you to smash women's faces, I suppose. Somebody or something that wants to make a man of you.

BILL [*blustering*] Mike a menn o me! Aint Aw a menn? eh? Oo sez Aw'm not a menn?

BARBARA. Theres a man in you somewhere, I suppose.

(II, 280)

In the same scene she urges Bill to "come with us . . . to brave manhood on earth and eternal glory in heaven" (II, 281). By the end of the play Barbara has decided to get "rid of the bribe of heaven" (III, 339), but it does not seem to have played a very significant role in her soul-saving while she was in the Salvation Army. Her desire is not so much to ensure Bill Walker's entry into heaven as to make him behave decently on earth. This is Shaw's own concept of religious conversion, expressed, for example, in Tanner's account of his acquisition of the "moral passion" in the first act of *Man and Superman,* and dramatized in *The Shewing-Up of Blanco Posnet* (1909). The really religious people, Shaw wrote to Janet Achurch in 1895, "have dignity, conviction, sobriety and force"; religion "substitutes a profound dignity and self-respect for the old materialistic self." [5]

Barbara's way of converting Bill Walker to manhood is to make him aware that he is not yet a man: to awaken a sense of sin in him. This is akin to what Shaw considered part of his own role as an artist. "It annoys me to see people comfortable when they ought to be uncomfortable," he says in the Epistle Dedicatory to *Man and Superman;* "and I insist on making them think in order to bring them to conviction of sin" (p. viii). According to Shaw's Lamarckian view of evolution, life can progress only if individuals desire to improve, and it is therefore vital that they be made aware of the need for self-improvement. The giraffe will not make the effort to acquire a longer neck until it feels that its present neck is too short.

This religion of Barbara's is directly contrary to what Shaw regards as a principal element in conventional Christianity: the belief that one can be saved without changing one's behavior—by atonement, forgiveness, punishment, or vicarious redemption. In the section of the Preface entitled "Weaknesses of the Salvation Army,"

Shaw writes that he does not think that "the inexorability of the deed once done should be disguised by any ritual, whether in the confessional or on the scaffold. And here my disagreement with the Salvation Army, and with all propagandists of the Cross (which I loathe as I loathe all gibbets) becomes deep indeed. Forgiveness, absolution, atonement, are figments: punishment is only a pretence of cancelling one crime by another; and you can no more have forgiveness without vindictiveness than you can have a cure without a disease. You will never get a high morality from people who conceive that their misdeeds are revocable and pardonable, or in a society where absolution and expiation are officially provided for us all" (p. 225). It is when Christian redemption is unavailable that the ruffian feels obliged to cease to be a ruffian. Then, as Shaw puts it in the Preface to *Androcles and the Lion*, "the drive of evolution, which we call conscience and honor, seizes on [our] slips, and shames us to the dust for being so low in the scale as to be capable of them." The awakened conscience of the thief "will not be easy until he has conquered his will to steal and changed himself into an honest man by developing that divine spark within him which Jesus insisted on as the everyday reality of what the atheist denies" (p. 92). It is this divine spark that Barbara refers to when she says to Bill Walker, "Theres a man in you somewhere, I suppose."

The precise position of the Salvation Army on this key question of redemption is not made plain in the play, and the Preface is self-contradictory. After the passage quoted above about Shaw's deepest disagreement with the Salvation Army, Shaw says that Bill "finds the Salvation Army as inexorable as fact itself. It will not punish him: it will not take his money. It will not tolerate a redeemed ruffian: it leaves him no means of salvation except ceasing to be a ruffian" (p. 225). This is the way in which *Barbara* treats him in the play, but the Salvation Army's policy is left unclear. One does notice, however, that Jenny Hill asks Barbara whether she might take some of the money which Bill offers "for the Army" (II, 293), and that Bill's conversion is frustrated—or at least postponed—when he sees that the Salvation Army accepts the money of Bodger and Undershaft, thus apparently offering them automatic salvation instead of demanding a real moral conversion. Shaw also remarks in the Preface that members of the Salvation Army "questioned the verisimilitude of the play, not because Mrs Baines took the money, but because Barbara refused it" (p. 219). The implication of both Preface and play is—although neither makes this entirely explicit—that Barbara's religion is, all through the play, different from that of the Salvation Army in that she alone uncompromisingly rejects the conventional Christian concept of salvation.

III

A reading of *Major Barbara* that based itself on the Preface might see Undershaft as one of the ideal heroes of Shaw's plays and as Shaw's spokesman in this play. For in the Preface he is presented as if he were the *raisonneur* of the play, who demonstrates the inadequacies of the points of view of the other characters, particularly of Barbara. The Preface implies that the play is about the justified triumph of Undershaft's gospel over that of Barbara and the Salvation Army. We have seen that Cusins, who is Undershaft's chief opponent in the climactic debate of the final act, is barely mentioned in the Preface.

In the play itself, of course, Undershaft is by no means an unattractive character. Part of his attractiveness lies in his power, and it is important to recognize just what is the nature of this power, and what its limitations are. His power is mainly of three different kinds. There is his will to survive, the power that enabled him to say as a young man, "Thou shalt starve ere I starve." There is the religious power which he shares with Barbara—the energy, vitality, and instinctive grip over others that come from the conviction that one is serving a just and irresistible purpose. Then there is the power of weapons, of which he is the manufacturer and symbol, and the power of money, of which he is the possessor. These qualities are, for the most part, what I called in discussing *Man and Superman* Philistine qualities. There are some elements of the Realist in Undershaft —his argumentative powers, his consciousness of his role, and his desire to change the world (although these last two, as we shall see, are equivocal)—but his leading characteristics are those of the Philistine, of Ann and Violet in *Man and Superman*. The principal differences between Undershaft and Ann and Violet are that he manifests these characteristics in the marketplace rather than the drawing room, and that he is more articulate than they. But while he is more articulate, what he articulates is a point of view very close to theirs. He believes, as Ann does, in the primacy of the acquisitive will. Much of his philosophy is an elaboration of Ann's remark to Octavius that "the only really simple thing is to go straight for what you want and grab it." Like Ann—and like Nietzsche's aristocrats—he is the beast of prey, stopping at nothing to get what he wants. His methods are more direct than those of Ann and Violet, as he is a man of business rather than a lady of leisure, but unscrupulous, predatory instincts dominate the behavior of all three. Buying the Salvation Army is to the marketplace as a chase across Europe or secrecy about one's marriage is to the drawing room.

Like Ann and Violet, Undershaft is able to get his own way: his overpowering of Cusins is directly comparable to Ann's overpowering of Tanner. In both cases there is the suggestion of some instinctive irresistible force. We have seen the way in which Ann overcomes Tanner, in spite of his desire to escape: she is an incarnation of the Life Force. In *Major Barbara* Undershaft overcomes Cusins not only with arguments but also with a comparable energy, which is called by Cusins Dionysiac (Dionysos being his name for the Life Force). Here is part of the scene between them at the Salvation Army shelter.

CUSINS. . . . Barbara is quite original in her religion.

UNDERSHAFT [*triumphantly*] Aha! Barbara Undershaft would be. Her inspiration comes from within herself.

CUSINS. How do you suppose it got there?

UNDERSHAFT [*in towering excitement*] It is the Undershaft inheritance. I shall hand on my torch to my daughter. She shall make my converts and preach my gospel—

CUSINS. What! Money and gunpowder!

UNDERSHAFT. Yes, money and gunpowder. Freedom and power. Command of life and command of death.

CUSINS [*urbanely: trying to bring him down to earth*] This is extremely interesting, Mr Undershaft. Of course you know that you are mad.

UNDERSHAFT [*with redoubled force*] And you?

CUSINS. Oh, mad as a hatter. You are welcome to my secret since I have discovered yours. But I am astonished. Can a madman make cannons?

UNDERSHAFT. Would anyone else than a madman make them?
And now [*with surging energy*] question for question. Can a sane
man translate Euripides?

CUSINS. No.

UNDERSHAFT [*seizing him by the shoulder*] Can a sane woman
make a man of a waster or a woman of a worm?

CUSINS [*reeling before the storm*] Father Colossus—
Mammoth Millionaire—

(II, 286–287)

Cusins, who is never entirely overcome by Undershaft, recovers; but
at the end of the act he prepares to march off with Undershaft, leaving Barbara behind, with the words "Dionysos Undershaft has de-
scended. I am possessed" (II, 299). J. I. M. Stewart objects to Cusins'
behavior here: "At the moment of Barbara's utmost despair he has
thrown himself so irresponsibly into an ironic Dionysiac masquer-
ade that we retain very little interest in him." [6] But Cusins is not a
fool; he *is* possessed by an irresistible power, as Pentheus is in *The
Bacchae*.[7] That this was Shaw's intention in these scenes is shown
not only in the text, but also in his instructions to Louis Calvert,
who created the role of Undershaft at the Court Theatre in 1905.
Undershaft's speech to Mrs. Baines near the end of the act about the
destructiveness of his weapons is, he says, "sort of a fantasia played
on the nerves of . . . [Cusins] and Barbara by Machiavelli-Mephi-
stopheles. All that is needed to produce the effect is steady concentration, magnetic intensity." [8] In another letter Shaw points out to
Calvert that once Undershaft decides that Cusins is the man he is
looking for, he "takes the lead in the conversation and dominates
Cusins at once. It all goes on in a steady progression of force." This
letter also tells Calvert how to play the last part of Act III: "And
now for the main point, on which the fate of the play depends. If
you once weaken or soften after 'Come, come, my daughter: don't
make too much of your little tinpot tragedy,' we are all lost. Undershaft must go over everybody like Niagara from that moment.
There must be no sparing of Barbara—no quarter for any one.
His energy must be proof against everybody and everything . . .
You must sweep everything before you until Lady B. knocks you off
your perch for a moment; and even then you come up buoyant the
next moment with your conundrum . . . Conviction and courage:

that is what he must be full of, and there is no room for anything smaller or prettier." [9] Shaw sees Undershaft less as a debater than as a man of magnetic intensity and overwhelming energy which captivates Cusins as Ann captivates Tanner.[10]

Like Ann and Violet, too, Undershaft represents the forces of the real world. Money is common to both plays as a symbol of the actual, physical, and immediate. The parallel in *Major Barbara* to sex, which Ann represents, is Undershaft's gunpowder. Just as sex is (along with money) the basic reality of the private, drawing room life which is the *milieu* of *Man and Superman,* so gunpowder (along with money) is the basic reality of the public, political life which is the *milieu* of *Major Barbara.* Undershaft may be a religious figure in that he possesses the Dionysiac energy I have been discussing, but this energy, like Ann's, is devoted to the immediate and the practical.

Undershaft, although he has a much stronger grasp of the world than Barbara or Cusins, is less highly evolved than either of them. His religious vision does not extend as far as Barbara's, and his political vision does not extend as far as Cusins'. In both cases, his vision does not extend to the spiritual; it does not go beyond money and gunpowder.

Like Barbara, he talks about saving souls, but what he means by this is not what Barbara means. Undershaft claims that he has saved the souls of his employees, as he has saved Barbara's soul, by giving his men adequate food, clothing, and shelter. He evidently feels that a man is saved if he has been saved from poverty. He cannot see the need for further evolution beyond material well-being, as Barbara can. Although he describes the lives of his employees with ironic detachment, he does not appear to be dissatisfied with the level of civilization that they have attained: "I dont say, mind you, that there is no ordering about and snubbing and even bullying. The men snub the boys and order them about; the carmen snub the sweepers; the artisans snub the unskilled laborers; the foremen drive and bully both the laborers and artisans; the assistant engineers find fault with the foremen; the chief engineers drop on the assistants; the departmental managers worry the chiefs; and the clerks have tall hats and hymnbooks and keep up the social tone by refusing to associate on equal terms with anybody. The result is a colossal profit, which comes to me" (III, 315). This society is very far from Shaw's ideal. In his essay "The Impossibilities of Anarchism" (1891), for example, he says that in our present, capitalist society snobbery flourishes at all levels except among the very poor. "The moment you rise into the higher atmosphere of a pound a week [wages at the Undershaft foundry begin at thirty shillings], you find that envy, ostentation, tedious and insincere ceremony, love of petty titles, precedences and dignities, and all the detestable fruits of inequality of condition, flourish as rankly among those who lose as among those who gain by it." [11] Undershaft is evidently not disturbed by the "detestable fruits of inequality of condition"; because his employees are not poor, he feels that they are saved.

Barbara's view—and Shaw's view—is that Undershaft has provided not salvation, but the necessary precondition of salvation. Barbara will build on the foundations which her father has provided, and try to convert the men to something beyond Philistine, bourgeois, snobbish individualism. What attracts Barbara to the cannon works are "all the human souls to be saved: not weak souls in starved bodies, sobbing with gratitude for a scrap of bread and treacle, but fullfed, quarrelsome, snobbish, uppish creatures, all standing on their little rights and dignities, and thinking that my father ought to be greatly obliged to them for making so much money for him—and so he ought. That is where salvation is really wanted" (III, 339). An early draft of this speech makes Barbara's concept of her new role more explicit: "I want to begin where hunger and cold and misery leave off. Anybody can convert a starving man: I want to convert prosperous ones. And I will. These souls here shall have the sulkiness and the quarrelling and the uppishness taken out of them by Major Barbara. She will teach them to live with one another, I promise you." [12] What satisfies Undershaft clearly does not satisfy Barbara. In fact, she implies not only in Act I but also near the end of the play, after she has heard his gospel, that he himself is in need of salvation. When Lady Britomart orders her children to come home with her because Undershaft is "wickeder than ever," Barbara replies, "It's no use running away from wicked people, mamma . . . It does not save them" (III, 332). Undershaft apparently does not feel in need of salvation; he seems to feel no need to develop beyond his Nietzschean individualism, with its self-seeking and its contempt for the common people ("the common mob of slaves and idolaters"—see II, 287). Precisely what Barbara would want Undershaft and his employees to become is not stated explicitly in the play—Shaw, as usual, is concerned more with direction than with goal—but what the play does make clear is that Undershaft's concept of salvation represents only a step on the way to salvation.

His political vision, which is closely related to his religious views, is similarly limited. His society of "saved" men, as we have seen, is a society of individualists: men who have no concept of the community as an organic whole with common goals. His own political philosophy is one of extreme individualism. He is proud of the fact that he never gives his employees orders, that the community at Perivale St. Andrews is self-regulating, without any need for external compulsion (see III, 315). His remedy for poverty is for individual poor men to decide to cease to be poor—to act on their own, as he has done, in demanding money from society. If every man behaved as I did, he claims (and Shaw argues in the Preface), then poverty would disappear: "*I* was an east ender. I moralized and starved until one day I swore that I would be a full-fed free man at all costs; that nothing should stop me except a bullet, neither reason nor morals nor the lives of other men. I said 'Thou shalt starve ere I starve'; and with that word I became free and great. I was a dangerous man until I had my will: now I am a useful, beneficent, kindly person. That is the history of most self-made millionaires, I fancy. When it is the history of every Englishman we shall have an England worth living in" (III, 330). It may be true that a nation of Andrew Undershafts would be superior to a nation of Peter Shirleys, but is there much point in urging every man to act as Undershaft has acted? Undershaft is a rare type: he has the enormous force of will to determine not to be poor. In *The Intelligent Woman's Guide to Socialism,* Shaw writes that "in great social questions we are dealing with the abilities of ordinary citizens: that is, the abilities we can depend on everyone except invalids and idiots possessing, and not with what one man or woman in ten thousand can do" (p. 172). And in *Major Barbara* Undershaft himself propounds an environmentalist view of society: economic factors determine human conduct. Poverty is in all ways debilitating; it "strikes dead the very souls of all who come within sight, sound, or smell of it" (III, 329). Undershaft's individualist argument that the solution to the problem of poverty is for the poor to determine, as he has done, not to be poor, is confuted by his own statements on the effects of poverty, which are illustrated in the scene in the Salvation Army shelter. It is also confuted by his own practice: he does not preach to the poor to act as he has done, but gives them jobs with adequate pay. The only person within the play who ceases to be poor is Peter Shirley, and this is not because he has declared "Thou shalt starve ere I starve," but because Undershaft's foundry has employed him. And the foundry can employ only a small proportion of the nation's working class: it is not a real solution to the problem of poverty. The play shows both the best and the worst effects of capitalism, and clearly implies that the blighted lives of the unfortunates at the Salvation Army shelter are more representative than those of the comfortable residents of Undershaft's garden city.

Undershaft, then, has achieved neither the religious nor the political goals of the play. He has not saved souls, in Barbara's and Shaw's sense, and he has not abolished poverty. Nor has he put an end to war. The Armorer's Faith—"to give arms to all men who offer an honest price for them, without respect of persons or principles" (III, 326)—has caused him to provide only the means for the waging of war, not the means for its abolition. His weapons serve no higher purpose of his own, but the lower purposes of "the most rascally part of society," as Cusins points out (III, 327). Undershaft seems to be quite unaware of these limitations, and yet he is drawn to Barbara and Cusins, who may be able to accomplish what he has not accomplished. His attitude toward them is contradictory: some of his speeches suggest that he sees them as followers, who will carry on his work for him. But in other speeches he challenges them to do work which is profoundly different from his own, and which would entail the overthrow of himself, his foundry, his class, and his gospel.

He tells Cusins in Act II that Barbara will be his follower, that she will give up her religion for his:

UNDERSHAFT . . . I shall hand on my torch to my daughter. She shall make my converts and preach my gospel—

CUSINS. What! Money and gunpowder!
UNDERSHAFT. Yes, money and gunpowder. Freedom and power.
Command of life and command of death.

(p. 287)

In Act III he continues to talk as if Barbara must give up her religion and practice his. He says, as we have seen, that he has saved
the souls of his men; if this is the case, then there is no place for
Barbara's religion at the cannon works. But on the following page he
issues his challenge to Barbara: not to give up her religion for his,
but to preach her own gospel to his employees. "Try your hand on
my men," he says; "their souls are hungry because their bodies are
full" (III, 330). The change now is to be not from one religion to
another but from the hungry to the well-fed, in line with Shaw's
view that material well-being must precede spiritual improvement.[13]
Yet Undershaft is contemptuous of Barbara's concept of salvation:

CUSINS. I . . . want to avoid being a rascal.
UNDERSHAFT [*with biting contempt*] You lust for personal
righteousness, for self-approval, for what you call a good conscience, for what Barbara calls salvation, for what I call patronizing
people who are not so lucky as yourself.

(III, 333)

Undershaft, then, invites Barbara to convert his men to a religion
that he appears to reject, a religion that could supplant his own.

His challenge to Cusins contains a similar contradiction. It is not
clear whether he intends him to carry on precisely as he himself has
done, or to bring about a new era at the cannon works. The particular question is whether Cusins will remain true to the Armorer's
Faith: whether he will sell weapons to anyone who can pay for
them, or whether he will provide them only to those who will use
them for the benefit of mankind. Undershaft insists that Cusins
"must keep the true faith of an Armorer, or you dont come in here"
(III, 326). But then on the next page he says to him: "If you good
people prefer preaching and shirking to buying my weapons and
fighting the rascals, dont blame me" (III, 327). That Undershaft is
inviting Cusins to gain control of the weapons in order to fight the
rascals is clear from his final challenge to him, "Dare you make war

on war? Here are the means" (III, 334). Now, one cannot both sell weapons only to those who can pay for them and at the same time make war on war. If you are loyal to the Armorer's Faith, then you continue to sell arms to the ruling classes—that is, to those who now have them anyway—and society does not change significantly.

These contradictions can be partly accounted for by the fact that Undershaft, a master of irony, is unscrupulously and cleverly appealing to Barbara and Cusins on their own terms. "It is through religion alone that we can win Barbara," [14] he tells Cusins in the scene in Act II in which he declares that she will preach his gospel of money and gunpowder (p. 286). Similarly, it is only through high-minded political goals that he can win Cusins. And so he invites Barbara to save the souls of his men and challenges Cusins to make war on war, confident that once they have joined the foundry they will succumb to the spirit of the place and continue as he has done.

But the contradictions are not entirely explained in this way. For they are connected not only with Undershaft's conscious irony, but with contradictions within his own mind of which he is not conscious. His hatred of poverty is genuine. "I hate poverty and slavery worse than any other crimes whatsoever," he says. "And let me tell you this. Poverty and slavery have stood up for centuries to your sermons and leading articles: they will not stand up to my machine guns. Dont preach at them: dont reason with them. Kill them" (III, 331). This is not ironic but impassioned; Undershaft sounds here like a serious revolutionary, and soon after this he is saying to Cusins, "Come and make explosives with me. Whatever can blow men up can blow society up" (III, 331).

Undershaft considers himself bound by the Armorer's Faith, as he considers himself bound by the firm's Antonine tradition of inheritance. He and his six predecessors have all been true to the Armorer's Faith, with the result that poverty and slavery have stood up not only to the sermons and leading articles written by people like Barbara and Cusins but to the seven generations of Andrew Undershafts. What is needed now—and Undershaft seems unconsciously to recognize this—is a new Andrew Undershaft who will reject the Armorer's Faith and sell arms only to those who will use them to fight against war, poverty, and slavery. The play implies that at some level he knows that he himself is inadequate for the task of creating a better society: that powers very different from his own are required as well. In Act II, in his first Dionysiac conversation with Cusins, he proposes an alliance between himself, Cusins, and Barbara: "I am a millionaire; you are a poet; Barbara is a savior of souls. What have we three to do with the common mob of slaves and idolaters? . . . We three must stand together above the common people: how else can we help their children to climb up beside us?" (pp. 287–288). The implication here, whether Undershaft consciously intends it or not, is that the three of them together might be able to do what he alone cannot do. And there are other hints in the play that Undershaft has some sense of his limitations. He tells Lady Britomart that the cannon works "does not belong to me. I belong to it" (III, 321); and he admits to Cusins that he has no power of his own (III, 327). Even more significant is his challenge to Barbara and Cusins, which follows Cusins' statement that Undershaft has no power: "If you good people prefer preaching and shirking to buying my weapons and fighting the rascals, dont blame me. I can make cannons: I cannot make courage and conviction" (III, 327). In this speech he is saying in effect that he must rely on "good people" like Barbara and Cusins to reform society, that he cannot do it alone.

Undershaft shows an awareness of the value of dialectical conflict in his desire for strong opponents. He tells Barbara near the end of the play that he loves only his "bravest enemy. That is the man who keeps me up to the mark" (III, 334).[15] When Mrs. Baines mentions that in 1886 the poor broke the windows of clubs in Pall Mall, Undershaft replies, *"gleaming with approval of their method,"* that this forced the rich to contribute to the relief of poverty (II, 294).

He also tells Mrs. Baines that he is giving money to the Salvation Army "to help you to hasten my own commercial ruin." "It is your work to preach peace on earth and goodwill to men . . . Every convert you make is a vote against war" (II, 298). He is, of course, being ironic; his purpose in giving the money is to win Barbara from the Salvation Army. But there is a double irony here. By bringing Barbara and Cusins into his cannon works, he *is* hastening his ruin, in that he is handing over the works to people whose val-

ues are profoundly different from those on which the foundry rests.
And this is what, at his deepest level, he may wish to do.

Undershaft's position is like that of Wotan in Wagner's *Ring of
the Nibelung.* Wotan, bound by his treaty with Fafnir, is unable to
accomplish his own goal, the retrieval of the ring from him, just as
Undershaft, bound by the Armorer's Faith, is unable to fight poverty. Wotan's desire for a hero who will not be bound by the god's
treaty and will be able to carry out the deed which he himself cannot is comparable to Undershaft's desire for Cusins [16] to succeed him
at the foundry. The relevance of this parallel between Wotan and
Undershaft is made clear by the way in which Shaw discusses *The
Ring* in *The Perfect Wagnerite.* Before he begins his analysis of
The Valkyre he tells his readers that "above all, we must
understand—for it is the key to much that we are to see—that
the god, since his desire is toward a higher and fuller life, must long
in his inmost soul for the advent of that greater power whose first
work, though this he does not see as yet, must be his own undoing"
(p. 190). Wotan, Shaw says earlier, looks for a higher race which
will "deliver the world and himself from his limited powers and disgraceful bargains." "On every side he is shackled and bound, dependent on the laws of Fricka [17] and on the lies of Loki, forced to traffic
with dwarfs [the instinctive, predatory, lustful, greedy people] for
handicraft and with giants [the patient, toiling, stupid, respectful,
money-worshipping people] for strength" (p. 184).[18] This reminds
one of Cusins' statement, which Undershaft does not really deny,
that Undershaft is driven by the cannon works, which in turn is
driven "by the most rascally part of society, the money hunters, the
pleasure hunters, the military promotion hunters" (III, 327). Undershaft's reply, which is the invitation to Cusins and Barbara to use
his weapons to "fight the rascals," is comparable to Wotan's hope
that a hero will defy those who limit his power.

IV

In selecting Cusins as his successor, Undershaft is in a sense putting into practice his view that his best friend is his bravest enemy;
he chooses his opposite—his anti-self.[19] Cusins is humane, hates
war, loves the common people, refuses to accept the Armorer's Faith,
and—contrary to the Undershaft tradition—is middle class, of

respectable background, and highly educated. According to Shaw, Undershaft decides on Cusins' merit in Act II, just before the first Dionysiac scene. Shaw wrote to Calvert, "The change comes from the line 'And now to business.' Up to that, Undershaft has been studying Cusins and letting him talk. But the shake-hands means that he has made up his mind that Cusins is the man to understand him; and he therefore takes the lead in the conversation and dominates Cusins at once." [20] What has presumably impressed Undershaft is not that Cusins has agreed with any of his views (which he hasn't) but that Cusins has declared, in reply to Undershaft's implied objections to him as a suitor for Barbara, that nothing will stop him from marrying her. And just before the handshake, Cusins responds to Undershaft's "You are a young man after my own heart" with "Mr Undershaft: you are, as far as I am able to gather, a most infernal old rascal" (II, 286). This is the way in which Cusins refers to Undershaft for the rest of the play, and while he is incapable of defending his own point of view against Undershaft's energy and arguments, he insists until the end of the play that he loathes Undershaft's principles. In reply to G. K. Chesterton's statement (in his book on Shaw) that Cusins puts up an "incredibly weak fight" against Undershaft's arguments, Shaw wrote, "As to the professor making no fight, he stands up to Undershaft all through so subtly and effectually that Undershaft takes him into partnership at the end of the play." [21]

The most important difference between Cusins and Undershaft is the difference between the kind of power that each possesses and represents. Undershaft's power, as we have seen, is in the main akin to that of Ann and Violet in *Man and Superman*. Cusins' power is like that of Tanner [22] and Don Juan: the power of imagination and intellect. Shaw's usual view of professors of Greek was not very favorable, but Cusins is based on Gilbert Murray, a close friend whom Shaw admired and respected. He says in the play's prefatory note on Murray that his "English version of The Bacchae came into our dramatic literature with all the impulsive power of an original work" (p. 202), and in *Major Barbara* itself Cusins is presented as a poet, an artist, a thinker (which the true Shavian artist always is). Like all of Shaw's Realists, he has a desire to improve the world around him. As a teacher of Greek he has tried to do this in Tanner's way, through thought, through spirit. He says in the play that his purpose in teaching Greek was to "make spiritual power" (III, 336), and this is amplified in an earlier draft, with the addition to Cusins' speech of the statement that "I am no mere grammarian: if I had not believed that our highest faculties would kindle and aspire at the touch of Greek poetry and Greek thought, I should never have wasted an hour in a class room." [23] In the final version of the play Shaw let the audience infer Cusins' sense of high purpose as a teacher of Greek from the sentence about "spiritual power" and from Cusins' character as a whole.

Cusins' interest is not confined to the university classroom. He tells Undershaft in Act II that his attachment to the Salvation Army is genuine, in the sense that the Salvation Army inspires people with joy, love, and courage: "It picks the waster out of the public house and makes a man of him: it finds a worm wriggling in a back kitchen, and lo! a woman!" (p. 284). And he objects to Undershaft's contemptuous dismissal of "the common mob of slaves and idolaters." "Take care!" he replies. "Barbara is in love with the common people. So am I" (II, 287). This love of the common people is a characteristic which Cusins shares with his original. Gilbert Murray wrote of himself that as Professor of Greek at Glasgow he tried to combine "an enthusiasm for poetry and Greek scholarship with an almost equal enthusiasm for radical politics and social reform." But he found that the two causes did not always go well together. "Throughout history it has been hard to combine the principles of culture and of democracy, the claims of the few who maintain and raise the highest moral and intellectual standards with those of the masses who rightly do not want to be oppressed." [24] Whereas Gilbert Murray felt that he was able to reconcile these two principles, Cusins is forced to choose one or the other. He chooses the claims of "the masses who rightly do not want to be oppressed"; he decides that it is better to give weapons to the many than civilization to the few. It is not that civilization is necessarily useless, but that it can affect only a minority, while the mass of society is left in the condition of the unfortunates in the Salvation Army shelter. "The world can never be really touched by a dead language and a dead civilization. The people must have power; and the people cannot have Greek." The only kind of power that can be of use to the majority is not the higher power of the spirit but the primitive, physical power of gunpowder.[25] "As a teacher of Greek I gave the intellectual man weapons against the common man. I now want to give the common man weapons against the intellectual man. I love the common people. I want to arm them against the lawyers, the doctors, the priests, the literary men, the professors, the artists, and the politicians, who, once in authority, are more disastrous and tyrannical than all the fools, rascals, and impostors.[26] I want a power simple enough for common men to use, yet strong enough to force the intellectual oligarchy to use its genius for the general good" (III, 336–337).

In the language of *The Quintessence of Ibsenism,* Cusins, the Realist, wants to provide the common people with Philistine power to use against the Idealists—an idea which is prefigured in Shaw's Preface (1900) to *Three Plays for Puritans.* If "the democratic attitude becomes thoroughly Romanticist," he predicts there, "the country will become unbearable for all realists, Philistine or Platonic. When it comes to that, the brute force of the strong-minded Bismarckian man of action, impatient of humbug, will combine with the subtlety and spiritual energy of the man of thought whom shams cannot illude or interest. That combination will be on one side; and Romanticism will be on the other" (p. xx). The implication in Cusins' speech is that the really dangerous people are not those with no ideas—the money hunters, the pleasure hunters, the military promotion hunters—but those with the wrong ideas. Cusins' speech presents the same pattern that we found in *Man and Superman:* the Realist will use aimless Philistine power for a higher purpose, and the real enemy of progress is the Idealist. Cusins will use gunpowder as Tanner will use sex, although Tanner's role is more passive, and he is largely unconscious of it.

In *Man and Superman* the dangers of Idealism are made to seem much greater in the discussion in the Hell Scene than they are in the presentation of life in the Comedy. Similarly, Cusins' discussion here of the misuse of spiritual power has little basis in the rest of the play. The only significant Idealists in the play are Stephen and Lady Britomart, and neither of them seems to represent much of a threat to society. Stephen, as the aspiring politician, comes closest to Cusins' speech, but Undershaft's statement in the first part of Act III that *"I am the government of your country"* (p. 312), which is confirmed in the second part of the act when the political man is the only member of the visiting party who praises the cannon works unreservedly, would seem to dispose of the political Idealist as an important factor. What one gathers from the play as a whole is that there is no effective "government of your country," that control is in the hands of those who have no social goals: that society is not guided by any purpose, good or bad, but by the primitive acquisitive instincts of those in whom these instincts are strongest. Both *Man and Superman* and *Major Barbara* tell us about the danger of Idealist illusions but make us feel that Philistine power is much more significant. It is not until *Saint Joan* that Shaw's intellectual fear of Idealism becomes something deeply enough felt to be given dramatic expression in characters like the Inquisitor, Cauchon, and de Stogumber. Cusins' speech, in fact, applies much more directly to *Saint Joan* than to *Major Barbara.* It would seem more to the point to arm the common people against the Inquisitor than against Stephen Undershaft.

In spite of this element of contradiction, Cusins' aims are basically clear enough. He will try to create a society which is run for the benefit of the majority by providing the common people with weapons so that they can insist on such a society. Only the threat of revolution, the play implies, will cause the ruling classes to do something about the state of society. In determining to arm the common people, Cusins is determining to reject the Armorer's Faith: he will provide weapons for that part of the community which without his intervention would never acquire them. When Undershaft first tells him of the Armorer's Faith, which (says Undershaft) he must keep if he is to succeed to the cannon works, he unhesitatingly rejects it: "As to your Armorer's faith, if I take my neck out of the noose of my own morality I am not going to put it into the noose of yours. I shall sell cannons to whom I please and refuse them to whom I please. So there!" Undershaft's reply is that "from the moment when you become Andrew Undershaft, you will never do as you please again" (III, 326–327). So one is left, as one is in so many of Shaw's plays, with a conflict which will continue after the play ends; Cusins intending to depart from the Armorer's Faith, and struggling against Undershaft, "the place," and presumably the "rascals" for whom the weapons are now produced. Whether or not he succeeds fully, a vital step has been taken: the man of intellect has united with the physical power of the Philistine world.

As in *Man and Superman,* this is in one sense a defeat for the man of intellect and in another sense a victory. It is a defeat in that the intellectual life is given up for the Philistine life: the teaching of Greek for the manufacture of cannons—as in *Man and Superman* the philosopher's activities are given up for those of the father and husband. But as Tanner's submission to Ann may also be seen as a step toward the control of Ann's kind of power by Tanner, so in *Major Barbara* Cusins submits to the foundry so that he can control it. Despite his agreement with Barbara's comment that he will have no power when he enters the foundry (III, 336), his next speeches, about arming the common people, indicate that he plans to exercise a power which Undershaft has never had: the power of directing the weapons which are made at the foundry. He will put the power of thought to practical use, and his power, like Tanner's, will increase rather than diminish when it combines with that of the Philistine world.

Neither Cusins' kind of power nor Undershaft's is of much use when it exists alone. Undershaft's view that spiritual power without cannons is impotent ("If you good people prefer preaching and shirking to buying my weapons and fighting the rascals, dont blame me") is balanced by Cusins' view that cannons without spiritual power are impotent. His remark to Undershaft that *"You* have no power" (III, 327) equates the maker of cannons with the cannons themselves; the Armorer's Faith reduces Undershaft to an instrument. "I have more power than you, more will" (III, 327), Cusins claims; that is, at least I have the power of mind which designs, seeks conscious goals, and is not a blind force with no purpose of its own. The mild-mannered professor of Greek has more significant power than the tough millionaire cannon manufacturer. This is the same kind of paradox that one finds in *Candida,* in which Marchbanks turns out to be stronger, more manly, and more religious than Morell. Shaw wrote to Gilbert Murray while he was writing Act III, "I have taken rather special care to make Cusins the reverse in every point of the theatrical strong man. I want him to go on his quality wholly, and not to make the smallest show of physical robustness or brute determination. His selection by Undershaft should be a puzzle to people who believe in the strong-silent-still-waters-run-deep hero of melodrama. The very name Adolphus Cusins is selected to that end." [27]

But although Cusins' kind of power may be more meaningful than Undershaft's, Cusins has done no more than Undershaft to improve society. Each of them has benefited only a relatively small number of people: Cusins his students, Undershaft his employees. And the improvement they have caused in these people has been only partial: Cusins has improved only men's minds, while Undershaft has improved only men's bodies. Cusins and Undershaft, when acting separately, have achieved little of real significance. Only when the spiritual and the material join together can society be improved. "Society cannot be saved until either the Professors of Greek take to making gunpowder, or else the makers of gunpowder become Professors of Greek" (III, 334).

Even this combination of Cusins and Undershaft is not sufficient, however. Cusins, in taking over the foundry, will try to provide "the people" with weapons and hence money, but this could only bring the population up to the level of the employees at the foundry. He would be using his spiritual power in giving the weapons a purpose, a direction, but in order to do this he is giving up the making of spiritual power. In order for men to be saved as well as fed, Barbara's power is required.

Barbara, like Cusins and Undershaft, has been almost—but not quite—ineffectual when working by herself. She does have an effect on Bill Walker, and the play implies that although her attempt to save his soul is frustrated by Undershaft, she has brought about a real change in him. When Barbara tells Bill that she will replace his pound, he replies, in a suddenly improved voice and accent, that he will not be bought by her (II, 301). And when in the next act she reproaches Undershaft for taking Bill Walker's soul from her, he convinces her that Bill's soul is not entirely lost:

UNDERSHAFT. Does my daughter despair so easily? Can you strike a man to the heart and leave no mark on him?
BARBARA [*her face lighting up*] Oh, you are right: he can never be lost now: where was my faith?

(III, 316)

Bill Walker, however, is quite unlike the others whom Barbara is trying to save at the Salvation Army shelter. He has come to the shelter not to beg bread but to demand his girl-friend. He is not noticeably hungry or poor; and he has been able to save two pounds "agen the frost" (II, 292). In fact, he is not very different from Undershaft's "fullfed, quarrelsome, snobbish, uppish" employees, and it is therefore most significant that Barbara converts him, while she has no effect whatever on the others at the shelter, who have come only to satisfy their bodily hunger.[28]

Neither Barbara nor Cusins, then, can have much effect on society while relying exclusively on spiritual power. They (and all those higher beings who want to improve society, of whom Barbara and Cusins are symbolic) must ally themselves with Undershaft, and the forces that he represents. And Undershaft cannot have much effect on society while he relies exclusively on physical power; he needs Barbara and Cusins as much as they need him. What is required is a marriage of intellectual power, religious power, and physical power. This is the real meaning of the alliance which Undershaft proposes in Act II, although no single character in the play is fully aware of the implications of the synthesis. It is left (as usual in Shaw's plays) for the audience to draw the threads together.

Nothing less than a fusion of all three will achieve the implicit goal of the play: a nation of what Barbara would call the saved—a nation of fully developed men and women. Cusins and Barbara without Undershaft would achieve no significant results: political advance is impossible without weapons and religious advance is impossible without money. Cusins and Undershaft without Barbara would achieve, as we have seen, only a nation of Philistines—an extension of the society at the foundry. Barbara and Undershaft without Cusins would achieve only a minority of the saved. Barbara recognizes this: when Undershaft challenges her to convert his employees, her (unanswered) reply is, "And leave the east end to starve?" (III, 330).

The aspect of this union which the play concentrates on is the decision of the two characters with spiritual power to unite with Undershaft: his need for the two of them is only implied, as Ann's dependence on Tanner is indicated only in the Hell Scene of *Man and Superman*. The counterpart in *Major Barbara* of the Hell Scene is the crucial scene between Barbara and Cusins near the end of the play, for it is here that the importance of the more highly developed person is made apparent. Barbara and Cusins seem at the beginning of this scene to have been utterly defeated by Undershaft; but now both of them declare triumphantly that they have found their new purpose, and their speeches in this scene should make it plain that the victory in *Major Barbara* is not Undershaft's alone, just as the Hell Scene should make it plain that the victory in *Man and Superman* is not Ann's alone. Neither Barbara nor Cusins is really converted to Undershaft's gospel of money and gunpowder. They retain their own goals, but see that money and gunpowder are necessary if these goals are to be attained. They see that the higher can be achieved only through the lower. This is an idea which is found in many forms in *Major Barbara.* "Then the way of life lies through the factory of death?" Cusins asks after Barbara has discovered her new role at the end of the play; and Barbara replies, "Yes, through the raising of hell to heaven and of man to God, through the unveiling of an eternal light in the Valley of The Shadow" (III, 339). Similarly, the way of the spirit lies through the flesh (Barbara will convert the well-fed) and the way of peace lies through the sword (Cusins will "make war on war," using weapons to create a world in which war would presumably disappear). The idea is also made explicit in Cusins' defense to Barbara of Undershaft's weapons.

BARBARA. Is there no higher power than that [*pointing to the shell*]?
CUSINS. Yes; but that power can destroy the higher powers just as a tiger can destroy a man: therefore Man must master that power first.

(III, 337)

This is parallel to Barbara's realization that although there is a higher power than money, men must have money first.

Cusins' analogy between Undershaft's weapons and the tiger calls to mind Blake's treatment of wild, destructive power in the *Songs of Experience.* The imagery of Blake's "The Tyger" is that of the foundry, with particular emphasis on fire ("My sort of fire purifies," says Undershaft in Act I, p. 260). And Blake's poem evokes the combination of terror and attraction that Shaw intends Undershaft and his weapons to produce in Cusins and in the audience—although Blake can create a much greater sense of terror than Shaw. If we assume that Blake's tyger represents the power necessary to overthrow the fallen world of Experience, then the parallel between the poem and the play becomes closer still. Maurice Bowra, who interprets the poem in this way, says that Blake

sought some ultimate synthesis in which innocence might be wedded to experience, and goodness to knowledge . . . The true innocence is not after all that of the *Songs of Innocence,* but something which has gained knowledge from the ugly lessons of experience and found an expanding strength in the unfettered life of the creative soul . . .

Blake knows well that such a consummation will not come simply from good will or pious aspirations and that the life of the imagination is possible only through passion and power and energy. That is why he sometimes stresses the great forces which lie hidden in man and may be terrifying but are none the less necessary if anything worth while is to happen . . . The tiger is Blake's symbol for the fierce forces in the soul which are needed to break the bonds of experience.[29]

Almost everything which Bowra says here about Blake applies precisely to *Major Barbara.* The tiger, like Undershaft, symbolizes a force from which "good men" recoil, but without which progress is impossible.

This same emphasis on the necessity of the terrifying is found in *The Marriage of Heaven and Hell.* That "the tygers of wrath are wiser than the horses of instruction" (Plate 9) is exactly what Cusins discovers in *Major Barbara. The Marriage of Heaven and Hell* asserts, like *Major Barbara,* that both forces are necessary: heavenly controlling power and hellish violent, destructive power must exist together. And in both works the heavenly is the conventionally good, while the hellish is the conventionally evil.[30] *The Marriage of Heaven and Hell* tries to break down and confuse rigid distinctions between heaven and hell, good and evil, soul and body. It is not true, says the voice of the Devil, that "Energy, call'd Evil, is alone from the Body; & that Reason, call'd Good, is alone from the Soul." The truth is that "Energy is the only life, and is from the Body; and

Reason is the bound or outward circumference of Energy" (Plate 4). Barbara makes a similar discovery: "Turning our backs on Bodger and Undershaft is turning our backs on life . . . There is no wicked side [of life] : life is all one" (III, 338).

Blake's technique of ironic reversal of heaven and hell is an important element in *Major Barbara*. Undershaft is the representative of hell: Cusins calls him the Prince of Darkness, a devil, Mephistopheles, a demon, an infernal old rascal; and says that at the Salvation Army meeting the "brazen roarings" of his trombone "were like the laughter of the damned" (III, 305). He calls the foundry "this Works Department of Hell," and Barbara says before the visit that she has "always thought of it as a sort of pit where lost creatures with blackened faces stirred up smoky fires and were driven and tormented by my father" (III, 314). The foundry, which is the center of hellish activity in the play, turns out to be heavenly ("It only needs a cathedral to be a heavenly city instead of a hellish one," Cusins observes, III, 318); while the center of heavenly activity, the Salvation Army shelter, is truly hellish. Undershaft's hell —his diabolical assertive values, his money, and his gunpowder —is the true road to heaven.[31] "You may be a devil; but God speaks through you sometimes," Barbara says after her father has dispelled her despondency about Bill Walker's soul (III, 316). This parallels Cusins' exclamation near the end of the play that "the way of life lies through the factory of death."

Blake, it is true, values hellish energy more than Shaw does, but both of them present hell as a state just as necessary as heaven in our imperfect world. The unpleasant or frightening cannot be dismissed as evil; Stephen and Lady Britomart are the equivalent of Blake's "Bibles or sacred codes" (Plate 4)—the representatives of conventional absolute morality, whose position is demolished in both works. The moral of the final act of *Major Barbara*, Shaw wrote to Gilbert Murray, "is drawn by Lomax 'There is a certain amount of tosh about this notion of wickedness.' "[32] Morality in both *Major Barbara* and *The Marriage of Heaven and Hell* is relative to the situation and to the individual: "There is only one true morality for every man; but every man has not the same true morality" (Undershaft in *Major Barbara*, I, 262); "One Law for the Lion & Ox is Oppression" (*The Marriage of Heaven and Hell*, Plates

22–24).[33] *Major Barbara* asserts the necessity of accepting and combining good and evil, heaven and hell; and the best brief statement of its central idea is the aphorism from *The Marriage of Heaven and Hell:* "Without Contraries is no progression. Attraction and Repulsion, Reason and Energy, Love and Hate, are necessary to Human existence" (Plate 3).

IV

John Bull's Other Island

Most of Shaw's characters are representative of a temperament, a profession, a social type, or a nationality, but *John Bull's Other Island* (1904) is the first of his plays in which characters are overtly symbolic. It is followed in this respect by *Getting Married* (1908), *Misalliance* (1909–10) and—above all—*Heartbreak House* (1916–17). *John Bull's Other Island* was written, at Yeats's request, "as a patriotic contribution to the repertory of the Irish Literary Theatre" (Preface, p. 13), and it is about the Irish national temperament in contrast with the English. The Irish characters in the play represent various aspects of the Irish temperament, and Broadbent is Shaw's symbolic Englishman. Shaw said in defense of the play at the time of its first production, "Just consider my subject—the destiny of nations! Consider my characters—personages who stalk on the stage incarnating millions of real, living, suffering men and women. Good heavens! I have had to get all England and Ireland into three hours and a quarter. I have shown the Englishman to the Irishman and the Irishman to the Englishman, the Protestant to the Catholic and the Catholic to the Protestant." [1]

Much of what *John Bull's Other Island* has to say about English and Irish temperaments is implicit in the passage from the Epistle Dedicatory to *Man and Superman* in which Shaw is talking about the success of the prosaic man: "From the day I first set foot on this foreign soil I knew the value of the prosaic qualities of which Irishmen teach Englishmen to be ashamed as well as I knew the vanity of the poetic qualities of which Englishmen teach Irishmen to be proud. For the Irishman instinctively disparages the quality which makes the Englishman dangerous to him; and the Englishman instinctively flatters the fault that makes the Irishman harmless and amusing to him" (p. xvi). This is in essence Doyle's point of view in *John Bull's Other Island,* and its precise relevance to the play can be seen if one applies it, for example, to the relationship between Broadbent and Keegan in Act IV. The play is intended as a corrective to English illusions about the Irish and Irish illusions about the English, so that each nation will see its own faults and the other's virtues.

The difference between Irish and English, for Shaw, is chiefly the difference between intelligence and stupidity, brain and body. "I am a typical Irishman," he wrote in 1902, "that is to say, a person with all the objectionable positive qualities of an Englishman, but with a certain nimbleness of mind, vividness of intellectual consciousness, and unbeglamored common sense produced partly by the climate of Ireland and partly by the eighteenth century environment which still exists in that country." [2] This is fundamentally the view of the Irish in *John Bull's Other Island.* "We Irishmen were never made to be farmers," Doyle says in Act III. "We're like the Jews: the Almighty gave us brains, and bid us farm *them,* and leave the clay and the worms alone" (p. 129). Doyle, like Shaw, is keenly aware of the danger of mental activity: that it can make people ineffectual, unable to cope with real life. This is the basis of his contempt for the Irish: "Oh, the dreaming! the dreaming! the torturing, heart-scalding, never satisfying dreaming, dreaming, dreaming, dreaming! [*Savagely*] No debauchery that ever coarsened and brutalized an Englishman can take the worth and usefulness out of him like that dreaming. An Irishman's imagination never lets him alone, never convinces him, never satisfies him; but it makes him that he cant face reality nor deal with it nor handle it nor conquer it: he can only sneer at them that do, and [*bitterly, at Broadbent*] be 'agreeable to strangers,' like a good-for-nothing woman on the streets. [*Gabbling at Broadbent across the table*] It's *all* dreaming, *all* imagination" (I, 84–85). Ireland is for Doyle a Heartbreak House, a land of dreams, imagination, and thought which has lost contact with the real world.

This, however, is only the negative side of the Irish mental activity, emphasized for the benefit of the play's intended Irish audiences (who were to find themselves castigated by the Irishman Doyle and praised by the Englishman Broadbent). When writing for the English, Shaw was more apt to emphasize the Irishman's cleverness in contrast with the Englishman's stupidity, as he does in the 1906 "Preface for Politicians" (which makes this contrast so strongly as to contradict the play; see especially "Our Temperaments Contrasted," pp. 17–22). In the music criticism which he wrote in the 1890's, one finds statements like the following:

[Villiers Stanford's] dullness is all the harder to bear because it is the restless, ingenious, trifling, flippant dullness of the Irishman, instead of the stupid, bovine, sleepable-through dullness of the Englishman.

[The Irishman in England] may end in founding a race of cultivated Irishmen whose mission in England will be to teach Englishmen to play with their brains as well as with their bodies; for it is all work and no play in the brain department that makes John Bull such an uncommonly dull boy.

The English brain is so dense that it is only by a strenuous and most desperately serious effort that the Englishman can set his intellect in action, a feat so easy to the Irishman that he is constantly doing it merely to amuse himself, and so acquires a playful intellectual manner as naturally as the Englishman acquires a ponderous and solemn one.[3]

What these passages and Doyle's denunciation of dreaming have in common is the view that the Irishman's vitality is intellectual.

The Englishman's vitality, on the other hand, is physical; his world is the material world. Broadbent is introduced to us in a stage direction as *"a robust, full-blooded, energetic man in the prime of life"* (I, 72), and one of the most memorable exchanges in the play brings out the distinction between his temperament and that of the Irishman Keegan.

BROADBENT [*with conviction*] . . . I find the world quite good enough for me: rather a jolly place, in fact.
KEEGAN [*looking at him with quiet wonder*] You are satisfied?
BROADBENT. As a reasonable man, yes. I see no evils in the

world—except, of course, natural evils—that cannot be reme-
died by freedom, self-government, and English institutions. I think
so, not because I am an Englishman, but as a matter of common
sense.

KEEGAN. You feel at home in the world, then?

BROADBENT. Of course. Dont you?

KEEGAN [*from the very depths of his nature*] No.

BROADBENT [*breezily*] Try phosphorous pills. I always take them
when my brain is overworked. I'll give you the address in Oxford
Street.

(IV, 152)

No passage in Shaw's writings presents so strikingly the Philistine
temperament as opposed to that of the Realist. In his foolishness and
in his commitment to obsolete ideas Broadbent may resemble Idealists like Ramsden and Lady Britomart, but his most important qualities, in the context of *John Bull's Other Island,* are Philistine ones;
he is the representative, and a contented inhabitant, of the physical
world, the world of flesh. One notes that he is the one character in
the play who has a considerable interest in food. His first thought as
Tim Haffigan is about to appear in Act I is that "he'll want tea"
(p. 73), and he is filled with consternation when he learns that he
is not going to be given dinner on his arrival at Cornelius Doyle's
house (II, 105). A subsequent stage direction here dwells on the
ample contents of the tea which he is given, and observes that *"his
fears of being starved"* have been replaced by the *"misgiving that he
is eating too much"* and that he goes off afterward *"full fed, happy
and enthusiastic"* (II, 108–109). The next morning he asks his
valet why he was given no porridge for breakfast (III, 116–117).
His response when he is told that Nora has gone home (after her
angry rejection of Doyle) is that he must feed her up (IV, 167); and
his whole concept of their relationship is that of the Philistine:
"First love," he tells her, "is only a little foolishness and a lot of curiosity: no really self-respecting woman would take advantage of it.
No, my dear Nora: Ive done with all that long ago. Love affairs always end in rows. We're not going to have any rows: we're going to
have a solid four-square home: man and wife: comfort and common
sense" (IV, 162).

Broadbent also has the Philistine's stupidity, which, as we have seen, Shaw regarded as a major English characteristic. When Broadbent says that he always takes phosphorous pills when his brain is overworked, the joke lies not only in his lack of understanding of Keegan, but in his lack of understanding of himself. His brain is never overworked. He does not think, and like Ann in *Man and Superman* he responds to others' thinking by reducing it to his own level, the level of the practical and the mundane, as he does in the exchange with Keegan that I have quoted. In fact, almost every major speech by Keegan or Doyle in the play is followed by an anticlimactic comment by Broadbent that reveals his incapacity to understand an idea, his lack of contact with the life of the mind. At the conclusion of Doyle's long impassioned speech on dreaming, for example, he replies: "Never despair, Larry. There are great possibilities for Ireland. Home Rule will work wonders under English guidance." Like Tanner after Ann's replies, Doyle is *"pulled up short"* here (I, 85–86). Even more reminiscent of Ann is Broadbent's reply to Doyle's analogy between the Englishman and the caterpillar: "Now you know, Larry, that would never have occurred to me. You Irish people are amazingly clever. Of course it's all tommy rot; but it's so brilliant, you know! How the dickens do you think of such things! You really must write an article about it: they'll pay you something for it. If Nature wont have it, I can get it into Engineering for you: I know the editor" (I, 90). Like Ann, Broadbent sees Doyle's speech not as the expression of an idea, but only as clever talk, and he is interested in the practical use to which such brilliance could be put, just as Ann thinks of Tanner's ability to talk as a qualification for a political career. And he offers practical assistance: he knows the editor of *Engineering,* as he knows "the address in Oxford Street."

This lack of understanding makes Broadbent totally invulnerable to intellectual opposition. Keegan's trenchant, prophetic indictment of capitalist efficiency at the end of the play, for example, does not disturb him at all. Keegan is made utterly ineffectual by Broadbent's lack of comprehension. Broadbent does not defend himself, because he is not aware that he is being attacked. Instead, he replies earnestly: "Too true, Mr Keegan, only too true. And most eloquently put. It reminds me of poor Ruskin: a great man, you know. I sympathize. Believe me, I'm on your side. Dont sneer, Larry: I used to read a lot of Shelley years ago. Let us be faithful to the dreams of our youth [*he wafts a wreath of cigar smoke at large across the hill*]" (IV, 174). This is just what Shaw saw as the public's response to himself, and to all revolutionary thinkers. "Even I," he writes in the Epistle Dedicatory to *Man and Superman,* "as I force myself, pen in hand, into recognition and civility, find all the force of my on-slaught destroyed by a simple policy of non-resistance." He complains that no matter how violent his language and revolutionary his opin-ions, the public accepts him—in just the way in which Broadbent accepts Keegan. "Instead of exclaiming 'Send this inconceivable Sa-tanist to the stake,' the respectable newspapers pith me by announcing 'another book by this brilliant and thoughtful writer.' And the ordinary citizen, knowing that an author who is well spo-ken of by a respectable newspaper must be all right, reads me, as he reads Micah, with undisturbed edification from his own point of view" (p. xxxiii). Far from being checked by Keegan, Broadbent is encouraged and inspired by him in his plan to develop Rosscullen along efficient English lines. His last words in the play are addressed to Doyle: "I feel sincerely obliged to Keegan: he has made me feel a better man: distinctly better. [*With sincere elevation*] I feel now as I never did before that I am right in devoting my life to the cause of Ireland. Come along and help me to choose the site for the hotel" (IV, 177). Broadbent quite sincerely interprets Keegan's curse on his activities as a blessing; he listens to Keegan "with undisturbed edifi-cation from his own point of view."

Broadbent's incapacity to grasp ideas is a limitation, but clearly at the same time it is part of his strength. In Broadbent, Shaw is showing the Englishman at his most absurd, while in Keegan he is showing the Irishman at his most noble and saintly, and he is point-ing out that on the level of immediate practical usefulness Broad-bent must be preferred to Keegan. In the words of the Epistle Dedi-catory to *Man and Superman,* he is demonstrating "the value of the prosaic qualities of which Irishmen teach Englishmen to be ashamed" and "the vanity of the poetic qualities of which English-men teach Irishmen to be proud." In a list of instructions that he prepared in 1904 for producers of *John Bull's Other Island,* Shaw wrote that "the object of the play is to teach Irish people the value of an Englishman as well as to shew the Englishman his own absurdities"; [4] and the play's Preface elaborates on this: "Writing the play for an Irish audience, I thought it would be good for them to be shewn very clearly that the loudest laugh they could raise at the expense of the absurdest Englishman was not really a laugh on their side; that he would succeed where they would fail; that he could inspire strong affection and loyalty in an Irishman who knew the world and was moved only to dislike, mistrust, impatience and even exasperation by his own countrymen; that his power of taking himself seriously, and his insensibility to anything funny in danger and destruction, was the first condition of economy and concentration of force, sustained purpose, and rational conduct" (pp. 13–14).

That English Philistine stupidity is of value is also asserted in the Comedy in *Man and Superman,* and this parallel between the two plays is brought out in a letter from Shaw to the American critic James Huneker. This was written five months before *John Bull's Other Island* was begun, and its comments on the Englishman are directly relevant to the play. Shaw says that people like Huneker are prevented by their ignorance of English life and their anti-English prejudice from understanding and appreciating many of his characters. These include his "specifically English women": Blanche Sartorius in *Widowers' Houses,* Vivie Warren in *Mrs Warren's Profession,* Lady Cicely Waynflete in *Captain Brassbound's Conversion,* "and, above all, Ann Whitefield and Violet Robinson in the Superman drama (Ann being my most gorgeous female creation)." "I tell you," he says to Huneker, "you dont appreciate the vitality of the English," and he continues: "The stupidity, peculiar to the Englishman, which prevents him from knowing what he is doing, is really a stroke of genius on his part and is far more voluntary than the bright American thinks. Cromwell said that no man goes further than the man who doesnt know where he is going; and in that you have the whole secret of English success. What is the use of being bright, subtle, witty, genial, if these qualities lead to the subjection and poverty of India and Ireland, and to the political anarchy and corruption of the United States? What says my beautiful, vital, victorious, odious-to-all-good-Americans Miss Ann Whitefield? 'The only really simple thing is to go straight for what you want and grab it.' " [5] In *John Bull's Other Island,* this letter is echoed in

Doyle's comments in Act I about Broadbent as a combination of idiot and genius.[6] The Englishman, Doyle says, is like the caterpillar, who "instinctively makes itself look exactly like a leaf; so that both its enemies and its prey may mistake it for one and think it not worth bothering about." The Englishman "instinctively makes himself look like a fool, and eats up all the real fools at his ease while his enemies let him alone and laugh at him for being a fool like the rest. Oh, nature is cunning! cunning!" (I, 89–90). As in *Man and Superman,* the Philistine is likened to a predatory animal who conquers with instinctive genius. The parallel to Broadbent's apparent idiocy is Ann's pose as a dutiful daughter—although Ann is conscious of her strategy.

Broadbent, like Ann and Violet, is the successful character in his play. Shaw's original title for the play was "Rule Britannia," which he rejected only because he thought it was "too frankly a jest," [7] and ironically Britannia does rule, in a way most inimical to what the Irish characters in the play (except Doyle) conceive as their real interests—but Britannia in the person of a Home Ruler who is devoting his life to the cause of Ireland. What the play is about, from the point of view of plot, is the Englishman's conquest of Ireland. Broadbent swallows up the parliamentary seat, he swallows up Nora, and he swallows up the land. It is this third conquest which is most emphasized in the discussion at the end of the play. Characteristically, Shaw stresses in *John Bull's Other Island* economic rather than political factors. The important question according to the play is not who governs Ireland but who owns it. The only two characters who actually declare themselves in favor of Home Rule are the two Englishmen, Broadbent and his valet Hodson. And the Broadbent who will affect Ireland is not the Home Ruler but the capitalist. His idiotic talk is of no consequence; what are of consequence are his Philistine virtues: his money, his practical knowledge, and his efficiency. "The world belongs to the efficient," he tells Keegan near the end of the play (IV, 173), and earlier in this discussion he says: "The fact is, there are only two qualities in the world: efficiency and inefficiency, and only two sorts of people: the efficient and the inefficient. It dont matter whether theyre English or Irish. I shall collar this place, not because I'm an Englishman and Haffigan and Co are Irishmen, but because theyre duffers, and I know my way about" (IV, 170).

The conquest of the land was mostly accomplished before Broadbent's visit to Ireland, and so the action of the play is more concerned with his conquest of the parliamentary seat and of Nora. These victories are a result not of his efficiency, but of his self-confidence and—primarily—his simple acquisitiveness. "You will get into parliament because you *want* to get into it enough to be prepared to take the necessary steps to induce the people to vote for you," Keegan tells him (IV, 149); he has what Shaw calls in the passage I quoted from the Preface "economy and concentration of force." As the Epistle Dedicatory to *Man and Superman* puts it, "The secret of the prosaic man's success, such as it is, is the simplicity with which he pursues [his] ends"—money and marriage (p. xvi).[8] Thus after Keegan has expressed his terrible vision of this world as hell, Broadbent's only reaction is to ask Cornelius, "Has he a vote?" (IV, 153); and Broadbent is (unconsciously) unscrupulous in his use of Nora for campaigning. His conquest of Nora is a good symbol of England's domination over Ireland, and it is one of the play's many reversals of the expectations of an Irish Nationalist audience that Cathleen ni Hoolihan marries an English capitalist. Broadbent acquires Nora mainly because he is determined to acquire her, even before he has set foot in Ireland. As a suitor he lacks dignity and tact, but he is effective. Although he is not at all the sort of person she wants as a husband, his energy and determination make resistance impossible. Once again in Shaw, the dreamer cannot cope with the man of the world.

Nora's other, more reluctant suitor, Doyle, says to her after her engagement to Broadbent that "I'm an Irishman, and he's an Englishman. He wants you; and he grabs you. *I* want you; and I quarrel with you and have to go on wanting you" (IV, 166). Doyle's attraction to Nora, like his attraction to dreams, is in fact outweighed by revulsion, but this speech emphasizes the neat parallel that exists between Doyle and Broadbent both in their public and in their private activities. We have the opportunity to compare in Act III their respective approaches to the electorate, and in Act IV their respective approaches to Nora. In each case Doyle is self-conscious, honest, and diffident; then he retires gracelessly, leaving the field to Broadbent, who woos energetically and although he makes a fool of himself is successful. In both politics and love acquisitive stupidity is more effective than diffident intelligence.

The three major characters in the play represent three levels of spirituality. Broadbent and Keegan are at the two extremes: Broadbent, the Englishman, is completely of this world, while Keegan, the Irishman, is not of this world at all. Doyle, the Irishman living in England, lies between one extreme and the other. That he is more a man of mind and spirit than Broadbent is clear from the stage direction which introduces him: *"Mr Laurence Doyle is a man of 36, with cold grey eyes, strained nose, fine fastidious lips, critical brows, clever head, rather refined and goodlooking on the whole, but with a suggestion of thinskinnedness and dissatisfaction that contrasts strongly with Broadbent's eupeptic jollity"* (I, 78).[9] What this might remind one of is the description, in the Hell Scene of *Man and Superman,* of Don Juan, who has *"a more critical, fastidious, handsome face, paler and colder"* than Tanner's (III, 84); and Doyle is in some ways not unlike Juan. His impatient response to Broadbent's cant in Act I, for example, is comparable to Juan's response to the Devil; and Broadbent speaks of Doyle as the Devil speaks of Juan. He calls him cold-blooded (I, 80) and heartless (IV, 161), and he tells Nora that he would not have made a suitable husband for her: "You dont know Larry as I do, my dear. He has absolutely no capacity for enjoyment: he couldnt make any woman happy. He's as clever as be-blowed; but life's too earthly for him: he doesn't really care for anything or anybody" (IV, 163).[10] Doyle also shares with Juan a dissatisfaction with his surroundings, and in spite of his contempt for dreaming he has his own dream of heaven: a country, as he tells Broadbent in Act I, where the facts are not brutal and dreams not unreal (p. 92). Keegan's heaven is also a country where opposites are reconciled: State and Church, work and play, worshipper and worshipped, humanity and divinity; and in the candidacy scene Doyle's speech about a saintly Ireland brings out more directly his similarity to Keegan: "I would have Ireland compete with Rome itself for the chair of St Peter and the citadel of the Church; for Rome, in spite of all the blood of the martyrs, is pagan at heart to this day, while in Ireland the people is the Church and the Church the people." Father Dempsey responds to this by saying, "Whisht, man! youre worse than mad Pether Keegan himself" (III, 130).

But at the end of the play Doyle rejects Keegan; he displays only hostility and contempt toward dreams of heaven and the vision of a saintly Ireland:

KEEGAN. In the accounts kept in heaven, Mr Doyle, a heart purified of hatred may be worth more than even a Land Development Syndicate of Anglicized Irishmen and Gladstonized Englishmen.

LARRY. Oh, in heaven, no doubt. I have never been there. Can you tell me where it is?

KEEGAN. Could you have told me this morning where hell is? Yet you know now that it is here. Do not despair of finding heaven: it may be no farther off.

LARRY [*ironically*] On this holy ground, as you call it, eh?

KEEGAN [*with fierce intensity*] Yes, perhaps, even on this holy ground which such Irishmen as you have turned into a Land of Derision.

(IV, 175)

Doyle's hostility to Keegan here is really a hostility to an aspect of himself. He has rejected the possibility of heaven—of a better world—and has decided to ally himself firmly with the forces of this world. Finding that facts and dreams cannot be reconciled, he chooses facts, and represses his religious nature so that he can remain in the world of facts. The ferocity of his denunciation of dreaming in Act I reflects his determination not to give way to this side of his nature. In fact, in the denunciation itself one can see this repressed side; the stage direction near the beginning of the speech tells us that Doyle is *"going off into a passionate dream"* (I, 84).

Whereas Doyle has rejected dreams for action, Keegan has rejected action for dreams. He is the saintly character in the play who has withdrawn completely from the world. He is introduced as *"a man with the face of a young saint"* (II, 95), and we first see him speaking, in imitation of St. Francis, to a grasshopper. Shaw wanted his superiority to common humanity to be emphasized in production. In his "Instructions to the Producer" he pointed out that Keegan "is a man of ascetic refinement and distinction, compared with whom an English Archbishop would seem only a respectable family butler." [11]

In the play itself, Keegan with his ascetic refinement and distinction is contrasted with the Roman Catholic Church's official representative in Rosscullen, Father Dempsey. One of the several sets of contrasting scenes in the play occurs at the beginning of Act II, where Keegan is immediately succeeded on the stage by Father Dempsey, who appropriately enters conversing with Broadbent— appropriately, because of all the Irish characters he is the only one who is really similar to Broadbent. Like Broadbent, and most unlike Keegan, he is a contented man who finds this world good enough for him. *"He is a priest neither by vocation nor ambition, but because the life suits him,"* says the stage direction which introduces him; he is *"on the whole, an easygoing, amiable, even modest man as long as his dues are paid and his authority and dignity fully admitted"* (II, 102). The Philistine concern with money suggested here is illustrated in the candidacy scene, where he says that Rosscullen's member of parliament ought to be wealthy enough so that he can be "a help to the Church instead of a burden on it" (III, 126); and his support of Broadbent seems to be largely connected with the latter's presumed wealth. Father Dempsey's values are frankly expressed in his remark to Cornelius while they are considering Broadbent's desirability as a candidate: "You might find out from Larry, Corny, what his means are. God forgive us all! it's poor work spoiling the Egyptians, though we have good warrant for it; so I'd like to know how much spoil there is before I commit meself" (III, 135). His Philistine nature is brought out in other ways in the play, too. In the scene in which he first appears, for example, there is the discussion of the Round Tower:

> FATHER DEMPSEY. . . . .D'ye see the top o the Roun Tower there? thats an antiquity worth lookin at.
> BROADBENT [*deeply interested*] Have you any theory as to what the Round Towers were for?
> FATHER DEMPSEY [*a little offended*] A theory? Me!
>
> (II, 103)

This first encounter ends with Father Dempsey's remark to Broadbent, "If theres anything I can do for you in this parish, let me know" (II, 106). His realm is not that of theory but of practical assistance.

We find a similar pattern, then, in the two businessmen in the play on the one hand and the two priests on the other. The difference between the mundane Broadbent and the more spiritual Doyle has its parallel in the difference between Father Dempsey and Keegan. But Keegan, I have suggested, is more spiritual than Doyle. While Doyle chooses facts, whether they are brutal or not, Keegan chooses dreams, whether they are unreal or not. His religion is presented as a kind of higher Catholicism, a revival of what was best in medieval Catholicism [12] (certain aspects of which were very congenial to Shaw's own mind); this religion is contrasted in the play with the conventional, unthinking institutional Catholicism of Father Dempsey and the superstitious debased Catholicism of Patsy Farrell. The main doctrine of Keegan's religion is that of the *Civitas Dei*, the transformation of the earth, which he sees as hell, into a heaven. His religion, like Barbara Undershaft's, is less otherworldly than it sounds; both use the language of traditional Christianity to talk about the elevation of men and society. He makes this clear in the exchange with Doyle which I have quoted. "Could you have told me this morning where hell is?" he asks. "Yet you know now that it is here. Do not despair of finding heaven: it may be no farther off." His vision of heaven, which he proclaims shortly after this, at the end of the play, is social and political, in spite of the theological language in which it is expressed. "In my dreams [heaven] is a country where the State is the Church and the Church the people: three in one and one in three. It is a commonwealth in which work is play and play is life: three in one and one in three. It is a temple in which the priest is the worshipper and the worshipper the worshipped: three in one and one in three. It is a godhead in which all life is human and all humanity divine: three in one and one in three" (IV, 177).[13] This is what Barbara calls "the raising of hell to heaven and of man to God" [14] and it means a perfected human society—and in *John Bull's Other Island,* a perfected Ireland in particular.

The phrase "island of the saints" was clearly very much in Shaw's mind when he thought of Ireland in connection with *John Bull's Other Island* (the title itself could suggest this). " 'The island of the saints' is no idle phrase," he writes in the Preface. "Religious genius is one of our national products; and Ireland is no bad rock to build a Church on" (p. 36). This idea is expressed in the play by both Doyle, in his speech in the candidacy scene, and by Keegan. To Keegan, Ireland is a potential heaven which has been debased by its people into a hell. He refers to the "dead heart and blinded soul of the island of the saints" (IV, 168), and tells Doyle that heaven might be found "on this holy ground which such Irishmen as you have turned into a Land of Derision." Broadbent, he says, is an ass who "comes to browse here without knowing that the soil his hoof touches is holy ground" (IV, 172).

Keegan's vision of heaven is what Shaw would call truly religious, and it is to be contrasted with other attitudes toward heaven in the play: with Father Dempsey's conventional heaven, which is reached (he tells Matthew Haffigan) by thinking "o the sufferins of the blessed saints" (III, 132); with Doyle's cynical rejection of heaven at the end of the play; and, most important, with Broadbent's concept of heaven. The first of the several references to heaven in the play comes, like the first hint of a theme in a symphony, during the conversation between Broadbent and Tim Haffigan in Act I:

> BROADBENT. Have you ever heard of Garden City?
> TIM [*doubtfully*] D'ye mane Heavn?
> BROADBENT. Heaven! No: it's near Hitchin.
>
> (p. 76)

The garden city, rather than the child's picture that he describes at the end of the play, is Broadbent's concept of heaven. It is the highest form of life of which he can conceive, just as Undershaft can see no better kind of society than the one which he has created at his garden city in Perivale St. Andrews. Broadbent promises Keegan that he will "take Ireland in hand": "I shall bring money here: I shall raise wages: I shall found public institutions: a library, a Polytechnic (undenominational, of course), a gymnasium, a cricket club, perhaps an art school. I shall make a Garden city of Rosscullen: the round tower shall be thoroughly repaired and restored" (IV, 171). It is this speech which should be set against Keegan's vision of heaven at the end of the play, just as Broadbent's division of men into the ef-

ficient and the inefficient should be set against Keegan's division of
men into the saved and the damned (IV, 175). These religions, with
their propounders, constitute the two poles of the play.

At the end of his climactic speech on heaven, Keegan says of his
vision that "it is, in short, the dream of a madman" (IV, 177); these
are his final words in the play. The man of vision is frequently described in Shaw's writings as a madman. In the Epistle Dedicatory
to *Man and Superman,* for example, Shaw writes that the world
which we find in books is "not the main world at all: it is only the
self-consciousness of certain abnormal people who have the specific
artistic talent and temperament"; and "the man whose consciousness
does not correspond to that of the majority is a madman" (p. xxi).
The Preface to *Major Barbara* contains the same equation in reverse,
in a reference to "the fact that lunacy may be inspiration in disguise,
since a man who has more brains than his fellows necessarily appears as mad to them as one who has less" (p. 204). Madness is
mentioned in connection with inspired characters in both of these
plays as well: Undershaft says that he, Cusins, and Barbara are mad;
and Tanner is described by Shaw as *"prodigiously fluent of speech,
restless, excitable (mark the snorting nostril and the restless blue
eye, just the thirty-secondth of an inch too wide open), possibly a little mad."* [15] But Keegan is madder than any of these characters; his
inspiration sets him off much more completely from the world. The
character in Shaw's plays whom he most resembles is Captain Shotover in *Heartbreak House* (which is anticipated in several important ways by *John Bull's Other Island*). Like Shotover, Keegan
really is treated by the world as a madman, and he is much more
isolated from it than (say) Tanner, Cusins, or Barbara. He has been
unfrocked by his Church, and the influence that he might have had
as a priest is enjoyed by the Philistine Father Dempsey. In spite of
Cornelius' statement that "theres lotsle vote the way he tells them"
(IV, 153), Keegan has no significant, spiritual influence over anyone. Patsy Farrell worships him in an ignorant, superstitious way,
and so really does Broadbent. These are the only two characters in
the play who regard him as anything like a saint, and neither has
the slightest understanding of his vision. Nora respects him, and recognizes his insight ("He'd see through me as if I was a pane o
glass," she tells Broadbent, IV, 165), but she does not share his vi-

sion of heaven and hell, and her destiny, in any case, is to marry Broadbent and live in London, depriving Keegan of his one consolation in Rosscullen (see his comment on her, IV, 153). The person with whom Keegan has most in common is Doyle, and Doyle is the only character in the play, apart from Father Dempsey, to show actual hostility toward him. It is this hostility that leads Keegan to say to Broadbent at the end of the play, with a bitter resignation like that of Shotover: "You see, Mr Broadbent, I only make the hearts of my countrymen harder when I preach to them: the gates of hell still prevail against me. I shall wish you good evening. I am better alone, at the Round Tower, dreaming of heaven" (IV, 176). Unlike Tanner, Barbara, and Cusins, who enter the real world at the end of the other two plays, Keegan goes off by himself; at the end of the play he returns to what he was doing at his first appearance, dreaming of heaven in solitude.

II

"Live in contact with dreams and you will get something of their charm: live in contact with facts and you will get something of their brutality. I wish I could find a country to live in where the facts were not brutal and the dreams not unreal" (I, 92). It is in this speech of Doyle's, near the end of the first act, that the central theme of *John Bull's Other Island* is stated. The play is about the relationship between brutal, stupid English facts and charming, ineffectual Irish dreams; and the question which it asks is: Can there be a marriage between the two, such as Doyle desires? Can there be a "third empire, in which the twin-natured shall reign?"

The play does contain two minor unions between England and Ireland, two marriages of contraries. The most obvious of these is the marriage between Broadbent and Nora. The symbolic nature of this union is implied in Shaw's introductory comment on Nora. She is *"an incarnation of everything in Ireland that drove* [Doyle] *out of it";* and the Irish qualities that she particularly symbolizes are suggested in the reference to *"the absence of any symptoms of coarseness or hardness or appetite in her, her comparative delicacy of manner and sensibility of apprehension, her fine hands and frail figure, her novel accent, with the caressing plaintive Irish melody of her speech."* These qualities, while commonplace to Irish eyes, give Nora a charm for *"the inhabitants of fatter-fed, crowded, hustling and bustling modern countries"*—that is, for Broadbent, to whom she appears ethereal (II, 99). As he says to her, "The Englishwoman is too prosaic for my taste, too material, too much of the animated beefsteak about her. The ideal is what I like" (IV, 162). Clearly their union is a marriage between England and Ireland, flesh and spirit. But it is not quite the kind of union that occurs in *Man and Superman* and *Major Barbara,* for it is simply a swallowing-up of spirit by flesh rather than a union leading to fruitful interaction. Broadbent and the world which he represents will not be changed by the marriage; it is Nora who will be "fed up" by him, and forced to become part of the world of brutal facts. A few lines before Broadbent's statement that he "must feed up Nora," Doyle explains to her what her new role will be: "Play your new part well, and there will be no more neglect, no more loneliness, no more idle regrettings and vain-hopings in the evenings by the Round Tower, but real life and real work and real cares and real joys among real people: solid English life in London, the very centre of the world. You will find your work cut out for you keeping Tom's house and entertaining Tom's friends and getting Tom into parliament" (IV, 166–167). And Broadbent has already introduced her to her immediate duties as a candidate's wife and compelled her to perform some of them.

In the speech in which Broadbent tells Nora about his lack of interest in English women, he adds that Doyle's taste is just the opposite from his own: "He likes em solid and bouncing and rather keen about him. It's a very convenient difference; for weve never been in love with the same woman" (IV, 162). Doyle's preference for solidity is revealed in the play not only in his lack of enthusiasm for Nora, but in his attraction to Broadbent himself. It is their partnership which is the other marriage of contraries in the play. "I want Ireland to be the brains and imagination of a big Commonwealth," Doyle says in Act I (p. 88), and he has acted accordingly by becoming the brains and imagination of the firm of Doyle and Broadbent. Shaw's comment on their partnership in the Preface provides a good statement of the "third empire" theme that I am examining in the middle plays. He is replying to the English supposition that Doyle is a failure as an engineer and Broadbent a success. "I should say, myself, that the combination was probably much more effective than either of the partners would have been alone. I am persuaded further—without pretending to know more about it than anyone else—that Broadbent's special contribution was simply the strength, self-satisfaction, social confidence and cheerful bumptiousness that money, comfort, and good feeding bring to all healthy people; and that Doyle's special contribution was the freedom from illusion, the power of facing facts, the nervous industry, the sharpened wits, the sensitive pride of the imaginative man who has fought his way up through social persecution and poverty" (pp. 14–15).

This applies to the play in that the play asserts the value of both Broadbent's Philistine qualities and Doyle's Realist qualities, but in the play it is Broadbent who is presented as very much the dominant member of the partnership. He is insensible to Doyle's clearheaded criticism of him in Act I; he takes Nora and the parliamentary seat from Doyle in Acts III and IV; and it is he rather than Doyle who makes the decisions about the Rosscullen land. By the time of the climactic debate that concludes the play Doyle has become simply the advocate of the Philistine efficiency that Broadbent represents. This is emphasized in the stage business at the end of the play. Broadbent ends an exchange between Doyle and Keegan by coming between them, saying "Take care! you will be quarrelling presently. Oh, you Irishmen, you Irishmen!" Here Doyle is linked with Keegan as an Irishman. But Doyle moves away, and *"presently strolls back on Keegan's right"* (IV, 175). Now the Englishman standing between Irishmen has given way to the saint standing between businessmen; Doyle is linked with Broadbent. Then Keegan leaves the two of them standing together (both of them smoking cigars), and goes up the hill toward the Round Tower. The final word of the play, as in *Man and Superman* and *Major Barbara,* is given to the apparently victorious Philistine. "Come along," says Broadbent to Doyle, "and help me to choose the site for the hotel" (IV, 177). All of this emphasizes that the union of Doyle and Broadbent is, like the union of Nora and Broadbent, one in which the Philistine dominates entirely. Doyle has become part of Broadbent's world. "In the main it is by living with you and working in double harness with you than I have learnt to live in a real world and not in an imaginary one . . . I should never have done anything without

you," Doyle tells Broadbent in Act I, and he adds: "All my friends
are either Englishmen or men of the big world that belongs to the
big Powers. All the serious part of my life has been lived in that atmosphere: all the serious part of my work has been done with men
of that sort" (p. 87).

The real union between facts and dreams would be a union between Broadbent and Keegan. Such a combination could produce an
intelligent, divine efficiency with Broadbent's power serving Keegan's vision. This union is impossible, however, within the context
of the play: the two characters are so totally different from each
other that they could never join together. They have less in common
than Barbara and Cusins have with Undershaft in *Major Barbara:*
Keegan is more remote from the world than Barbara and Cusins,
and Broadbent has nothing of Undershaft's understanding of the religious temperament. And of course the literal marriage of *Man and
Superman* is not possible here.

Instead of a union between Broadbent and Keegan, we have in
John Bull's Other Island the immediate total triumph of Broadbent, with the promise of the eventual supersession of his values by
Keegan's. As in the other two plays, the Philistine's triumph represents an improvement over the present situation; to this extent, the
play presents Broadbent in a favorable light. Doyle argues that it is
better to have Broadbent than the peasant farmer Haffigan owning
the land, and that Broadbent's action is preferable to Keegan's
dreaming. To Keegan, Broadbent's garden city is not a heaven but a
hell—"And our place of torment shall be as clean and orderly as
the cleanest and most orderly place I know in Ireland, which is our
poetically named Mountjoy prison," he says in reply to Broadbent's
speech about his plan to transform Ireland—but nevertheless
even Keegan admits that Broadbent's efficiency is preferable to the
mere talk of the Irish party. "Well, perhaps I had better vote for an
efficient devil that knows his own mind and his own business," he
says, "than for a foolish patriot who has no mind and no business"
(IV, 172).

But, as in the other two plays, the triumph and the superiority of
the Philistine may be temporary. Shaw's comments in the Preface on
Broadbent's value are parallel to the section of the Epistle Dedicatory to *Man and Superman* in which he says that the prosaic man's

vitality "may muddle successfully through the comparatively tribal stages of gregariousness" but will prove disastrous for "nineteenth century nations and twentieth century commonwealths" (p. xvi). Here is the relevant section on Broadbent:

I do not say that the confidence of the Englishman in Broadbent is not for the moment justified. The virtues of the English soil are not less real because they consist of coal and iron, not of metaphysical sources of character. The virtues of Broadbent are not less real because they are the virtues of the money that coal and iron have produced. But as the mineral virtues are being discovered and developed in other soils, their derivative virtues are appearing so rapidly in other nations that Broadbent's relative advantage is vanishing. In truth I am afraid (the misgiving is natural to a by-this-time slightly elderly playwright) that Broadbent is out of date. The successful Englishman of today, when he is not a transplanted Scotchman or Irishman, often turns out on investigation to be, if not an American, an Italian, or a Jew, at least to be depending on the brains, the nervous energy, and the freedom from romantic illusions (often called cynicism) of such foreigners for the management of his sources of income. At all events I am persuaded that a modern nation that is satisfied with Broadbent is in a dream. Much as I like him, I object to be governed by him, or entangled in his political destiny. I therefore propose to give him a piece of my mind here, as an Irishman, full of an instinctive pity for those of my fellow-creatures who are only English.

(p. 15)

In this passage Shaw is at once praising and depreciating Broadbent's qualities; they are valuable, but only "for the moment." In the play the praise comes from Doyle and the depreciation from Keegan. Keegan, in spite of his statement that Broadbent is preferable to foolish patriots, nonetheless holds him and his values in the greatest contempt. He sees further than anyone else in the play and does not accept efficiency for its own sake but considers what its goal is—what interests it is serving. Just as Cusins is aware that the efficient Undershaft serves the worst elements in society, so Keegan says that Broadbent spends his life "efficiently serving the cupidity of base money hunters" (IV, 174). He accuses him of being like an ass who "wastes all his virtues—his efficiency, as you call it —in doing the will of his greedy masters instead of doing the will of Heaven that is in himself. He is efficient in the service of Mammon, mighty in mischief, skilful in ruin, heroic in destruction" (IV, 172). He predicts, with inspired insight, that all of the effort of Broadbent and his fellow land developers will lead only to the enrichment of "your English and American shareholders," who will "spend all the money we [Irish] make for them very efficiently in shooting and hunting, in operations for cancer and appendicitis, in gluttony and gambling." "For four wicked centuries," he concludes, "the world has dreamed this foolish dream of efficiency; and the end is not yet. But the end will come" (IV, 174). The empire of the flesh will be succeeded by the empire of the spirit; and Ireland will fulfill its destiny as the island of the saints. At present Ireland is the island of the traitors, those who betray the proper purpose of their country, but "the day may come when these islands shall live by the quality of their men rather than by the abundance of their minerals; and then we shall see" (IV, 172–173).

Man and Superman and *Major Barbara* (written respectively before and after *John Bull's Other Island*) also predict that the empire of the flesh will not last, but in these two plays its triumph, like that of capitalism in Marx's view of history, is itself a necessary step toward its own overthrow. That is why the immediate victories of Ann and Undershaft are presented as a cause for rejoicing; they will—or at least may—lead to the ultimate victory of Tanner and Don Juan, Cusins and Barbara. But Broadbent's triumph represents no such necessary step; it is in no sense a gain for Keegan. Keegan's values may be triumphant one day, but Broadbent's triumph does not contribute toward this.

John Bull's Other Island therefore lacks the jubilant conclusion of the other two plays; there is no significant union of opposing forces. Indeed, as Shaw wrote to Granville Barker, "There is no ending at all: only a transcendental conversation." [16] What the transcendental conversation does, I think, is to present Broadbent and Keegan so that the audience is made aware of the virtues and defects of each, and a perfect balance is maintained between them. Doyle adds the weight to Broadbent's side that makes it impossible to value Keegan more. Keegan denounces Broadbent and Doyle in what are the most moving and impressive speeches of the play, but against his judgment on them must be set Doyle's judgment on him:

KEEGAN . . . I am better alone, at the Round Tower, dreaming of heaven. [*He goes up the hill*].
LARRY. Aye, thats it! there you are! dreaming! dreaming! dreaming! dreaming! [17]

Keegan replies that "every dream is a prophecy: every jest is an earnest in the womb of Time" (IV, 176), and then proclaims his vision of heaven. If the play ended with this, then Keegan would be left with the advantage, but it is followed by an exchange between Doyle and Broadbent which brings out the dreamer's limitations. He talks about heaven, but does nothing to help bring it into existence; and his contemporaries learn nothing from him.

BROADBENT [*looking after him affectionately*] What a regular old Church and State Tory he is! He's a character: he'll be an attraction here. Really almost equal to Ruskin and Carlyle.
LARRY. Yes; and much good *they* did with all their talk!
(IV, 177)

Broadbent and Doyle go off to choose the site for their hotel, while Keegan ascends to his tower to dream of heaven. The world of facts and the world of dreams remain totally separate, the efficiency of the one vitiated by its lack of divine purpose, and the nobility of the other vitiated by its impotence.

One is left, then, at the end of the play, with Doyle's discontent —wishing for a country in which the facts are not brutal and the dreams not unreal, but feeling that such a union is impossible. And the audience is unlikely to choose, as Doyle does, Broadbent's real garden city over Keegan's dream of heaven. We remain torn between the two, recognizing that neither by itself is adequate.

V

The Doctor's Dilemma and Pygmalion

The intellect of man is forced to choose
Perfection of the life, or of the work.

These lines, from Yeats's poem "The Choice," incapsulate a theme
that is basic to both *The Doctor's Dilemma* and *Pygmalion.* In each
of these plays we are forced to choose between a character who embodies perfection of the work—a dedicated professional, an artist
—and other characters who possess the human qualities that he
signally lacks. This choice is made as difficult as possible, for a careful balance is maintained between the inhuman professionals, Dubedat in *The Doctor's Dilemma* and Higgins in *Pygmalion,* and the
unprofessional human beings who are placed beside them.

The idea that there is something inhuman or antisocial about the
man who is dedicated to his work is one which is found frequently
in Shaw's writings. He declares in the Epistle Dedicatory to *Man and
Superman* that the man of genius is "an atrocious egotist in his dis-
regard of others" (p. xx); and in the Hell Scene the Devil says of
the Life Worshippers (like Rembrandt) that "there is something unnatural about these fellows"; and he warns the Statue: "Beware of
the pursuit of the Superhuman: it leads to an indiscriminate contempt for the Human" (III, 129). Tanner's speech to Octavius, in
Act I of the Comedy, about the unscrupulousness of the artist is an
expansion, in his own hyperbolic language, of the same point. The
true artist, Tanner says, will sacrifice those around him for the sake
of his art. "Since marriage began, the great artist has been known as
a bad husband. But he is worse: he is a child-robber, a blood-sucker,

a hypocrite, and a cheat" (p. 23). Shaw applied the same kind of language to himself in 1912, the year in which he began *Pygmalion,* in a letter to Eliza's original, who was to play the role two years later. "Shut your ears tight against this blarneying Irish liar and actor," he warned Mrs. Patrick Campbell. "He will fill his fountain pen with your heart's blood, and sell your most sacred emotions on the stage. He is a mass of imagination with no heart. He is a writing and talking machine that has worked for nearly forty years until its skill is devilish . . . I pray still that you, great actress as you are, are playing with him as he is playing with you. He cares for nothing really but his mission, as he calls it, and his work. He is treacherous as only an Irishman can be: he adores you with one eye and sees you with the other as a calculated utility." [1]

In reviewing a memoir of Wagner in 1891, Shaw wrote that it showed him "defying all the regulation categories by which we distinguish admirable from despicable characters, and yet throughout all standing out consistently as a great and lovable man." [2] Here is one of the ways in which an artist may deviate from normal human behavior: by defying our moral conventions. It is Dubedat's way. The other is discussed in Shaw's own brief memoir of William Morris, where he says that Morris was "a wise and great man *sub specie eternitatis;* but he was an ungovernable man in a drawingroom. What stimulated me to argument, or at least repartee, made him swear"; and he adds later that though Morris was "rich in the enormous patience of the greatest artists, he went unprovided with the small change of that virtue which enables cooler men to suffer fools gladly." [3] This sounds very much like Higgins. While Dubedat lacks ordinary human morals, Higgins lacks ordinary human manners. Both of these characteristics arise from a respect for their work which is so great that it excludes respect for other people as human beings. In *Caesar and Cleopatra,* Caesar says to the Sphinx, "I am he of whose genius you are the symbol: part brute, part woman, and part god—nothing of man in me at all" (I, 102). Dubedat and Higgins are part brute, part child, and part god—with little of man in them at all (although neither comes close to Caesar's greatness). Ridgeon refers to Dubedat as a "clever brute" in the final act of *The Doctor's Dilemma,* and in *Pygmalion* Eliza three times calls Higgins a brute. They are brutes in their total lack of consideration for others. Dubedat, we are told in a stage direction, *"is as natural as a cat: he moves among men as most men move among things"*; while Higgins is described as a man *"of the energetic, scientific type, heartily, even violently interested in everything that can be studied as a scientific subject, and careless about himself and other people, including their feelings."* [4]

II

Dubedat, in *The Doctor's Dilemma,* is brought to mind not only by Tanner's speech to Octavius about the immorality of the artist, but by one of his Maxims for Revolutionists: "There are no perfectly honorable men; but every true man has one main point of honor and a few minor ones" [5]—except that Dubedat lacks the few minor ones. His only point of honor is the artistic one; his only devotion is to his profession. His priorities are demonstrated at the beginning of Act III, when his wife is begging him not to borrow money from other people:

MRS DUBEDAT. Promise.
LOUIS [*putting on a touch of paint with notable skill and care and answering quite perfunctorily*] I promise, my darling.

(p. 129) [6]

He will not stop borrowing, even though it gives his wife pain, and he will not feel the slightest guilt about his actions. His artistic conscience is so clear that he does not require any other sort of conscience to preserve his self-respect. Having lived a life which is disgraceful from the ordinary moral point of view, he dies the death of a saint, confident that he has lived according to his faith—which he has.[7] "I'm not afraid," he says in his last moments, "and not ashamed . . . I know that in an accidental sort of way, struggling through the unreal part of life, I havnt always been able to live up to my ideal. But in my own real world I have never done anything wrong, never denied my faith, never been untrue to myself. Ive been threatened and blackmailed and insulted and starved. But Ive played the game. Ive fought the good fight. And now it's all over, theres an indescribable peace. [*He feebly holds his hands and utters his creed*]: I believe in Michael Angelo, Velasquez, and Rembrandt;

in the might of design, the mystery of color, the redemption of all things by Beauty everlasting, and the message of Art that has made these hands blessed. Amen. Amen" (IV, 163).

Max Beerbohm, reviewing the first production of *The Doctor's Dilemma* in 1906, made the objection that one could not believe in Dubedat as a great artist. This is, he said, partly because of the fact that his work is actually displayed on the stage, which Beerbohm thought injudicious on Shaw's part ("The posthumous 'one man show' is a revelation of his versatility. Dubedat seems to have caught, in his brief lifetime, the various styles of *all* the young lions of the Carfax Gallery. Budding genius is always, I know, imitative; but not so frantically imitative as all that"), and also because Dubedat's personality is not that of the great artist.[8] But how much of a genius is Dubedat supposed to be? Although he is clearly very talented, nothing in the play suggests that he is to be taken as a Michelangelo, or even a potential Michelangelo. There is, I think, a good reason for this. If Dubedat were one of the world's great artistic geniuses, then we could have little hesitation about thinking him more valuable than the other characters in the play, in spite of his moral failings. And Shaw, as I said at the beginning of this chapter, wants our choice to be as difficult as possible. Therefore he weighs the scales evenly, giving Dubedat much to recommend him, but not so much that the balance is upset.

The one immoral feature of *Don Giovanni,* Shaw wrote twelve years before *The Doctor's Dilemma,* "is its supernatural retributive morality. Gentlemen who break through the ordinary categories of good and evil, and come out at the other side singing Fin ch' han dal vino and La ci darem, do not, as a matter of fact, get called on by statues, and taken straight down through the floor to eternal torments; and to pretend that they do is to shirk the social problem they present. Nor is it yet by any means an established fact that the world owes more to its Don Ottavios than to its Don Juans." [9] It is this last question that we are to consider in *The Doctor's Dilemma.* Dubedat is a Don Juan figure; he is in fact closer to Mozart's Don Juan than Tanner in *Man and Superman* is in that he really does lead an immoral life. And he comes "out at the other side" delivering the finest "aria" of the play: his death speech. (In Act III the doctors are in the position of the Statue: "Think of your position," Sir Patrick Cullen warns him. "You can defy the laws made by men; but there are other laws to reckon with. Do you know that youre going to die?" p. 140). The Don Ottavio of the play is Blenkinsop, in that he is the decent, conventional man, who contrasts with Dubedat in every respect. He is as honest as Dubedat is dishonest, and as scrupulous about money as Dubedat is unscrupulous: he refuses to borrow one and fourpence for his train fare home from Richmond in Act II. But even this honesty is not entirely a point in his favor: in this scene it makes him a tedious and uncomfortable companion, in contrast to Dubedat, who is always agreeable and fascinating, and especially when he is at his most scoundrelly, as in his conversation with Ridgeon in Act III, when he suggests that Ridgeon should blackmail his patients into having their portraits painted by him. And, more important, Dubedat is a talented painter, while it is made plain that Blenkinsop is not of much use as a doctor.[10] This is the point that Ridgeon makes in the discussion with Sir Patrick Cullen at the end of Act II: "It's not an easy case to judge, is it? Blenkinsop's an honest decent man; but is he any use? Dubedat's a rotten blackguard; but he's a genuine source of pretty and pleasant and good things" (p. 126). Ridgeon seems to prefer Dubedat, and he echoes Shaw's comment on Don Juan and Don Ottavio: "I'm not at all convinced that the world wouldnt be a better world if everybody behaved as Dubedat does than it is now that everybody behaves as Blenkinsop does" (p. 127). Sir Patrick is firmly on the side of the honest Blenkinsop, and argues that men and women are more important than pictures. "Suppose you had this choice put before you," he says to Ridgeon, "either to go through life and find all the pictures bad but all the men and women good, or to go through life and find all the pictures good and all the men and women rotten. Which would you choose?" (p. 126). The conflict is between aesthetic and moral values: should one choose beauty or goodness? Ridgeon and Sir Patrick agree that the desirable solution would be a marriage of these contraries:

RIDGEON. It would be simpler if Blenkinsop could paint Dubedat's pictures.
SIR PATRICK. It would be simpler still if Dubedat had some of

Blenkinsop's honesty. The world isnt going to be made simple for you, my lad: you must take it as it is. Youve to hold the scales between Blenkinsop and Dubedat. Hold them fairly.

(pp. 126–127)

As in the other plays which I have examined, valuable qualities are divided between opposing characters, and here no combination of the complementary characters is possible. Ridgeon (we are asked to believe) can take only one more tuberculosis patient, and must decide whether to save Dubedat or Blenkinsop, whose claims are made to seem equal.[11]

On the surface, it looks as if this dilemma is the center of the play. But in fact it is lost sight of in the last three acts, as is Blenkinsop himself (who does not appear on the stage after Act II and is hardly mentioned). Ridgeon's choice in Act III is more to let Dubedat die than specifically to save Blenkinsop, and it is made with reference to Dubedat's wife, Jennifer, more than to Dubedat himself. The main dilemma of the play, I think, is not Ridgeon's choice between Dubedat and Blenkinsop, but the choice that *we* must make between Dubedat and all the doctors.

The doctors are honorable men: the only doubtful case is that of Ridgeon himself. The others, like Blenkinsop, do their best in life. Even Walpole, who could be taken at first glance as a charlatan, sincerely believes in the efficacy of his surgical operations, and his motive is not avarice: he is eager, for example, to operate on Dubedat in order to make Jennifer happy (see I, 95).[12] But our judgment on the doctors as a group will inevitably have to do less with their honor than with their professional competence, since it is mainly in their professional role that the play presents them. As professional men, they are hardly very impressive; *The Doctor's Dilemma* is in the tradition of Molière's satires on doctors. The one medical treatment in the play that we are supposed to regard as sound is Ridgeon's opsonin treatment, and not one of the other doctors takes any serious interest in it. Sir Patrick Cullen, although he is the most sensible man in the play, dismisses it as gammon, and has no use for new discoveries in general; Cutler Walpole, the successful surgeon, calls it simple rot; Blenkinsop confesses to Ridgeon, "I'm ashamed to say I havnt a notion what your great discovery is" (I,

100); and B.B., the Court physician Sir Ralph Bloomfield Bonington, who thinks that he is taking up the treatment and pushing it, completely misunderstands it. Schutzmacher, the general practitioner who has prospered and retired, does not mention the treatment, but it is clear that it would not interest him if he were still in practice: he explains to Ridgeon that while in practice he treated every case with Parrish's Chemical Food. Similarly, Walpole treats every case by removing the patient's nuciform sac (that is, vermiform appendix), Blenkinsop by prescribing a pound of ripe greengages every day half an hour before lunch, and B.B. by inoculating to kill "the germ." [13]

At the end of the first act, then, the only doctor who is left with any claim to the status of a true professional man is Ridgeon.[14] And Ridgeon murders his patient (by the rather novel method of entrusting him to the care of one of the nation's most eminent physicians), after having deliberately misled the patient's wife into believing that only the other doctor could cure him. In the last act Jennifer accuses Ridgeon of being a callous vivisector to whom living things have no souls; doctors like him, she says, "blind themselves to the souls of animals; and that blinds them to the souls of men and women. You made a dreadful mistake about Louis; but you would not have made it if you had not trained yourself to make the same mistake about dogs. You saw nothing in them but dumb brutes; and so you could see nothing in him but a clever brute" (V, 172–173). Taken together with the comments on vivisection in the Preface, this speech appears to have the stamp of Shaw's own authority on it, but, in reality, as an analysis of Ridgeon's conduct in the play it could scarcely be further from the truth. It was not the callous detachment of the doctor but the emotional involvement of the man that caused him to "murder" Dubedat. When, at the end of Act II, Ridgeon finds that he is forced to choose between Dubedat and Blenkinsop, with the knowledge that the one he rejects will die, he tells Sir Patrick Cullen that the choice is complicated by the fact that he wants to marry Jennifer. Sir Patrick gives the advice that a conscientious doctor would presumably follow: "Well," he says, "you must choose as if she didnt exist: thats clear." To this Ridgeon replies, "Is that clear to you? Mind: it's not clear to me. She troubles my judgment" (pp. 127–128). His precise motivation in allowing

Dubedat to die is not made explicit in the play, but what is made reasonably plain is that his decision is based largely on his human feelings about Jennifer rather than a detached assessment of Dubedat's worth in relation to Blenkinsop: "The doctor . . . kills the young artist for the sake of the lovely wife," Shaw wrote to Arnold Daly in December 1907.[15] Ridgeon confesses to Jennifer near the end of the play that he put her husband into B.B.'s hands "because I was in love with you" (V, 174); he is partly motivated, then, by the hope that Jennifer as a widow might marry him. Probably more important is his altruistic desire to protect Jennifer, whom he loves, from the disillusionment with her husband which he thinks will be inevitable if he lives. This is the one point of Sir Patrick's to which Ridgeon assents at the end of Act II, and it is the consideration on his mind when he actually turns Dubedat over to B.B. at the end of Act III. Added to these two factors is his anger (another human passion) at Dubedat's impudence during the course of the visit in this act—and a specific desire to save Blenkinsop plays a role as well, although not apparently a major one.

When Jennifer responds to his confession that he allowed her husband to die because he was in love with her by saying, "In lo— You! an elderly man!" Ridgeon cries, "Dubedat: thou art avenged!" (V, 174).[16] One's general impression in the final act is just this, that Dubedat is avenged: that he emerges victorious, and that his victory is Ridgeon's ignominious defeat. We learn, for example, that both of Ridgeon's principal motives in allowing Dubedat to die were based on a lack of understanding of Jennifer: she would never have considered marrying the "elderly" Ridgeon, and one gathers that her belief in Dubedat's greatness is indestructible, so that she would never have become disillusioned with him. It looks near the end of the play as if Ridgeon is going to crush her when he tells her "the truth" about Dubedat—that he was "the most entire and perfect scoundrel, the most miraculously mean rascal, the most callously selfish blackguard that ever made a wife miserable." But Jennifer is not at all crushed; she seems to have known all along about his moral deficiencies; and this has simply not affected her worship of him.

JENNIFER . . . And [*with a gentle reassuring movement towards him*] dont think that you have shocked me so dreadfully. I know

quite well what you mean by his selfishness. He sacrificed everything for his art. In a certain sense he had even to sacrifice
everybody—

RIDGEON. Everybody except himself. By keeping that back he lost
the right to sacrifice you, and gave me the right to sacrifice him.
Which I did.

JENNIFER [*shaking her head, pitying his error*] He was one of
the men who know what women know: that self-sacrifice is vain
and cowardly.

RIDGEON. Yes, when the sacrifice is rejected and thrown away.
Not when it becomes the food of godhead.

(V, 176–177)

Jennifer's defense of Dubedat is a good one, and we feel that she,
who is Dubedat's representative, has the better of the argument.
This feeling is reinforced by the play's final disclosure, which brings
on Ridgeon his crowning humiliation, when he learns that Jennifer
has already remarried in obedience to Dubedat's wishes. Whereas at
the beginning of the play Jennifer was struggling to gain access to
the newly knighted physician in his consulting room, to beg him for
his professional services, now the scene has changed to Dubedat's
home ground, his one-man show, from which Ridgeon withdraws
awkwardly after he has been unable even to buy any of Dubedat's
paintings because Jennifer's new husband has bought them all for
her. The artist who was faithful to his profession (if to nothing else)
is posthumously triumphant over the doctor who has been unfaithful
to his by putting human above professional considerations.

The scoundrel Dubedat, then, turns out to be the only man in the
play who possesses both competence and integrity as a professional
man. He is the only man on whose work (as opposed to his life) we
can make a totally favorable judgment. And his work, as shown in
the play, has been of more value to other people than that of any of
the doctors. While the doctors have killed their fellow men either
through incompetence or (in Ridgeon's case) by deliberate intention,
he, as an artist, has given his fellow men pleasure through his professional skill and devotion. And, one might add, he has "made his
wife the happiest woman in the world"—as she herself testifies
(V, 176).

This is not to say that one's final judgment is completely in Dubedat's favor. His "perfection . . . of the work" does not excuse the

gross imperfection of his life. One is disposed to agree with Ridgeon's statement at his death that "the most tragic thing in the world is a man of genius who is not also a man of honor" (IV, 165). The play suggests that life is complicated for us by the fact that different desirable qualities are not found united in a single person. The well-intentioned doctors are incompetent professionally; the only doctor who is really competent betrays his professional responsibility by deliberately allowing his patient to die for personal reasons; and the only man who is both professionally capable and professionally scrupulous is in his moral life an unmitigated scoundrel.

III

The first point to be grasped about Henry Higgins in *Pygmalion* is that he is, like Dubedat, an artist—as the title of the play implies. He makes a graceless flower girl into a graceful lady, as the sculptor Pygmalion created a beautiful statue out of shapeless stone.[17] Higgins does this by teaching her how to speak correctly and beautifully; phonetics is to be regarded in this play as an artistic as well as scientific pursuit, and elegant speech is to be seen as a valuable accomplishment. Eliza as a lady in Act IV is perhaps less happy than she was as a flower girl—people who are transformed into a higher state usually are not happy in Shaw's plays—but she is superior. (This is perhaps clearer on the stage, where one actually hears the improvement in speech and sees the corresponding improvement in appearance.) The importance and value of the training that Higgins gives to Eliza is stated explicitly in the play in his reply to his mother's charge that he and Pickering are a pair of babies playing with their live doll: "Playing!" he exclaims, "The hardest job I ever tackled: make no mistake about that, mother. But you have no idea how frightfully interesting it is to take a human being and change her into a quite different human being by creating a new speech for her. It's filling up the deepest gulf that separates class from class and soul from soul" (III, 256).[18] Similarly, Shaw in the Preface stresses the crucial role which the phonetician ought to play in society. "The reformer we need most today," he writes, "is an energetic phonetic enthusiast: that is why I have made such a one the hero of a popular play" (p. 195). And later: "If the play makes the public aware that there are such people as phoneticians, and that they are among the most important people in England at present, it will serve its turn" (p. 198).

Shaw's Pygmalion regards other people not in human terms, but as so much stone to be used for his higher purposes. Therefore he simply cannot understand the concern expressed by Mrs. Pearce and his mother over Eliza's personal future. Mrs. Pearce, on the other hand, understands his lack of concern very well: "Of course I know you dont mean her any harm," she says to him; "but when you get what you call interested in people's accents, you never think or care what may happen to them or you" (II, 225). His behavior to Eliza all through the play is never unkind, but it is always unfeeling. He never tries to hurt her feelings; it is just that he cannot conceive of her (or anyone else) as having any feelings to be hurt.

> PICKERING [*in good-humored remonstrance*] Does it occur to you, Higgins, that the girl has some feelings?
> HIGGINS [*looking critically at her*] Oh no, I dont think so. Not any feelings that we need bother about. [*Cheerily*] Have you, Eliza?
> LIZA. I got my feelings same as anyone else.
> HIGGINS [*to Pickering, reflectively*] You see the difficulty?
> PICKERING. Eh? What difficulty?
> HIGGINS. To get her to talk grammar. The mere pronunciation is easy enough.
>
> (II, 223)

To Higgins, Eliza is merely a thing to be taught (in Acts II and III); then a thing which has been taught (in Act IV); and finally a thing which it would be agreeable and useful to have around the house (in Act V). A human being is not an end in himself with an individual personality that ought to be respected, but the raw material out of which something higher can be made. In Act II Higgins justifies the proposed experiment with Eliza on the ground that "the girl doesnt belong to anybody—is no use to anybody but me" (p. 222), and when in Act V Eliza tells him that Freddy loves her and would make her happy, he replies, "Can he make anything of you? Thats the point" (p. 291).

For Eliza this is not the point at all; she wants a husband who will love and respect her as she is, not one who will make something of her. The fact that Higgins puts forward this particular objection to Freddy reflects his lack of understanding of Eliza. In this lack of human understanding Higgins is like Tanner: he is a master only in his own higher intellectual pursuit, while in dealing with other people (especially women) he is frequently a blunderer. All through the final act Higgins reveals how little he has learned about Eliza during his months of close association with her. When she finally demonstrates that she has become independent of him, he still thinks that she will return to Wimpole Street as a companion: "Now youre a tower of strength: a consort battleship," he says to her. "You and I and Pickering will be three old bachelors together instead of only two men and a silly girl" (V, 294). It would be difficult to imagine terms more ludicrously inappropriate to Eliza, or less likely to appeal to her, than "consort battleship" and "old bachelor."

The key words in *Pygmalion* are gentleman and lady: they are used over and over again, with different meanings.[19] In the first act, for example, the Bystander says of Higgins, "E's a genleman: look at his bə-oots" (p. 205), while Eliza says of him, "He's no gentleman, he aint, to interfere with a poor girl" (p. 207). In Act II she says to him, "Well, if you was a gentleman, you might ask me to sit down, I think," and she objects to being called a baggage when she has "offered to pay like any lady" for Higgins to enable her to become a "lady in a flower shop" (p. 217). Later she tells Higgins that she wouldn't have eaten his chocolate, "only I'm too ladylike to take it out of my mouth" (p. 224). In Act V the entrance of the newly enriched, formally attired Doolittle is preceded by this dialogue:

> THE PARLORMAID. Mr Henry: a gentleman wants to see you very particular. He's been sent on from Wimpole Street.
> HIGGINS. . . . Who is it?
> THE PARLORMAID. A Mr Doolittle, sir.
> PICKERING. Doolittle! Do you mean the dustman?
> THE PARLORMAID. Dustman! Oh no, sir: a gentleman.
>
> (p. 275)

Doolittle is identified as a gentleman by his dress, as Higgins was at the start of the play. All of these references (and others) to ladies and gentlemen provide a background to Eliza's well-known speeches to Pickering in Act V about what constitutes ladies and gentlemen: "It was from you that I learnt really nice manners; and that is what makes one a lady, isnt it? You see it was so very difficult for me with the example of Professor Higgins always before me. I was brought up to be just like him, unable to control myself, and using bad language on the slightest provocation. And I should never have known that ladies and gentlemen didnt behave like that if you hadnt been there. . . . You see, really and truly, apart from the things anyone can pick up (the dressing and the proper way of speaking, and so on), the difference between a lady and a flower girl is not how she behaves, but how she's treated." I shall always be a flower girl to Professor Higgins, because he always treats me as a flower girl, and always will; but I know I can be a lady to you, because you always treat me as a lady, and always will" (pp. 283, 284). Ladies and gentlemen, according to Eliza, are people with "really nice manners" (which include proper speech) and the self-respect that comes from being treated respectfully by others.

In the final act Eliza wishes to humiliate Higgins, and therefore she dismisses his role in her education as trivial and says that it was Pickering who really taught her to be a lady. This is unfair to Higgins, without whom she would still be a flower girl. It is true that Pickering has the good manners that Higgins so conspicuously lacks, and it is also true that he was necessary (although not sufficient) for her transformation. But it was Higgins who conceived the bold idea of transforming Eliza in the first place, and it was his professional skill and perseverance which enabled her to learn to speak—a vital accomplishment for her which she treats too lightly in Act V. Higgins and Pickering are, like Dubedat and Blenkinsop in *The Doctor's Dilemma*, complementary characters, each of them possessing the opposite of the other's qualities and defects. Whereas Dubedat and Blenkinsop force us to consider the relative value of creative genius and moral virtue, Higgins and Pickering force us to consider the relative value of creative genius and good manners. Pickering's manners are as good as Higgins' are bad: Pickering is the perfect gentleman. But Higgins, though no more a real gentleman than Doolittle the dustman is, possesses qualities of a very different kind, which Pickering lacks: like Dubedat, he is the true professional and (as I have noted) artist. The difference between the two characters is brought out in the printed version of the play in the first act, where Pickering is designated "the Gentleman" and Higgins "the Note Taker" (and it is significant in this act that Higgins, who treats Eliza without any consideration, is nevertheless the one who gives her the "large" sum of money). At the beginning of Act II Higgins' professional nature is emphasized by contrast with Pickering; the act begins as Higgins' demonstration of his art ends.

HIGGINS [*as he shuts the last drawer*] Well, I think thats the whole show.

PICKERING. It's really amazing. I havnt taken half of it in, you know.

HIGGINS. Would you like to go over any of it again?

PICKERING . . . No, thank you: not now. I'm quite done up for this morning.

HIGGINS . . . Tired of listening to sounds?

PICKERING. Yes. It's a fearful strain. I rather fancied myself because I can pronounce twenty-four distinct vowel sounds; but your hundred and thirty beat me. I cant hear a bit of difference between most of them.

(II, 215)

It is this professional quality of Higgins to which Eliza principally owes her transformation. We can be certain that Pickering by himself would not have undertaken the experiment, and, as he tells Eliza in Act V, "He [Higgins] taught you to speak; and I couldnt have done that, you know." To this she replies merely, "Of course: that is his profession" (V, 283). For her the only significant acts are those which are done from human, personal motives; she cannot see anything noble or praiseworthy in what a man does as his work. (She tells Higgins that she does not want Freddy to have to work when he is her husband.) We, however, are in a position to see the value in both Pickering's human gentlemanliness and Higgins' zeal and ability, and there is no easy choice to be made between them.

Although Higgins and Pickering are deliberately contrasted characters whose qualities we are to judge in relation to each other, the two of them do not come into conflict at any point in the play; the conflict is between Higgins and Eliza, and it is out of this relationship that the play grows. Eliza is of course a much more complex character than Pickering: whereas the description *"an elderly gentleman of the amiable military type"* (I, 203) leaves little more to be said about him, she cannot be described so easily. For *Pygmalion* is concerned not simply with ladies and gentlemen, but with the relationship between this type and women and men (a higher type) and girls and boys (a lower type); and Eliza passes through all three of these stages. She begins in Acts I and II as a flower *girl;* in Acts III and IV she is a lady; and by the end of the play she has become a woman. We have here an ingenious version of the Pygmalion myth: Pygmalion/Higgins makes the stone/girl into a statue/lady, which Venus/the Life Force causes to come alive as a woman.

The interesting part of this development, both in the original myth and in Shaw's handling of it, is the transformation of the statue into a woman. A valuable commentary on this process in *Pygmalion* is provided by a letter that Shaw wrote to the actress Florence Farr in 1891—twenty-one years before he wrote the play—while he was giving her elocution and voice lessons: "Prithee persevere with the speaking: I found with unspeakable delight last time that you were beginning to do it quite beautifully. There is much more to be done, of course, much ill usage in store for you, but success is now certain. You have reached the stage of the Idiotically Beautiful. There remain the stages of the Intelligently Beautiful & finally of the Powerfully Beautiful; & until you have attained the last you will never be able to compel me to recognize the substance of that soul of which I was shown a brief image by Nature for her own purposes." [21] This letter is indeed remarkable as an anticipation of *Pygmalion*—even its final sentence is echoed in Higgins' references to Eliza in Act V as a soul and as a part of humanity "that has come my way and been built into my house" (p. 289). And the progression that Shaw sets out in the letter corresponds exactly to Eliza's development in the last three acts of the play. In Act III, at Mrs. Higgins' At Home, she is Idiotically Beautiful; she is an artificial duchess, a live doll, a statue. The fact that she is now fit for the Eynsford Hills's society implies that many of the middle class never evolve beyond the statue stage, that they never become human. In Act IV she has reached the level of the Intelligently Beautiful; she is a lady not only in her accent and dress, but also in her possession of a new sensitivity, a delicacy of feeling that has hitherto been lacking. With this sensitivity she becomes aware that Higgins has no human feeling for her and regards her as a mere thing, and she therefore determines to be independent of him. This she achieves in a limited way in Act IV, when she reviles him bitterly and leaves Wimpole Street, and in a final, thorough way in Act V, when she repudiates his dominance exultantly, announcing that she will marry Freddy and support him by teaching phonetics as an assistant to Higgins' rival. The exchange that follows this declaration is the climax of the play:

HIGGINS [*rising in a fury*] What! That impostor! that humbug! that toadying ignoramus! Teach him my methods! my discoveries! You take one step in his direction and I'll wring your neck. [*He lays hands on her*]. Do you hear?

LIZA [*defiantly non-resistant*] Wring away. What do I care? I knew youd strike me some day. [*He lets her go, stamping with rage at having forgotten himself, and recoils so hastily that he stumbles back into his seat on the ottoman*]. Aha! Now I know how to deal with you. What a fool I was not to think of it before! You cant take away the knowledge you gave me. You said I had a finer ear than you. And I can be civil and kind to people, which is more than you can. Aha! [*Purposely dropping her aitches to annoy him*] Thats done you, Enry Iggins, it az. Now I dont care that [*snapping her fingers*] for your bullying and your big talk. I'll advertize it in the papers that your duchess is only a flower girl that you taught, and that she'll teach anybody to be a duchess just the same in six months for a thousand guineas. Oh, when I think of myself crawling under your feet and being trampled on and called names, when all the time I had only to lift up my finger to be as good as you, I could just kick myself.

HIGGINS [*wondering at her*] You damned impudent slut, you! But it's better than snivelling; better than fetching slippers and finding spectacles, isnt it? [*Rising*] By George, Eliza, I said I'd make a woman of you; and I have. I like you like this.

(V, 293-294)

This is the moment at which the sculptor sees with delighted amazement that his statue has come to life. Eliza is now Powerfully Beautiful: no longer a flower girl, more than a mere lady—a

woman, who has sufficient vitality and strength of will to face life
with courage and self-reliance.

Where does this leave Higgins? One point to be noted is that his
statement "I said I'd make a woman of you; and I have" is not quite
correct. He said he would make a lady, "a duchess," of her; it is the
Life Force inherent in Eliza herself that has enabled her to become a
woman (although Higgins has helped by bullying and offending her
to the point where she revolts against him). And if she is a woman,
what is he? According to the concept of "woman" which is implicit
in his speech to her, he is a man; he has already boasted of his own
self-reliance. But in other senses he is not a man: he is inhuman and
immature, which is to say that he is a brute rather than a man and
a boy rather than a man. (Dubedat, in *The Doctor's Dilemma,* is
called a brute by Ridgeon and a child by his wife.) Higgins is described in the stage direction that introduces him as *"rather like a
very impetuous baby"* (II, 215), and is treated as such by his
mother, for whom he feels a child's affection; and he himself says to
Pickering in Act II that he has "never been able to feel really
grown-up and tremendous, like other chaps" (p. 231). Whereas
Eliza has become by the end of the play both a lady and a woman,
Higgins is neither a gentleman nor (in important senses of the
term) a man.[22]

This does not mean, however, that Eliza is the outright victor. She
does, it is true, humiliate Higgins in the final act, particularly in the
last part. (It is interesting that both *Pygmalion* and *The Doctor's Dilemma* end with the humiliation of a man by a much younger
woman.) But Higgins, though humiliated by Eliza, is still superior
to her in significant ways. He is the creator of Eliza the lady, and
only as a lady could she have become a woman—or so the play
implies. He propounds an ideal, by which his own life is governed,
which Eliza can neither understand nor live by: the ideal of a cold
life of impersonal striving. Eliza, on the other hand, propounds *her*
ideal: a warm life of personal friendship and love. During the discussion between Higgins and Eliza in Act V, these two ideals, and
the characters who embody them, are beautifully balanced; only at
the end does Eliza seem to emerge triumphant—and even then one
feels that the issue has not been finally decided. During the discussion, we have the impression that Higgins is utterly vanquished,

then Eliza, then Higgins, and so on. With each speech an unexpected other side to the question springs into view. On the day on which *Pgymalion* opened in London, Shaw sent Mrs. Patrick Campbell a letter headed "FINAL ORDERS," which included the following: "If you have ever said to Stella [Mrs. Patrick Campbell's daughter] in her childhood 'I'll let you see whether you will. . . . obey me or not,' and then inverted her infant shape and smacked her until the Square (not to mention the round) rang with her screams, you will . . . . . . know how to speak the line 'I'll let you see whether I'm dependent on you.' There is a certain dragging intensity, also used in Act IV in 'YOU thank God etc,' which is wanted here to re-establish your lead after Higgins' long speech about science and classical music and so on. The author took care to re-establish it by giving Eliza a long and energetic speech in reply to him; but the ignorant slave entrusted with the part thought she knew better than the author, and cut out the speech as useless. Now she has got to do it the other way." [23]

The line "I'll let you see whether I'm dependent on you," which Shaw removed from the play when revising the scene for the film version, occurred shortly after Eliza's reply to Higgins' "science and classical music" speech. What Shaw is saying to Mrs. Patrick Campbell in the letter is that since she has dropped the "long and energetic speech" that he had provided to re-establish Eliza's lead (that is, the one beginning "Oh, you are a cruel tyrant," V, 292), she would have to re-establish it by giving special emphasis to the later speech. The phrase "re-establish your lead" neatly sums up Shaw's "tennis" technique in the last scene of *Pygmalion,* and in the debates which provide the climaxes of many of his other plays. (*John Bull's Other Island* offers a particularly good example.) Eliza and Higgins keep re-establishing their respective leads, until the play ends with no clear victory for either of them. The play does not take one side or the other; it leaves us valuing both Eliza's warm human qualities and Higgins' cold professional qualities, and it leaves us faced with the dilemma that arises from the incompatibility of these two sets of virtues, perfection of the life and of the work.

VI

Misalliance

Misalliance, observed Desmond MacCarthy, "may be regarded in a measure as a preliminary canter for the far finer *Heartbreak House*"; [1] and later critics have followed him in noting similarities between the two plays. Along with *Getting Married* (which was written the year before *Misalliance*), both of these plays stand out from most of Shaw's other works because of their lack of dependence on plot, which gives them an apparent, superficial formlessness. The characters in all three plays represent a great diversity of types; and in *Misalliance* we find particular types which recur in *Heartbreak House.* Johnny Tarleton, the capitalist without brains or ability in *Misalliance,* shares these characteristics with Mangan in *Heartbreak House;* Lord Summerhays in *Misalliance* and Sir Hastings Utterword In *Heartbreak House* both govern the Empire; and Hypatia Tarleton in *Misalliance,* like Hesione Hushabye in *Heartbreak House,* is one of Shaw's vital, dominating women (and the two of them are similar in appearance). Situations recur as well: in each play a weekend house party is interrupted by an unexpected descent from the sky (the airplane crashing into the greenhouse in *Misalliance* has its counterpart in *Heartbreak House* in the bombs landing in the gravel pit), and by the intrusion of a character of a lower class than the others who is bent on committing a crime. [2]

There is also a similarity between the two plays which is more fundamental than any of these, and that is their atmosphere of frustration and restlessness. This is more pronounced in *Heartbreak House,* which is much more a play of atmosphere in any case, but in both plays we have the sense of strong energies that cannot find any satisfying expression, and which therefore run to talk and to sexual pursuit, which Shaw sees as very limited forms of activity. The speech in *Misalliance* that is closest to *Heartbreak House* is Lina's denunciation near the end of the play: "Old pal," she says to Tarleton, "this is a stuffy house. You seem to think of nothing but making love. All the conversation here is about love-making. All the pictures are about love-making. The eyes of all of you are sheep's eyes. You are steeped in it, soaked in it: the very texts on the walls of your bedrooms are the ones about love. It is disgusting. It is not healthy. Your women are kept idle and dressed up for no other purpose than to be made love to. I have not been here an hour; and already everybody makes love to me as if because I am a woman it were my profession to be made love to" (p. 195). Lina's description is in fact truer of the Hushabyes' house than it is of the Tarletons', for in *Misalliance* love-making is not quite as central and pervasive as she suggests. But the speech is valid as a comment on the waste of energy in the world of the play; most of the characters in *Misalliance,* with the notable exception of the outsiders Lina and Percival, lead unfulfilled lives.

The character in whom the mood of frustration has its main focus is Hypatia.[3] She says repeatedly how bored she is with the life at her father's house, and whereas Lina is disgusted with the sexual pursuit, she is driven nearly mad by the talk: "If you all sat in silence," she says to Lord Summerhays, "as if you were waiting for something to happen, then there would be hope even if nothing did happen. But this eternal cackle, cackle, cackle about things in general is only fit for old, *old,* OLD people. I suppose it means something to them: theyve had their fling. All I listen for is some sign of it ending in something; but just when it seems to be coming to a point, Johnny or papa just starts another hare; and it all begins over again; and I realize that it's never going to lead anywhere and never going to stop. Thats when I want to scream" (p. 135). Phrases like "something to happen" and "nothing did happen" remind one of the dialogue between Mazzini Dunn and Captain Shotover in the last part of *Heartbreak House;* and Hypatia's speech also anticipates Ellie Dunn's remark just before their dialogue: life, Ellie says, "cant go on for ever. I'm always expecting something. I dont know what it is; but life must come to a point sometime" (III, 136–137). Hypatia wants something to happen; or, as her father puts it, she "has always wanted some adventure to drop out of the sky" (p. 148; see also p. 141). Her desire, like Ellie's, is satisfied, although the disturbing implications of the bombing in *Heartbreak House* are totally absent from *Misalliance,* which is altogether a much less disturbing (and important) play.

The airplane in *Misalliance* brings what Hypatia really wants: an attractive man whom she can marry. She is a classic example of the Shavian Philistine, and, as with Ann Whitefield in *Man and Superman,* her primitive motivation is suggested by the repeated mention of animals in connection with her. "How I envy the animals!" she says to Lord Summerhays (p. 134); and when he calls her a "glorious young beast" she declares that this phrase expresses exactly what she likes to be (pp. 138–139). In her approach to Joey Percival she fulfills admirably this ideal which she has set up for herself. The stage direction describing the first step in her campaign of pursuit says that *"Hypatia, excited, mischievous, her eyes glowing, runs in, precisely on his trail"* (p. 158).[4] A few minutes later she is chasing him out into the woods, and when Percival becomes the pursuer she fights like a wild cat (as she boasts to the others afterward) (p. 189). Her outlook on life is best expressed in her demand to her father to enable her to marry Percival: "Papa: buy the brute for me" (p. 189); this combines the two Philistine concerns of *Man and Superman:* sex and money.

Whereas Hypatia lives with what she regards as a surfeit of talk and ideas, and wants action, her father leads an active life and regrets that he lacks the opportunity for more talk and ideas. This inverse relationship between them is noted in part by Hypatia herself: "Theres my father in the garden, meditating on his destiny," she says to Lord Summerhays. "All very well for him: he's had a destiny to meditate on; but I havnt had any destiny yet. Everything's happened to him: nothing's happened to me" (p. 135). Tarleton shares with Hypatia boundless and irrepressible energy, which is in his case both intellectual and sexual: the two seem closely related in him. And, as in the case of Hypatia, his inability to release all this energy in the sphere of society in which he finds himself—the underwear business—makes him restless and dissatisfied.[5] He says in the first part of the play, *"bouncing up, too energetic to sit still,"* "But I'm getting sick of that old shop. Thirty-five years Ive had of it: same blessed old stairs to go up and down every day; same old lot: same old game: sorry I ever started it now. I'll chuck it and try something else: something that will give a scope to all my faculties" (p. 127). We may well feel that Tarleton's faculties are better suited to the manufacture of underwear than to the writing of books on philosophical subjects, since his thinking is strictly amateur and ludicrously second-hand, but his frustration is nonetheless real.

If capitalism fails to satisfy the needs of a successful capitalist, what does it do for those who are lower down in its hierarchy? The answer to this question is provided by "Mr. Gunner," the clerk who threatens to kill Tarleton.

> TARLETON. . . . Ive a good deal of business to do still before I die. Havnt you?
> THE MAN. No. Thats just it: Ive no business to do. Do you know what my life is? I spend my days from nine to six—nine hours of daylight and fresh air—in a stuffy little den counting another man's money. Ive an intellect: a mind and a brain and a soul; and the use he makes of them is to fix them on his tuppences and his eighteenpences and his two pound seventeen and tenpences and see how much they come to at the end of the day and take care that no one steals them. I enter and enter, and add and add, and take money and give change, and fill cheques and stamp receipts; and not a penny of that money is my own: not one of those transactions has the smallest interest for me or anyone else in the world but him; and even he couldnt stand it if he had to do it all himself . . . Of all the damnable waste of human life that ever was invented, clerking is the very worst.

> (pp. 166–167)

In short, Gunner is suffering from the same complaint as Tarleton —lack of satisfying activity for his mental faculties, although Gunner's symptoms are much worse, for in him these faculties have gone utterly to seed. What *Misalliance* implies is that the capitalist system satisfies only underdeveloped, soulless people like Tarleton's son, Johnny, who is content with his life because his needs are so limited in range.

Lord Summerhays' position is comparable to that of Tarleton and Gunner, in that he too has no opportunity to exercise his talents. In his case, though, the unused talents (which are for governing) [6] are more genuine than those of the others, and the obstacle to their use is not capitalism but democracy. He has governed a colonial territory, apparently with great success, but now that he is retired he finds that there is no place for him in the English political system. Soon after Tarleton's speech about trying "something else . . . that will give a scope to all my faculties," Lord Summerhays says that he has nothing to do in England, and this exchange follows:

TARLETON . . . But theres lots for you to do here. You have a genius for government. You learnt your job out there in Jinghis-kahn. Well, we want to be governed here in England. Govern us.

LORD SUMMERHAYS. Ah yes, my friend; but in Jinghiskahn you have to govern the right way. If you dont, you go under and come home. Here everything has to be done the wrong way, to suit governors who understand nothing but partridge shooting (our English native princes, in fact) and voters who dont know what theyre voting about. I dont understand these democratic games; and I'm afraid I'm too old to learn. What can I do but sit in the window of my club, which consists mostly of retired Indian Civil servants? We look on at the muddle and the folly and amateurishness; and we ask each other where a single fortnight of it would have landed us.

(pp. 128–129)

II

While Tarleton and Lord Summerhays have abilities which they cannot put at the service of English society, their sons have little to contribute in the first place. Both fathers are disappointed in their sons, and with good reason. Tarleton, although he is foolish in his display of undigested reading, is nevertheless (we are led to believe) a good man of business and a public-spirited one, and he is at least interested in books and ideas. Johnny, on the other hand, is no good as a businessman, a point which is made by both his father and Bentley; nor is he public spirited: public work (like setting up free libraries), he tells Lord Summerhays, is "really a sort of laziness, getting away from your own serious business to amuse yourself with other people's" (p. 115); and his idea of a good book indicates his cultural level: "I like a book with a plot in it," he says to his father. "You like a book with nothing in it but some idea that the chap that writes it keeps worrying, like a cat chasing its own tail. I can stand a little of it, just as I can stand watching the cat for two minutes, say, when Ive nothing better to do. But a man soon gets fed up with that sort of thing. The fact is, you look on an author as a sort of god. *I* look on him as a man that I pay to do a certain thing for me. I pay him to amuse me and to take me out of myself and make me forget" (p. 129). To Johnny the test of any action is its return in personal profit or advantage. One of Shaw's least agreeable characters, he represents a clear decline in the Tarleton stock.[7]

Correspondingly, Bentley represents a decline in the Summerhays stock. Lord Summerhays is sensitive, as his reaction to Hypatia's crudeness demonstrates, but he is strong in public life and dignified in private life. Bentley has the sensitivity to a debilitating degree, and lacks the strength and manliness. The contrast between him and the utterly insensitive Johnny, with which *Misalliance* begins, is complete; they are deficient in precisely opposite directions. In one of the first speeches of the play, Bentley tells Johnny that his own brothers and sisters are the "quite pleasant, ordinary, do-the-regular-thing sort: all body and no brains, like you," while he himself, because he was born many years after them, "came out all brains and no more body than is absolutely necessary" (p. 109). This opposition between body and brain is frequently referred to in the early part of the play—in the scene between Bentley and Johnny, where it is actually dramatized, and in the scene in which Hypatia and her mother discuss Bentley. Hypatia contrasts Bentley with her other suitors, who one gathers have been of Johnny's type. Bentley, she says, at least "has some brains. He's not like all the rest. One cant have everything." She describes one of her former suitors, Jerry Mackintosh, as a "splendid animal" but a fool, and comments that "not one of them has as much brains in his whole body as Bentley has in his little finger." Her dilemma is of a kind that is important in other forms in Shaw's middle plays: "I can imagine all sorts of men I could fall in love with; but I never seem to meet them. The real ones are too small, like Bunny, or too silly, like Jerry" (pp. 121–123). She must choose between brainless matter and immaterial brain, and she wants both mental and physical distinction in a husband.

Hypatia and her mother agree that Bentley is deficient in physical distinction, and in fact he is deficient in other ways as well. Like Marchbanks, his excessive sensitivity about himself and unconscious callousness about the feelings of others make him a very trying person to have around—and he lacks Marchbanks' redeeming creative abilities.[8] Bentley is just as unsatisfactory in his way as his opposite, Johnny, is unsatisfactory in *his*.

see pg. 243

One possible direction in which *Misalliance* could have developed is toward a union of the opposing qualities of Johnny and Bentley. This goal might have been achieved by the marriage of Hypatia and Bentley, whose engagement is the basis of the play's plot. Hypatia is herself "a splendid animal," and such a marriage would have joined together the predominantly Philistine Tarleton stock with the intelligent Summerhays stock (as represented by Lord Summerhays and Bentley), and of course it would have crossed the middle class and the aristocracy—a union which Carlyle saw in 1867 in *Shooting Niagara: And After?* as offering the best hope for England.[9]

The idea of a marriage of contraries and its desirability are suggested in various ways in the first half of *Misalliance*. We have already seen that the opposition between Bentley, who is all brain, and Johnny and his type, who are all body, occupies an important place in this section of the play, and is the note on which the whole play opens. It is also evident in the early part of the play that people are attracted to their opposites. Not only is Hypatia attracted (albeit half-heartedly) to Bentley, but the vigorous Tarleton takes to this effete young man as well; they enter together when Tarleton first appears, and both Johnny and Bentley himself remark on their liking for one another. And then there is the attraction that Lord Summerhays felt toward Hypatia; he had proposed marriage to her, prompted by the "innocent impulse to place the delicacy and wisdom and spirituality of my age at the affectionate service of your youth for a few years, at the end of which you would be a grown, strong, formed—widow" (p. 137)—an idea that anticipates the union between Ellie Dunn and Captain Shotover in *Heartbreak House*.[10] In the political sphere, too, Lord Summerhays believes in uniting opposites: "To make Democracy work," he says to Tarleton, "you need an aristocratic democracy. To make Aristocracy work, you need a democratic aristocracy" (p. 129). Tarleton's belief that the Empire serves a useful purpose because it "averages out the human race. Makes the nigger half an Englishman. Makes the Englishman half a nigger" (p. 144) is based on the same general principle.

In the middle of *Misalliance,* however, the play's direction changes, with the arrival on the scene of Joey Percival and Lina Szczepanowska. Earlier Mrs. Tarleton has said of Bentley, "He's overbred, like one of those expensive little dogs. I like a bit of a mongrel myself, whether it's a man or a dog" (p. 121). Joey Percival is a bit of a mongrel in the sense that he possesses both brain and body: before his arrival Bentley says that he would not risk letting Hypatia meet Percival, for "who'd marry me, dyou suppose, if they could get my brains with a full-sized body?" (p. 128). Lina too is a mongrel, but in another way: she combines feminine attractiveness with masculine bravery and strength, a union which is reflected in Hypatia's designation of her as "the man-woman or woman-man or whatever you call her that came with you [Percival]" (p. 159).[11] (This combination in Lina of physical and spiritual superiority, and male and female qualities, is an anticipation of *Saint Joan.*)

Percival and Lina are the two outsiders of the play. While the Tarletons and the Summerhayses represent English families of the traditional middle-class and aristocratic types, Joey, who is half-Italian, was brought up by three fathers, and Lina, who is Polish, comes from a family in which it is a point of honor for some member to risk his or her life on each day of the year. Since they are the two characters who carry everything before them, we might feel, comparing them with Johnny and Bentley in particular, that the family systems of the English ruling classes do not produce the best results.

The superficial theme of *Misalliance* is the incompatibility of parents and children. A subtler and more interesting theme, I think, is the exhaustion of the two English ruling classes, the capitalist middle class and the aristocracy. Johnny and Bentley will never be the men their respective fathers are; the new generation will not be able to run England's factories and its Empire. And there is no hope to be found in a union of the middle class and the aristocracy, which might have been symbolized by a marriage between Hypatia and Bentley. Instead, both Hypatia and Bentley are carried off by the outsiders, against the wishes of their respective fathers. Joey scoops up Hypatia (as Tarleton puts it), and Lina literally carries Bentley off the stage and later persuades him to go up in the airplane with her. The outsiders, who have dropped down from the sky, are victorious. England's future lies neither with the Tarletons nor the Summerhayses, nor with a Carlylean composite of the two, but with people who belong to quite a different world.

VII

Heartbreak House

"Take a man and a woman at the highest pitch of natural ability and charm yet attained, and enjoying all the culture that modern art and literature can offer them; and what does it all come to?" Shaw is writing here of Rubek and Irene in Ibsen's *When We Dead Awaken;* the passage is from the chapter on Ibsen's later plays which he wrote for the second edition of *The Quintessence of Ibsenism,* published in 1913—the year he first conceived *Heartbreak House.*[1] Shaw's question is really more relevant to his own play than to Ibsen's: *Heartbreak House* is a study of the class of people which Mazzini Dunn in the play (and no doubt many others in real life) saw as "rather a favorable specimen of what is best in our English culture." These men and women are, Dunn tells them in the final act, "very charming people, most advanced, unprejudiced, frank, humane, unconventional, democratic, free-thinking, and everything that is delightful to thoughtful people" (III, 135). Much of what Dunn says here about the Heartbreakers is true, but by this point in the play we are in the mood to reply, "They may be very charming, most advanced, and the rest of it, but what does it all come to?" Certainly not "everything that is delightful to thoughtful people": the climax of Dunn's tribute we have no hesitation in rejecting. Shaw could have called his play, as Tolstoy called his study of this class, *Fruits of Culture* (or *Fruits of Enlightenment*). Shaw undoubtedly had Tolstoy's play in mind when he wrote *Heartbreak House;* he discusses it at the beginning of his Preface; and in a speech he delivered in 1920 at the Tolstoy Commemoration at Kingsway

Hall, he describes the play as "the first of the Heartbreak Houses, and the most blighting." [2]

What are the fruits of culture, as presented in *Heartbreak House?* What it all comes to is something very close to the hell of *Man and Superman*—and the play is full of references to hell, devils, and damnation. In Act I Hector, speaking of people like Boss Mangan and Randall Utterword, says that he must believe that the red light over their door is hellfire; and the evening light, seen through the glass doors of Heartbreak House, is described in a stage direction shortly before this speech as *"now very red"* (pp. 76, 74). The atmosphere of the play is that of the stuffy, cloying, disabling unreality from which Don Juan (like Hector Hushabye) wishes so desperately to escape. Much of what Juan says of hell in the Hell Scene of *Man and Superman* accurately describes Heartbreak House. Consider, for example, the following outburst which Juan addresses to the Devil: "Rather would I be dragged through all the circles of the foolish Italian's Inferno than through the pleasures of Europe. That is what has made this place of eternal pleasures so deadly to me . . . It is the success with which you have diverted the attention of men from their real purpose, which in one degree or another is the same as mine, to yours, that has earned you the name of The Tempter. It is the fact that they are doing your will, or rather drifting with your want of will, instead of doing their own, that makes them the uncomfortable, false, restless, artificial, petulant, wretched creatures they are" (III, 124). In the Hell Scene in *Man and Superman* we are never actually shown this drifting, and in the Comedy the atmosphere is not that of hell at all, but one of gaiety, in which the "diabolic," heartbroken Octavius is a ridiculed outsider. But *Heartbreak House* is a play specifically about drifting, both in terms of structure—its apparent formlessness is in marked contrast to the neatness of the Comedy in *Man and Superman*—and in terms of atmosphere. The dominant atmosphere of *Heartbreak House* emanates from those characters in the play who are most uncomfortable, false, restless, artificial, petulant, and wretched. One such character, though a minor one, is Randall Utterword—Randall the Rotter, on whom Lady Utterword, with complete justice, inflicts this description of himself: "You are," she says, "laziness incarnate. You are selfishness itself. You are the most uninteresting man on earth. You cant even gossip about anything but yourself and your grievances and your ailments and the people who have offended you" (II, 119). This is a description of the precise opposite of the heroic man as Juan conceives him in the Hell Scene, and as Shaw describes him in the "true joy in life" passage in the Epistle Dedicatory to *Man and Superman.*

Heartbreak House, like hell in *Man and Superman,* is "the home of the unreal" and a "Palace of Lies." Of all Shaw's plays, *Heartbreak House* has the most unreal, dreamlike atmosphere (again in contrast to the bright clarity of the Comedy in *Man and Superman*), and its plot—insofar as it can be said to have one—has to do with Ellie's discovery of the unreality of everything around her.

> ELLIE. There seems to be nothing real in the world except my father and Shakespear. Marcus's tigers are false; Mr Mangan's millions are false; there is nothing really strong and true about Hesione but her beautiful black hair; and Lady Utterword's is too pretty to be real. The one thing that was left to me was the Captain's seventh degree of concentration; and that turns out to be—
> CAPTAIN SHOTOVER. Rum.
>
> (III, 129)

Nothing is solid and real in Heartbreak House: not even the burglar, whose purpose is not to commit straightforward theft but to extract money from the inhabitants by telling them lies and exploiting their reluctance to have the truth told about themselves in court. As Mangan says, "The very burglars cant behave naturally in this house" (II, 103). Another good reflection of the spirit of lying and unreality in Heartbreak House is Hesione's remark to Mangan that "cruelty would be delicious if one could only find some sort of cruelty that didnt really hurt" (II, 98). Similarly, she looks for love affairs in which real love plays no part: she sets out to fascinate Mangan—and succeeds—although she finds him not only unattractive but actually repellent. The love affairs of her husband, Hector, have no more reality in them. Lady Utterword, he complains to Hesione, "has the diabolical family fascination. I began making love to her automatically. What am I to do? I cant fall in love; and I cant hurt a woman's feelings by telling her so when she falls in love with me. And as women are always falling in love with my moustache I get landed in all sorts of tedious and terrifying flirtations in which I'm not a bit in earnest." To which Hesione replies, "Oh, neither is Addy. She has never been in love in her life" (I, 73).

The very heartbreak at Heartbreak House is mostly unreal or superficial. As applied to most of the characters in the play, the term "heartbreak" means suffering which results from disappointment in love. No character seems to suffer unbearably from this. Mangan's suffering is the most painful, but then he is an outsider, and has not devoted his life to love affairs: his unreality lies (amply) in other directions. Randall is certainly made unhappy by his relationship with Lady Utterword, but his suffering is of little account when considered next to that of (say) Chekhov's characters—Masha or Konstantin in *The Seagull,* for example, or Voynitsky in *Uncle Vanya.* It could be argued that this reveals the limitation of Shaw as a dramatist in comparison with Chekhov, but the important point is surely that in *Heartbreak House* this limitation produces effects which are dramatically appropriate. Randall's heartbreak is superficial, like most of the other activity in Heartbreak House. When Hector accuses Lady Utterword of making Randall howl by twisting his heart, her reply puts the affair in its proper perspective: "That is because Randall has nothing to do but have his heart broken. It is a change from having his head shampooed" (III, 136). The love affairs and consequent heartbreak in the play are, for the most part, not deeply felt experiences, but merely ways of passing the time. The superficiality of the characters' experience is what the play wants to convey: the characters' lives, like those of the damned in *Man and Superman,* are without depth and solidity, because they are not fulfilling their real purposes.

The host and hostess at Heartbreak House are Hector and Hesione Hushabye [3] (Captain Shotover says that Heartbreak House is not his house, but only his kennel, III, 134); and it is they who are closest to Shaw's account in the Preface of "cultured, leisured Europe before the war." It is in them—especially in Hector—that the tragic misuse of valuable potential is most apparent. Hector is a Don Juan who finds that he is condemned to remain in hell; he cannot work to bring a better world into being because he is compelled by his wife to be her domestic pet. "It's a dangerous thing," says Captain Shotover, "to be married right up to the hilt, like my daughter's husband. The man is at home all day, like a damned soul in hell" (II, 110). This reminds one not only of the Hell Scene in *Man and Superman,* but more particularly of Tanner's remark to Octavius in the first act of the Comedy that a lifetime of domestic happiness would be hell on earth; [4] and perhaps the marriage of Hector and Hesione can be taken as a kind of sequel to *Man and Superman,* showing Tanner and Ann in middle age. One hopes not. But Hector's views on love and marriage sound in places very much like Tanner's, expressed with a bitterness bred of years of captivity. "Is there any slavery on earth viler than this slavery of men to women?" he exclaims in Act II (p. 121), as he watches Lady Utterword humiliate Randall; and at several points in the play he complains of his own slavery to Hesione. When Captain Shotover suggests that Hector should invent something, he agrees:

> HECTOR. . . . You are right: I ought to support my wife.
> MRS HUSHABYE. Indeed you shall do nothing of the sort: I should never see you from breakfast to dinner. I want my husband.
> HECTOR [*bitterly*] I might as well be your lapdog.
> MRS HUSHABYE. Do you want to be my breadwinner, like the other poor husbands?
> HECTOR. No, by thunder! What a damned creature a husband is anyhow!
>
> (I, 77–78)

Hector refers elsewhere to the fascinating Shotover sisters as demons and devils, and he is very much aware of his state of damnation, just as Juan is very much aware that he is in hell. Like Juan, he is suited for a life which is nobler, more creative, and more useful; his captivity in Heartbreak House prevents him from making use of his considerable powers. His capacity for invention is used in telling lies to amuse people; and his capacity for heroism is used in capturing the seedy, contemptible burglar (who wanted in any case to be captured) and in the self-destructive act of tearing down the curtains and turning on the lights so that the bombs will destroy the house. He spends most of his energies in being what Lady Utterword calls him in the third act, "a very fascinating gentleman whose chief occupation is to be married to my sister" (p. 135). Instead, he should be saving the country: this would be his way of going from hell to heaven.

The idea that the relationship between the Hushabyes looks back to the Comedy in *Man and Superman* is strengthened by the similarity between Hesione and Ann Whitefield. Like Ann, Hesione is fascinating, very vital, sexually alluring, flirtatious, and unscrupulous in her determination to have her own way. In this last respect she is more brutal and direct than Ann, but the similarity remains. In the first act, for example, she bullies Ellie into staying at the house by threatening to insult Ellie's father; and when Ellie says that her family's struggle to survive was at least dignified, she replies: "*I shouldnt have pulled the devil by the tail with dignity. I should have pulled hard— [between her teeth] hard*" (I, 54). This determined point of view is Ann's in *Man and Superman,* although Ann is more restrained in expressing it, because she is a hypocrite. Another passage in *Heartbreak House* in which we are reminded of Ann—and of Doña Ana—is Hesione's speech at the end of the first act. After the lamentation raised by her husband and father, she says: "What do men want? They have their food, their firesides, their clothes mended, and our love at the end of the day. Why are they not satisfied? Why do they envy us the pain with which we bring them into the world, and make strange dangers and torments for themselves to be even with us?" (p. 78). But Hesione is without the *raison d'être* of Ann: she has already had her children, and has found no other, proper use to make of her enormous vitality, which she therefore spends in pointless flirtations and attempts to dominate other people's affairs, such as those of her husband and Ellie. In this lack of purpose she is like Hector. Both of them are drifting with the Devil's want of will, instead of doing their own.

It is this drifting which precludes self-fulfillment that makes them, in Don Juan's words, "the uncomfortable, false, restless, artificial, petulant, wretched creatures they are." Both are dissatisfied with their lives, and indeed, seem on the verge of madness and despair. Hector curses the Shotover sisters and himself in words that recall Othello and Lear: "Fool! Goat!" he says of himself in Act I, striking himself on the chest (p. 72), and at the end of Act II, after the humiliation of Randall: "Poor wretch! Oh women! women!

women! [*He lifts his fists in invocation to heaven*] Fall. Fall and crush" (p. 122). Hesione in not overtly critical of herself or of the other Heartbreakers; her dissatisfaction takes the form of a fierce effort to stave off emotional collapse. "I warn you," she tells Ellie, "that when I am neither coaxing and kissing nor laughing, I am just wondering how much longer I can stand living in this cruel, damnable world" (II, 94).[5] And when Ellie names the house Heartbreak House, Hesione cries out, "Stop, Ellie; or I shall howl like an animal" (III, 134). What has upset Hesione at this particular point is presumably the fact that Ellie has told the truth about the house and about the lives of its inhabitants: "This silly house, this strangely happy house, this agonizing house, this house without foundations" (III, 134). One doubts whether the house is strangely happy for the Hushabyes, as it is for Ellie, but their lives are certainly agonizing and without foundations. This truth is most painful for Hesione to face; and one feels that much of the futile, pointless activity of the Heartbreakers is intended to prevent them from having to face the truth about themselves.

Here we come to the main paradox of Heartbreak House. It is a Palace of Lies where the truth, however devastating, cannot be suppressed. In this way it is closer to a conventional hell than is the hell of *Man and Superman,* for the Heartbreakers' attempts to lose themselves in a world of happy unreality fail miserably, leaving them confronting the unadorned fact that their lives are meaningless and worthless. In this house, says Hector, "our game is to find out the man under the pose" (II, 117)—and, he might have added, to compel him to find out himself. This game has succeeded so well by the bombing scene in the third act that everyone's pretenses and deceptions have been entirely torn away. "If ever two cultivated souls of the propertied middle class were stripped naked and left bankrupt, these two are," Shaw wrote of the Allmerses in Ibsen's *Little Eyolf;* [6] and this spiritual undressing is one of the major motifs of *Heartbreak House,* given a concrete expression when Mangan (like Lear) begins to take off his clothes in the final act. "Let's all strip stark naked," he says. "We may as well do the thing thoroughly when we're about it. Weve stripped ourselves morally naked: well, let us strip ourselves physically naked as well, and see how we like it. I tell you I cant bear this" (III, 130).[7]

The term "heartbreak" has different meanings when applied to different people in the play, and it affects different people in different ways, according to how deep their natures are. For the shallow Randall heartbreak is a matter of being scorned by Lady Utterword, which leads him to whine and cry like a child. For Hector, whose spirit and vision are greater, heartbreak is the realization that "we are useless, dangerous, and ought to be abolished" (III, 124), which leads him to destructive fury. For Ellie, heartbreak is a release from the trivial; it is "the end of happiness and the beginning of peace" (II, 108), and leads to marriage with Captain Shotover and her concept of life with a blessing.

Ellie's type of heartbreak is basic to the whole play, although only she appears to experience it, and only she and Shotover appear to understand it. Ellie defines this kind of heartbreak when talking about Mangan in Act II, but she is clearly thinking of her own experience rather than his. The speech occurs after Mangan breaks down while being tormented by Hesione.

LADY UTTERWORD. What an extraordinary way to behave! What is the matter with the man?

ELLIE [*in a strangely calm voice, staring into an imaginary distance*] His heart is breaking: that is all. [*The Captain appears at the pantry door, listening*]. It is a curious sensation: the sort of pain that goes mercifully beyond our powers of feeling. When your heart is broken, your boats are burned: nothing matters any more. It is the end of happiness and the beginning of peace.

(II, 108)

Mangan does not experience the burning of his boats in this way at all: for him it is a painful undressing which leaves him with nothing, because without superficial trappings he is nothing. His feelings are comparable in this sense to Lear's in the first two acts of Shakespeare's tragedy. For Ellie, on the other hand, as for most of the heroic characters in Shaw's plays, casting off burdensome trappings like love and happiness is an indispensable preliminary to finding something higher. Her feelings are closer to those of Lear at the end of *King Lear*.[8]

This theme of boat-burning and undressing has echoes all through the play. During Ellie's discussion with Captain Shotover in Act II, she explains that she has experienced heartbreak:

ELLIE. . . . I fell in love with Hector, and didnt know he was married.

CAPTAIN SHOTOVER. Heartbreak? Are you one of those who are so sufficient to themselves that they are only happy when they are stripped of everything, even of hope?

ELLIE . . . It seems so; for I feel now as if there was nothing I could not do, because I want nothing.

CAPTAIN SHOTOVER. Thats the only real strength. Thats genius. Thats better than rum.

(p. 115)

Elsewhere Shotover expresses the same idea in minor and offhand ways:

LADY UTTERWORD. Oh! What about *my* sheets?

THE CAPTAIN [*halting at the door*] Take my advice: air them; or take them off and sleep in blankets.

(I, 51)

MANGAN. This girl [Ellie] doesnt want to spend her life wondering how long her gloves will last.

CAPTAIN SHOTOVER [*passing through*] Dont wear any. I never do.

(II, 99)

A few lines after this last piece of advice Hector echoes Shotover's views: "Let us all go out into the night and leave everything behind us," he says (II, 100). This is just what they do in Act III, which takes place in the garden, and it is in this act that the last of their pretenses are thrown away and Mangan makes his speech about un-dressing, while beginning to do so. And it is in this act that Ellie announces her marriage to Captain Shotover—a marriage which represents a renunciation of the trivial things of this world, and which has taken place, Hector says, quoting Shelley, out in the night: "Their altar the grassy earth outspread, / And their priest the muttering wind" (III, 131).[9]

It is Ellie's journey to Shotover which is the main element of plot in *Heartbreak House*, and it brings together many of the play's other elements. Ellie begins the play as an innocent young girl who knows nothing of the world. She has been instructed by an Idealist

father, is infatuated by the handsome Hector, and is prepared for her
father's sake to marry the (supposedly) wealthy Mangan. During the
course of the play she moves from these three men, and the values
that they represent, to Shotover and his values.

In the first act she moves beyond Hector—beyond romantic
love and beauty, and beyond the world of the Heartbreakers, of
which Hector is a principal member. The scene in which she is
heartbroken by the discovery that she has been deceived is a memorable one.

> Mrs Hushabye [*laying Ellie down at the end of the sofa*] Now,
> pettikins, he is gone. Theres nobody but me. You can let yourself go.
> Dont try to control yourself. Have a good cry.
> Ellie [*raising her head*] Damn!
> Mrs Hushabye. Splendid! Oh, what a relief! I thought you were
> going to be broken-hearted. Never mind me. Damn him again.
> Ellie. I am not damning him: I am damning myself for being
> such a fool. [*Rising*] How could I let myself be taken in so? [*She
> begins prowling to and fro, her bloom gone, looking curiously older
> and harder*].
>
> (I, 61)

Ellie is broken-hearted, but not in a way which Hesione would recognize: she does not cry like Randall (or Octavius), but cuts off the
whole side of her life which has been betrayed; she moves beyond
the desire for romantic love and happiness. The difference between
her type of heartbreak and the Randall—Octavius type is brought out
in a speech to Hesione in the next act. Ellie says: "You dont suppose
I'm going to sit down and die of a broken heart, I hope, or be an
old maid living on a pittance from the Sick and Indigent Roomkeep-
ers' Association. But my heart is broken, all the same. What I
mean by that is that I know that what has happened to me with
Marcus will not happen to me ever again" (II, 94–95). Here she
is behaving like Vivie Warren, trying to protect herself against further betrayal by becoming hard and worldly. She decides on a love-
less match with Mangan, so that she will have money: "I shall not
have to spend most of my time wondering how long my gloves will
last, anyhow" (II, 95). But she moves beyond Mangan and the Gospel of Mammonism: her crucial discussion with Shotover in Act II

constitutes her second major conversion in the play. Ellie asks the Captain whether she should marry Mangan, and argues that she should, presenting a point of view that recalls *Major Barbara.* "It is just because I want to save my soul that I am marrying for money. All the women who are not fools do." Shotover's reply is that "if you sell yourself, you deal your soul a blow that all the books and pictures and concerts and scenery in the world wont heal" (II, 111)—that there are values higher and more important than material ones.

In this scene between Ellie and Captain Shotover he describes —without directly intending it—the three levels of life through which she moves in the play: "I see my daughters and their men living foolish lives of romance and sentiment and snobbery. I see you, the younger generation, turning from their romance and sentiment and snobbery to money and comfort and hard common sense. I was ten times happier on the bridge in the typhoon, or frozen into Arctic ice for months in darkness, than you or they have ever been. You are looking for a rich husband. At your age I looked for hardship, danger, horror, and death, that I might feel the life in me more intensely" (II, 113). These three levels are comparable to the hell, earth, and heaven of *Man and Superman,* and Ellie's journey— her pilgrim's progress—is from the romantic hell of Hector to the Mammonish earth of Mangan to the heaven of Captain Shotover, where the goal is to live more intensely and abundantly. These three stages, as we have seen in earlier chapters, form a recurring pattern in Shaw's middle plays. The way out of hell and into heaven in *Man and Superman* is through the earth—through childbearing. The way to the heaven of a society of the saved in *Major Barbara* lies through the solid, earthly realities of money and gunpowder. In *John Bull's Other Island* Ireland will move from its present hellish state to control by the earthly, wealthy Broadbent, and then—one hopes—to the heaven of Peter Keegan (although the earthly does not appear here to be a causal step toward the heavenly). The lower must precede the higher: this is the belief that underlies much of Shaw's thinking in the period I am considering.

The heaven of *Heartbreak House,* as in the earlier plays, is not at all clearly delineated. Ellie herself does not know what she means by "life with a blessing":

ELLIE [*her face lighting up*] Life with a blessing! that is what I want. Now I know the real reason why I couldnt marry Mr Mangan: there would be no blessing on our marriage. There is a blessing on my broken heart. There is a blessing on your beauty, Hesione. There is a blessing on your father's spirit. Even on the lies of Marcus there is a blessing; but on Mr Mangan's money there is none.
MANGAN. I dont understand a word of that.
ELLIE. Neither do I. But I know it means something.

(III, 132)

One clue to what it means is to be found in Captain Shotover's speech on happiness, to which Ellie's declaration is a response. "I tell you happiness is no good. You can be happy when you are only half alive. I am happier now I am half dead than ever I was in my prime. But there is no blessing on my happiness" (III, 132). Another clue may be found in a passage from Carlyle's *Past and Present,* which predicts that when the Gospel of Mammonism has been overthrown, and replaced by "a nobler Hell and a nobler Heaven" —by a truly religious sense of the world—then "by degrees, we shall again have a Society with something of Heroism in it, something of Heaven's Blessing on it." [10]

A life "with something of Heroism in it": that is the essence of Captain Shotover's heaven. It is significant that Ellie's speech about heartbreak as "the end of happiness and the beginning of peace" comes just shortly *before* her scene with Shotover late in Act II. For it is in this scene that she discovers that the full life is not one of peace but one that faces "hardship, danger, horror, and death." It is no good to live for money and happiness; one's goal must be to live more intensely, more abundantly, more heroically—to stretch one's vitality to the utmost.[11] One example of this sort of life is Shotover's youth as a sailor; another is hinted at in his speeches on navigation, which we will come to later.

Even in his dotage Captain Shotover is the most intense, heroic, vital person in the play; of all Shaw's prophetic characters he is, to my mind, the most convincing. The comments made by other characters in the play that he has supernatural abilities and that he has sold his soul to the devil in Zanzibar do not seem out of place. Hector calls him "that supernatural old man" (I, 71), and according to the burglar he "can divine water, spot gold, explode a cartridge in your pocket with a glance of his eye, and see the truth hidden in the heart of man" (II, 106). Mazzini Dunn is also affected by him: Shotover, he says, "is so fearfully magnetic: I feel vibrations whenever he comes close to me" (II, 87). Like Keegan, Shotover notices everything (as Ellie observes, II, 80), and he is right about everything —about Randall's age (I, 66), and Mangan's age and the fact that he will not marry Ellie (I, 65), for example; every word that he utters in the play is found to be essentially true, the result of an uncanny inspiration.

Ellie, in marrying Captain Shotover, finds her proper destiny and values: she embraces Shotover's concept of the heroic life, and leaves behind the values of Hector (as a lover), Mangan, and her father. In announcing her marriage, she declares: "Yes: I, Ellie Dunn, give my broken heart and my strong sound soul to its natural captain, my spiritual husband and second father" (III, 131–132). She has accepted Shotover as a husband, instead of Hector or Mangan, and he becomes her second father—a substitute for Mazzini Dunn, who represents the antithesis of Shotover's values. This is a moment comparable to Doña Ana's decision to try to follow Don Juan to heaven instead of remaining in hell, the home of the seekers for happiness, with the Devil; or Marchbanks' decision to go out bravely into the night instead of longing for romantic happiness with Candida. All of these characters must renounce happiness in order to live fully. That is the meaning of Ellie's reference to her broken heart and strong sound soul. One must break one's heart in order to find one's soul. Paradoxically, Ellie, in renouncing conventional happiness, finds a higher, truer happiness, while the Heartbreakers, in seeking for conventional happiness, only make themselves miserable.

The parallel between Ellie and Marchbanks is particularly close —although Ellie is the more effective character dramatically. Both begin as weak, deluded youths and end, after being disillusioned about love and happiness (and in Ellie's case money), as strong, inspired adults. At the beginning of *Heartbreak House*, Ellie's youth is emphasized, as is Marchbanks' in the first part of *Candida*. She is described in a stage direction as *"a pretty girl"* (I, 42), and by Shotover (whose initial descriptions are always an important clue to the nature of the character he is describing) as "young and attractive" (I, 43; the phrase "young and attractive" is used twice, and Shotover also calls her on the same page "this misguided and unfortunate young lady"). After her heartbreak in the first act, she *"begins prowling to and fro, her bloom gone, looking curiously older and harder";* and in Act II she says to Hesione, "Perhaps you dont understand why I was quite a nice girl this morning, and am now neither a girl nor particularly nice" (p. 94). In the third act it is her strength which is emphasized, in her reference to her "strong sound soul," in her remark to Mangan that she never wanted to marry him but only "to feel my strength: to know that you could not escape if I chose to take you," and in her statement to Hesione, "I know my strength now" (III, 131, 132). Like Marchbanks, she becomes aware of her real potential.

II

Ellie's marriage to Captain Shotover is a union of opposites: most obviously of youth and age. When, near the beginning of the play, Nurse Guinness tells Ellie that she has made an impression on Shotover (who has brought his special tea for her), the Captain says gloomily, "Youth! beauty! novelty! They are badly wanted in this house. I am excessively old" (I, 48). This implies a complementary relationship between Ellie and Heartbreak House, and in particular between her youth and Shotover's age. Ellie and Shotover each have what the other lacks: Shotover has the wisdom of age and Ellie has the energy of youth—and has her life ahead of her. And it is perhaps significant that she is able to dominate Mangan, while Shotover is not: she compels him to agree to marry her, in order "to feel my strength," and she hypnotizes him. One might think, then, that the union between Ellie and Shotover offers grounds for hope at the end of the play: that Ellie can somehow give substance and effect to Shotover's ideas, as Ann can ultimately do for Tanner's, and Undershaft for Barbara's and Cusins'. But this union does not dominate the end of the play in the way that the other unions dominate the endings of *Man and Superman* and *Major Barbara*. *Heartbreak House* ends not with the announcement of the marriage between

Ellie and Shotover but with the bombing scene, in which Ellie's role is highly ambiguous. She agrees with Hector that the house ought to be destroyed, suggesting to him that he should set fire to it, and with Hesione that the bombing is a glorious experience:

MRS HUSHABYE. But what a glorious experience! I hope theyll come again tomorrow night.
ELLIE [*radiant at the prospect*] Oh, I hope so.

(III, 142)

This is the last speech in the play, and while it could suggest that Ellie is putting into practice Captain Shotover's doctrine about living dangerously, it could equally suggest that she is naively inviting destruction. For in terms of the symbolic structure in *Heartbreak House,* the bombs are to be equated with the rocks which the sailor must at all costs avoid.

Another union of opposites in *Heartbreak House,* which offers no grounds for hope whatever, is the business relationship between Mazzini Dunn and Mangan. This is faintly reminiscent of the partnership between Doyle and Broadbent, in the sense that Dunn provides the brains and Mangan the worldliness. Dunn has the ideas, but he requires Mangan to see to the money. "Mangan is wonderful about money," he tells Hesione: "he thinks of nothing else. He is so dreadfully afraid of being poor. I am always thinking of other things: even at the works I think of the things we are doing and not of what they cost" (II, 89). This union certainly has no blessing on it; it is like a parody of the fruitful, vital unions in Shaw's earlier plays.

As in *John Bull's Other Island,* there are marriages of contraries in *Heartbreak House,* but not the one which is the most needful: between the powers that run the country on the one hand and Shotover and the Heartbreakers on the other. It is this aspect of the play—the separation of power and culture—that Shaw discusses in the Preface. Chekhov's plays, he says, "fitted all the country houses in Europe in which the pleasures of music, art, literature, and the theatre had supplanted hunting, shooting, fishing, flirting, eating, and drinking. The same nice people, the same utter futility. The nice people could read; some of them could write; and they were the only repositories of culture who had social opportunities of contact with our politicians, administrators, and newspaper proprietors, or any chance of sharing or influencing their activities. But they shrank from that contact. They hated politics. They did not wish to realize Utopia for the common people: they wished to realize their favorite fictions and poems in their own lives" (p. 4; see also "Revolution on the Shelf," pp. 5–6). Here is the divorce between intellect and power which is the main concern of *Man and Superman, Major Barbara,* and *John Bull's Other Island.* It is also, I believe, the main concern of *Heartbreak House.* The theme is not quite as obvious in this later play as in (say) *Major Barbara* because it is dealt with negatively: that is to say, the play shows us what the Heartbreakers *are* doing as a way of directing our attention to what they are *not* doing. We see the potential—and much needed— captains wasting their lives in the pursuit of personal happiness instead of navigating, instead of running the country. The central theme of *Heartbreak House* is the theme which bulks so large in Carlyle's jeremiads against nineteenth-century England: the idea that the governing classes do not govern.[12] "We sit here talking," Hector says in the final act, "and leave everything to Mangan and to chance and to the devil. Think of the powers of destruction that Mangan and his mutual admiration gang wield! It's madness: it's like giving a torpedo to a badly brought up child to play at earthquakes with" (III, 137).

If men like Hector remain imprisoned in Heartbreak House while men like Mangan run the country, then England will go on the rocks. Mangan is a Captain of Industry (the phrase is used three times in the second act); the country needs real captains, who will navigate. As Carlyle says in the first of his *Latter-Day Pamphlets,* "The Present Time" (a work to which *Heartbreak House* is probably much indebted): "Who would govern that can get along without governing? He that is fittest for it, is of all men the unwillingest unless constrained. By multifarious devices we have been endeavouring to dispense with governing; and by very superficial speculations, of *laissez-faire,* supply-and-demand, etc. etc. to persuade ourselves that it is best so. The Real Captain, unless it be some Captain of mechanical Industry hired by Mammon, where is he in these days? Most likely, in silence, in sad isolation somewhere, in remote obscurity; trying if, in an evil ungoverned time, he cannot at least govern himself. The Real Captain undiscoverable; the Phantasm Captain everywhere very conspicuous . . ." [13]

Mangan, the Phantasm Captain of mechanical Industry hired by Mammon, is based, as Shaw's letter to St. John Ervine quoted in note 12 to this chapter implies, on Lord Devonport,[14] a businessman who was Food Controller during part of the war. A. J. P. Taylor says of him that though he was "a great grocer, [he] was a failure at the ministry of food." [15] As Mangan, he becomes a symbol for Shaw of the public uselessness of the "practical businessman"—of the fact that the Captain of Industry is only a Phantasm Captain.

Mangan is perhaps the least agreeable character in Shaw's plays, with scarcely a single redeeming quality. When he complains to Hesione in Act II, "I'm a man aint I," she replies, "Oh no: not what I call a man. Only a Boss: just that and nothing else"; but it soon dawns on her that he is "a real person" with a Christian name and a mother, like other people. "You have a heart, Alfy," she tells him, "a whimpering little heart, but a real one" (p. 98). It is not like Shaw to create a character without *any* humanity: Mangan is a man, but only just a man. And while as a person he could attract some sympathy from us, especially as the victim of Ellie and Hesione, in his public, symbolic role he is utterly beyond redemption. Near the beginning of the Preface Shaw speaks of Tolstoy's hostile view of Heartbreak House—of cultured, leisured Europe: "He knew," Shaw writes, "that our utter enervation and futilization in that overheated drawing-room atmosphere was delivering the world over to the control of ignorant and soulless cunning and energy, with the frightful consequences which have now overtaken it" (p. 3). "Soulless" is the single word which best describes Mangan; he lacks that vitality of spirit which makes a character like Broadbent so appealing. But the step from Broadbent to Mangan is not quite as large as it might appear. Broadbent is redeemed for the audience because of his comic, absurd human qualities and because his business activities are presented as having some value. To Keegan, on the other hand, Broadbent is not funny but heartbreaking, and his activities as a businessman are worse than useless. (Keegan's analysis of Broadbent's business methods reappears as Mangan's cynical confession to Ellie at the beginning of Act II of *Heartbreak House*.) One could say that Mangan is a Broadbent who is seen exclusively from Keegan's point of view—as, indeed, one could say that *Heartbreak House* is pre-war England seen from Keegan's point of view.

In Blake's terminology, Broadbent could be called a Contrary, while Mangan is a Negation.[16] Broadbent's vitality could be made to serve divine purposes; what is needed is an interaction between him and Keegan. Mangan's "ignorant and soulless cunning and energy" are irredeemable; the only relationship between him and Captain Shotover can be one of killed and killer—or vice versa. Shotover sees this, and tells Hector that the purpose of his dynamite is "to kill fellows like Mangan . . . Are we to be kept for ever in the mud by these hogs to whom the universe is nothing but a machine for greasing their bristles and filling their snouts?" At present they are in effect killing us: they are, he says, "strangling our souls"; "We kill the better half of ourselves every day to propitiate them. The knowledge that these people are there to render all our aspirations barren prevents us having the aspirations" (I, 74–76).

Mangan's development in the play is directly antithetical to Ellie's: while Ellie progresses to womanhood, Mangan is stripped of all his pretenses to manhood; and at the end of the play Ellie has married Captain Shotover while Mangan has been killed by his dynamite. In Act I Mangan is seen as a millionaire Captain of Industry who has been kind and generous to Ellie's father. We learn at the beginning of the second act that his kindness and generosity are unreal (pp. 81–83), and then that he is a fraud as a Captain of Industry—that he does not in fact run his works (pp. 88–89). All that is left of him is his money, and of course in the third act it too turns out to be phantasmal (pp. 126–127). Mangan is truly a Phantasm Captain; he represents void, nullity. We never learn what it is he manufactures, and the organization that controls him is referred to only as "the syndicate" (III, 128). A stage direction describes him as *"about fiftyfive, with a careworn, mistrustful expression, standing a little on an entirely imaginary dignity, with a dull complexion, straight lustreless hair, and features so entirely commonplace that it is impossible to describe them,"* and Captain Shotover, in introducing him, describes him negatively: "Says his name is Mangan. Not ablebodied" (I, 63). Nor is he ableminded—which is what Shotover's statement really signifies. In a speech to

Ellie, which recalls Broadbent's remark about the pills he takes when his brain is overworked, Mangan says that macaroni is too rich for him: "I suppose it's because I have to work so much with my brain. Thats the worst of being a man of business: you are always thinking, thinking, thinking" (II, 80). Mangan uses his brain even less than Broadbent; for while Broadbent has general ideas, even if they are wrong ones, Mangan has none at all—he thinks only of himself. When the other men rush upstairs after the discovery of the burglar, he remains behind, with the reflection, "It aint my house, thank God" (II, 101).

Mangan, then, has no mind, no soul, no public spirit, no generosity, no great wealth, no managing ability. He has nothing; he is nothing. "I dont start new businesses," he tells Ellie; and "I take no risks in ideas" (II, 82). He also in this scene denies having acted (toward Mazzini Dunn) either out of kindness of heart or out of ill-nature (II, 81), as in the third act he denies having any money and then later denies that he is poor:

MANGAN. Dont you run away with this idea that I have nothing. I—

HECTOR. Oh, dont explain. We understand. You have a couple of thousand pounds in exchequer bills, 50,000 shares worth tenpence a dozen, and half a dozen tabloids of cyanide of potassium to poison yourself with when you are found out. Thats the reality of your millions.

MAZZINI. Oh no, no, no. He is quite honest: the businesses are genuine and perfectly iegal.

HECTOR [disgusted] Yah! Not even a great swindler!

MANGAN. So you think. But Ive been too many for some honest men, for all that.

LADY UTTERWORD. There is no pleasing you, Mr Mangan. You are determined to be neither rich nor poor, honest nor dishonest.

(III, 133–134)

It is, frighteningly, this nonentity who is the only character in the play to take a part in the running of the country. He is (like Lord Devonport) "the dictator of a great public department" (III, 127), where his achievements have been of a predictably negative kind: "Achievements? Well, I dont know what you call achievements; but

Ive jolly well put a stop to the games of the other fellows in the other departments. Every man of them thought he was going to save the country all by himself, and do me out of the credit and out of my chance of a title. I took good care that if they wouldnt let me do it they shouldnt do it themselves either. I may not know anything about my own machinery; but I know how to stick a ramrod into the other fellow's. And now they all look the biggest fools going" (III, 128). One could imagine nothing less like navigation than this.

Although Mangan is the only character in the play who "governs" England, there is another character who does not appear on the stage who has political power. This is Sir Hastings Utterword, "who has been governor of all the crown colonies in succession" (I, 46); he represents stupidity in imperial government, as Mangan represents stupidity in domestic government. Like Mangan, Sir Hastings Utterword is mindless and without imagination. He is introduced into the play (as Mangan is) by Captain Shotover: "I have a second daughter who is, thank God, in a remote part of the Empire with her numskull of a husband. As a child she thought the figurehead of my ship, the Dauntless, the most beautiful thing on earth. He resembled it. He had the same expression: wooden yet enterprising" (I, 44). This picture of Sir Hastings is confirmed by Randall, who says that his brother "has the gift of being able to work sixteen hours a day at the dullest detail, and actually likes it. That gets him to the top wherever he goes" (II, 116). We learn little more than this about Sir Hastings himself in the play, but we do learn more about his values through his wife, who represents them. Perhaps that is why there is no need for him to appear in the play in person.

Lady Utterword is the one character who has escaped from Heartbreak House, and Shaw's point is that what she has escaped to is certainly no better than what she has left. This point is made explicitly in the section of the Preface entitled "Horseback Hall" (pp. 4–5), and in the play itself the inadequacy of her values is apparent. They are the values of the mindless upper classes (as opposed to the cultured, thinking upper classes): in particular snobbery and conformity to the established social code. Lady Utterword is also the most practical, worldly person in the play: her ideal is not romantic adventure, but a comfortable life. It is she who has the common sense to ask Mangan in the last act, when they are discussing whether or not Ellie should marry him, how much money he actually has, and her comments all through the play are eminently sensible. But common sense is not enough. In *Heartbreak House* a character can be judged according to Captain Shotover's attitude toward him and according to his distance from Captain Shotover.[17] Shotover is hostile to Lady Utterword; and her distance from him is revealed in the fact that he refuses during the first act to recognize her as his daughter, and in a passage like the following, in which he is speaking to Mangan, who has threatened to leave the house.

CAPTAIN SHOTOVER. You were welcome to come: you are free to go. The wide earth, the high seas, the spacious skies are waiting for you outside.

LADY UTTERWORD. But your things, Mr Mangan. Your bags, your comb and brushes, your pyjamas—

(II, 100)

Here, in Lady Utterword's echoing cadence, we see the low prosaic mind in contrast with the lofty poetic one. The Utterwords are better people than Mangan, but their values will not save the country any more than Mangan's will.

The question is, what will save the country? The situation demands power of the right kind, and *Heartbreak House,* like *Major Barbara,* is much concerned with different types of power. At the lowest end of the scale there is the type of power that Mangan exercises in his great public department; this is power without any direction, purpose, or thought whatever, and it is the kind that is guiding—or rather failing to guide—England. Then there is Sir Hastings Utterword's kind of power, which is contemptuously dismissed by Captain Shotover:

LADY UTTERWORD. . . . Get rid of your ridiculous sham democracy; and give Hastings the necessary powers, and a good supply of bamboo to bring the British native to his senses: *he* will save the country with the greatest ease.

CAPTAIN SHOTOVER. It had better be lost. Any fool can govern with a stick in his hand. *I* could govern that way. It is not God's way.

(III, 129)

There is also power in the play of a non-public kind: Hector's power to attract women, Ellie's power to hypnotize Mangan, and the Shotover sisters' power to fascinate men. Nearer to the top of the scale would come Shotover's power over his sailors, which he gained by tricking them into believing that he had sold himself to the devil (see II, 111–112). Although this involves lying and appealing to superstition, nevertheless it was necessary because the crew consisted of degraded thieves who could otherwise be governed only by swearing and beating. This lying is more effective than Shotover's present means of attempting to deal with society's thieves, such as Mangan —his dynamite. Shotover's intention is a good one: to develop psychic power that will explode dynamite; in other words, to achieve Shaw's goal of the marriage of mental and physical power, so that a mind like Shotover's could have a real effect on society.[18] The power which Cusins attains at the end of *Major Barbara* is of a similar kind. But it is made quite clear in *Heartbreak House* that Shotover never will develop the necessary psychic power. He tells Hector that he will be able to kill "fellows like Mangan" when he has "attained the seventh degree of concentration," at which point Hector asks, "Whats the use of that? You never do attain it." Captain Shotover's answer is in effect an admission that Hector is right: all he can say is, "What then is to be done?" (I, 74–75).[19]

This is the question that dominates the last part of the play: "What then is to be done?" None of the kinds of power that we have seen in the play is adequate to save the country, and it may be significant that suggestions of the diabolic are attached to several of them. Of Mangan's power Hector says, "We sit here talking, and leave everything to Mangan and to chance and to the devil" (III, 137); and of Sir Hastings' power Captain Shotover says, "It is not God's way" (III, 129). Mangan calls Ellie a little devil shortly before she hypnotizes him (II, 84), and Hesione calls herself and her sister "the devil's granddaughters":

MRS HUSHABYE. Oh, *I* say it matters very little which of you governs the country so long as we govern you.

HECTOR. *We?* Who is we, pray?

MRS HUSHABYE. The devil's granddaughters, dear. The lovely women.

HECTOR . . . Fall, I say; and deliver us from the lures of Satan!

(III, 129)

And Shotover, in order to rule his sailors, had to pretend that he had sold himself to the devil.

What is needed is a kind of power which is not diabolic but divine. "To be in heaven is to steer," says Don Juan in a passage from the Hell Scene (III, 128) which is crucial both to *Man and Superman* and to *Heartbreak House.* The metaphor of the ship that needs steering, emphasizing the need for the guiding power of mind in human affairs, is a common one in Shaw's writings. It did not of course originate with Shaw; he would have found it, for example, in Plato's *Republic* (in the section on the philosopher ruler) and in the works of Carlyle. The use of the metaphor which is perhaps closest to its use in *Heartbreak House* is in *Past and Present,* in a passage which contrasts Carlyle's symbol of the contemporary politician, Sir Jabesh Windbag, with Cromwell, "the Ablest Man of England":

Windbag, if we will consider him, has a problem set before him which may be ranged in the impossible class. He is a Columbus minded to sail to the indistinct country of NOWHERE, to the indistinct country of WHITHERWARD, by the *friendship* of those same waste-tumbling Water-Alps and howling waltz of All the Winds; not by conquest of them and in spite of them, but by friendship of them, when once *they* have made-up their mind! He is the most original Columbus I ever saw. Nay, his problem is not an impossible one: he will infallibly *arrive* at that same country of NOWHERE; his indistinct Whitherward will be a *Thither*ward! In the Ocean Abysses and Locker of Davy Jones, there certainly enough do he and *his* ship's company, and all their cargo and navigatings, at last find lodgment.

Oliver knew that his America lay THERE, Westward Ho;— and it was not entirely by *friendship* of the Water-Alps, and yeasty insane Froth-Oceans, that he meant to get thither! He sailed accordingly; had compass-card, and Rules of Navigation,—older and greater than these Froth-Oceans, old as the Eternal God! [20]

Shotover's warning about the dire results of drifting is in reply to a character about whom I have so far said little: Mazzini Dunn. Dunn's significance in the play lies primarily in the fact that he more than anyone represents the ideas which are leading England to disaster—as Shotover represents the ideas which alone can save the country. And as Shotover's every remark in the play is right, Dunn is consistently wrong. He thinks that Mangan is dead when he is alive in Act II, and that Mangan will live when he is in fact killed in Act III: "Mangan and the burglar are acting very sensibly," he says, after they have hidden in the gravel pit with the dynamite during the bombing; "and it is they who will survive" (III, 141). He is the only person in the play who defends Mangan, and it is he (and people like him) who make Mangan possible by managing his works for him. Upon the arrival of the burglar—an event which puts most of the men in the play to the test—only Mangan behaves less impressively than Dunn, who almost shoots the burglar accidentally, and then plays into his hands by making the (well-intended) suggestion that he might set up as a locksmith (II, 102, 104). And it is Dunn who misjudges the Heartbreakers in the speech quoted at the beginning of this chapter.

For much of the play, Dunn is taken by Captain Shotover as his villainous ex-boatswain, who (somewhat incredibly) turns up in person in Act II as the burglar, Billy Dunn. Captain Shotover thus refers to Mazzini Dunn in a most hostile, unflattering way, suggesting that he is or was a drunkard (I, 63) and calling him "a thief, a pirate, and a murderer" (I, 69). Now on the face of it Captain Shotover could not be more mistaken: Mazzini Dunn is a lifelong teetotaler, and he is pre-eminently a "good man"—honest, respectable, likeable, kindly, and well intentioned. Superficially, no two men could be less alike than Mazzini Dunn and Billy Dunn. But Captain Shotover's judgments are a result not of madness but of profound insight. What he means by referring to Mazzini as a drunkard is made plain later in the play. "To be drunk," he tells Ellie in Act II, "means to have dreams; to go soft; to be easily pleased and deceived; to fall into the clutches of women" (p. 114); and Dunn fulfills this definition in all particulars but the last. Even more to the point is Shotover's speech to Ellie in the navigation scene, after Dunn has declared his tentative faith in Providence. To Ellie's suggestion that the way to stay off the rocks is to avoid rum, Shotover replies vehemently: "That is a lie, child. Let a man drink ten barrels of rum a day, he is not a drunken skipper until he is a drifting skipper. Whilst he can lay his course and stand on his bridge and steer it, he is no drunkard. It is the man who lies drinking in his bunk and trusts to Providence that I call the drunken skipper, though he drank nothing but the waters of the River Jordan" (III, 138). The reference to Mazzini Dunn here is unmistakable: it is he, the lifelong teetotaler, who is the real drunkard. There are, says the burglar in Act II, "two sets in the family: the thinking Dunns and the drinking Dunns, each going their own ways. I'm a drinking Dunn: he's a thinking Dunn" (p. 105). Paradoxically, Mazzini Dunn's thinking is more dangerous—more drunken—than Billy Dunn's (or Shotover's) ordinary drinking.

What of the rest of Captain Shotover's accusation? One could say that Mazzini Dunn is a thief in that he is part of the capitalist system (along with Mangan, who is called a burglar at the end of the play); that he is a pirate in that he is an obstacle to navigation, and that he is a murderer in two senses. First, he almost kills the burglar: "Shooting yourself, in a manner of speaking," the burglar says to him (II, 105), suggesting the self-destructive quality of Idealists like Dunn. Second—and most important—he is a murderer in that his ideas are leading to the slaughter of the war.

These disastrous ideas, upon which the whole play is an attack, are that "there is a great deal to be said for the theory of an overruling Providence, after all," and its corollary, that "nothing happens" (III, 137, 138). Shotover assails these illusions, in speeches which constitute the thematic center of the play:

CAPTAIN SHOTOVER. Every drunken skipper trusts to Providence. But one of the ways of Providence with drunken skippers is to run them on the rocks.

MAZZINI. Very true, no doubt, at sea. But in politics, I assure you, they only run into jellyfish. Nothing happens.

CAPTAIN SHOTOVER. At sea nothing happens to the sea. Nothing happens to the sky. The sun comes up from the east and goes down to the west. The moon grows from a sickle to an arc lamp, and comes later and later until she is lost in the light as other things are lost in the darkness. After the typhoon, the flying-fish glitter in the sunshine like birds. It's amazing how they get along, all things considered. Nothing happens, except something not worth mentioning.

ELLIE. What is that, O Captain, my captain?

CAPTAIN SHOTOVER [savagely] Nothing but the smash of the drunken skipper's ship on the rocks, the splintering of her rotten timbers, the tearing of her rusty plates, the drowning of the crew like rats in a trap.

HECTOR. And this ship that we are all in? This soul's prison we call England?

CAPTAIN SHOTOVER. The captain is in his bunk, drinking bottled ditch-water; and the crew is gambling in the forecastle. She will strike and sink and split. Do you think the laws of God will be suspended in favor of England because you were born in it?

HECTOR. Well, I dont mean to be drowned like a rat in a trap. I still have the will to live. What am I to do?

CAPTAIN SHOTOVER. Do? Nothing simpler. Learn your business as an Englishman.

HECTOR. And what may my business as an Englishman be, pray?

CAPTAIN SHOTOVER. Navigation. Learn it and live; or leave it and be damned.

ELLIE. Quiet, quiet: youll tire yourself.

MAZZINI. I thought all that once, Captain; but I assure you nothing will happen.

A dull distant explosion is heard.

HECTOR [*starting up*] What was that?

CAPTAIN SHOTOVER. Something happening [*he blows his whistle*]. Breakers ahead!

(III, 137–139)

Navigation is really Shotover's doctrine of living without happiness applied to public affairs. On the personal level, an individual has the choice between a purposeful life of striving and a life of easy happiness, of "yielding in the direction of the least resistance," of drifting with the Devil's want of will.[21] On the public level, society has the choice between organizing its affairs intelligently and being friendly toward the wind and waves while trusting to Providence to keep the nation on a safe course. It is this parallel which unifies *Heartbreak House,* and makes the disordered, drifting life of the house itself a symbol of the national life of England before the war.

Although Shotover can tell others that "happiness is no good," and can warn that England will go on the rocks if she continues to drift, he cannot live according to his own precepts. On the public level he cannot influence the direction of the nation, and on the private level he cannot give direction to his own life.

On the public level, he is in the line of Tanner, Cusins, and Keegan; and it is Keegan whom he most resembles. Like Keegan, he is cut off from the world of practical affairs; both are prophets without influence. Keegan's inability to control Broadbent is paralleled by Shotover's inability to control Mangan—although in a limited sense it is Shotover who kills Mangan (with his dynamite) at the end of the play. And he does influence Ellie and Hector, while Keegan influences no one. But Shotover feels himself a failure, in that he is too old to give his wisdom practical effect—and this is the main feeling that we are left with about him. He is in this sense like Sir Arthur Chavender, the prime minister in *On the Rocks* (1933), who says, "I see what has to be done now; but I dont feel that I am the man to do it" (II, 258). Both men know what is required to keep England off the rocks, but they can only stand back and hope that others will undertake the practical business of navigation, of which they themselves are incapable.

Shotover is not only unable to control others; but because of his old age he is unable to control himself. He is aware of the necessity of striving instead of drifting, but he feels in himself "the accursed happiness I have dreaded all my life long: the happiness that comes as life goes, the happiness of yielding and dreaming instead of resisting and doing, the sweetness of the fruit that is going rotten" (II, 114). In terms of the Hell Scene in *Man and Superman,* he feels himself sinking, as a result of old age, from heaven to hell, and he can do little to prevent this.

Of all Shaw's characters, Captain Shotover is the closest to a self-portrait. Shaw was fifty-seven when he first conceived *Heartbreak House* in 1913, and he evidently felt that his powers were waning. In this year he wrote to Gilbert Murray about work on which he was engaged at the time; and the note of dissatisfaction is obvious. Speaking of the new edition of *The Quintessence of Ibsenism,* Shaw said that he was growing old and that he thought the new material was "slushy" in places and perhaps sentimental, but that it was the best he could do, and it would have to stand as it was. He also wrote of the "Parents and Children" preface (which was later attached to *Misalliance*), saying that he intended it to be the last of his prefaces, and that he was having difficulty in finishing it; he complained that he kept cursing and repeating himself, and that he could not proceed to any constructive suggestion.[22] There is much of Captain Shotover in this letter: the feeling of being old, the fear of being slushy and sentimental (compare Shotover's reference to "the sweetness of the fruit that is going rotten"), the fear that one is not doing one's best work, and the feeling of inability to pursue a line of argument.

A letter that has even more of Captain Shotover in it is one that Shaw wrote earlier in the same year to Beatrice Webb about his differences with Clifford Sharp, the young editor of the newly founded *New Statesman,* who treated Shaw's contributions with scant respect, refusing in particular to publish his views on corporal punishment and vivisection. Shaw told Beatrice Webb of his plans to stop writing for the *New Statesman* in order to let the younger generation take it over. He spoke of the "Kiplingesque brutalitarianism of Sharp's generation," by which he meant, for example, lack of hostility to corporal punishment and vivisection and belief in what Asquith in a speech had called an "empirical basis" as opposed to "abstract rights." (This last question is in effect what Ellie and Captain Shotover disagree about in their discussion in Act II on whether Ellie should marry Mangan.) Shaw's letter continues:

If he [Sharp] really does believe in an empirical basis, and thinks the fuss about flogging a fuss about nothing, he is not of much use to me: in fact he will end up as my opponent. He is too young to see this; but I am an old bird, and know the symptoms. You see I am in my old difficulty: I can shew people this fact and that fact or this argument or that argument; but I cannot make them see the relative importance of them. When I want to make an unexpected rush and strike, they assure me that there is nothing much in my point, and go on flogging dead horses. And as I get old and petulant and spoilt, and have to work with the knowledge that I have only a few years more of any sort of vigor and power, I can no longer wait to persuade people. I must just fling the stuff at their heads and let them make what they can of it when it at last dawns on them that I was rather nearer the centre of the target and further off the moon than they thought.

Other passages in this letter also bring Captain Shotover to mind. Sharp, wrote Shaw, "is young, and must try all the things that we have tried in our youth before he finds out that they are just the intellectual amusements that disguise the fact that nothing is being done." Near the end of the letter he said of Sharp and J. C. Squire (who was the literary editor of the *New Statesman*), "They are

young and jolly: the time has come for me to be old and savage." 23
This letter echoes many of Captain Shotover's attitudes and phrases,
particularly in the scene in which Shotover attempts to convert the
younger generation, in the person of Ellie, to something higher than
a materialistic "empirical basis." "I cant argue," he tells her, in reply
to her reasons for wanting to marry Mangan: "I'm too old: my
mind is made up and finished." And later in this scene: "It confuses
me to be answered. It discourages me. I cannot bear men and
women. I *have* to run away. I must run away now"; and: "I cant
think so long and continuously. I am too old. I must go in and out"
(II, 111, 112, 113).

In the character of Captain Shotover Shaw has expressed the frustration and bitterness that he felt before and during the war. The
major cause of this frustration and bitterness, I think, was his feeling
that had people listened to him the war could have been avoided.
The bombing at the end of the play, like the war which broke out
between the time the play was first conceived and the time it was
written, is seen by him as the inevitable result of the attitudes and
behavior that he (and Shotover) had warned against. This is the pri-
mary significance of the bombing scene; it is a confirmation of Shotover's doctrine of the need to navigate and a fierce refutation of
Mazzini Dunn's antithetical view that "nothing happens."

At the superficial level the bombs are German, and the bombing
is a symbolic rendering of the outbreak of the war. When Hesione
exclaims that the sound in the sky is splendid: "it's like Beethoven,"
Ellie replies, "By thunder, Hesione: it *is* Beethoven" (III, 140). It is
Beethoven not only in sound (Hesione perhaps has in mind the
opening bars of the Fifth Symphony) but also in nationality (Beethoven, we may recall, is used in the Preface as a symbol of Germany, p. 19). It is noteworthy, however, that nowhere in the play is
there any explicit reference to Germany or to the war. The lack of
precise historical realism in *Heartbreak House* greatly disturbed
Desmond MacCarthy, who thought that the play must take place
during the war and that it presents an inaccurate picture of the
probable wartime behavior of its characters.24 The vagueness of historical background seems to me to be a deliberate technique on
Shaw's part, to contribute to the dreamy atmosphere of the whole

play, and more especially to give the bombing at the end a wider reference. It is a symbol of the outbreak of the war, but at the same time it is thunder from the heavens, a sign of divine wrath.[25] The war is to be taken as a divine judgment on England, on Europe, and—perhaps in the final analysis—on the human race. The view of history here is that of Carlyle (and the Old Testament), which sees historical calamities as signs that man has broken heaven's laws.[26] Shaw sees the war as a judgment on late nineteenth-century Darwinist England, as Carlyle saw the French Revolution as a judgment on eighteenth-century materialist France, and the forthcoming English revolution (should it occur) as a judgment on early nineteenth-century *laissez-faire* England. Carlyle's writings are full of warnings of the terrible consequences which will ensue if men persist in defying the laws of the universe. He writes, for example, in *Past and Present:* "Foolish men imagine that because judgment for an evil thing is delayed, there is no justice, but an accidental one, here below. Judgment for an evil thing is many times delayed some day or two, some century or two, but it is sure as life, it is sure as death! In the centre of the world-whirlwind, verily now as in the oldest days, dwells and speaks a God. The great soul of the world is *just.*" [27] The section of the Preface to *Heartbreak House* entitled "Nature's Long Credits" (pp. 7–8) is virtually a paraphrase of this passage, with the use of a characteristically Shavian medical analogy. In a passage from another work, Carlyle demonstrates what form divine chastisement would take in nineteenth-century England, and one again thinks immediately of *Heartbreak House:* "If help or direction is not given; if the thing called Government merely drift and tumble to and fro, no-whither, on the popular vortexes, like some carcass of a drowned ass, constitutionally put 'at the top of affairs, ['] —popular indignation will infallibly accumulate upon it; one day, the popular lightning, descending forked and horrible from the black air, will annihilate said supreme carcass, and smite *it* home to its native ooze again!" [28] It is in the light of passages like these that one should look at the apocalyptic ending to *Heartbreak House.* "Providence always has the last word," says Lady Utterword with unconscious prescience in Act II (p. 99); and this Providence turns out to be not Mazzini Dunn's divine protector of England, which blesses those who try to muddle through, but Carlyle's "great soul of the world," which Shaw (who is almost as fond as Carlyle of quasi-theological language) would call the Life Force.

Outside of the play itself, the section of the Preface about "The Wicked Half Century" [29] gives one insight into the nature of "the sins of which this war is the punishment" (Shaw's phrase in *What I Really Wrote about the War*, p. 281—from a newspaper article written in January 1918). By "The Wicked Half Century" Shaw means the half century of Darwinism which preceded and led to the war, and it is useful to connect the attitudes which the play presents unfavorably with Shaw's view of Darwinism "in the ethical sphere": "the banishment of conscience from human affairs, or, as Samuel Butler vehemently put it, 'of mind from the universe' " (Preface, p. 9). More important, Shaw sees the drifting which Captain Shotover denounces as a product of Darwinism. This comes out particularly in the Preface (1921) to *Back to Methuselah,* which discusses much that is implicit in *Heartbreak House.* Here Shaw argues that the war was the outcome of Darwinist materialism, which led statesmen and nations to act from unprincipled, irreligious, selfish stupidity (like Mangan's) rather than intelligent foresight (like Shotover's: "Look ahead," Shotover tells Ellie in Act II, p. 110). Darwinism produces this kind of behavior because it denies the importance of individual responsibility and individual striving. In discussing the effect of Darwinism on public life, Shaw refers to the type of statesman who tricks the people "into furthering his personal ambition and the commercial interests of the plutocrats who own the newspapers and support him on reciprocal terms" in the belief that "if everyone takes the line of least material resistance the result will be the survival of the fittest in a perfectly harmonious universe. Once produce an atmosphere of fatalism on principle, and it matters little what the opinions or superstitions of the individual statesmen concerned may be. A Kaiser who is a devout reader of sermons, a Prime Minister who is an emotional singer of hymns, and a General who is a bigoted Roman Catholic may be the executants of the policy; but the policy itself will be one of unprincipled opportunism; and all the Governments will be like the tramp who walks always with the wind and ends as a pauper, or the stone that rolls down the hill and ends as an avalanche: their way is the way to destruction" (p. lxv). These last two similes suggest drifting, and this particular image is in fact used in the Preface to *Back to Methuselah,* when Shaw speaks of the Darwinist behavior of the Western Powers after the war; they are, he says, "drifting and colliding and running on the rocks, in the hope that if they continue to do their worst they will get Naturally Selected for survival without the trouble of thinking about it" (p. lxviii).[30]

The bombing, then, signifies heaven's displeasure with English —and European—drifting. But it also signifies something even more alarming: heaven's displeasure with man himself. When the sound of the bombing is first heard early in the third act, different characters interpret it in different ways, according to their particular manner of seeing the world. Mangan, to whom the world is a place in which to make money, interprets the sound in a commercial context; he thinks it is a goods (freight) train. Hesione, to whom the world is—or ought to be—a place in which to enjoy love and beauty, hears the sound as "a sort of splendid drumming in the sky." Hector, to whom the world is a resented prison, comes closest to the truth. The sound is, he says, "heaven's threatening growl of disgust at us useless futile creatures. [*Fiercely*] I tell you, one of two things must happen. Either out of that darkness some new creation will come to supplant us as we have supplanted the animals, or the heavens will fall in thunder and destroy us" (pp. 123–124).

This speech reflects a real fear which Shaw had in the period of the war that man as a species might no longer be viable. The war and its aftermath, he writes in the Preface to *Back to Methuselah,* "confirmed a doubt which had grown steadily in my mind during my forty years public work as a Socialist: namely, whether the human animal, as he exists at present, is capable of solving the social problems raised by his own aggregation, or, as he calls it, his civilization" (p. x). If man cannot find the remedy for his deficiencies, that does not mean that no remedy will be found. "The power that produced Man when the monkey was not up to the mark, can produce a higher creature than Man if Man does not come up to the mark . . . Nature holds no brief for the human experiment: it must stand or fall by its results. If Man will not serve, Nature will try another experiment" (p. xv). Within *Back to Methuselah* itself, this fear is given expression in the second play of the cycle, *The Gospel of the Brothers Barnabas,* when the Creative Evolutionist brothers tell the politicians Burge and Lubin about the alternative to their theory of longevity.

CONRAD. Well, some authorities hold that the human race is a failure, and that a new form of life, better adapted to high civilization, will supersede us as we have superseded the ape and the elephant.

BURGE. The superman: eh?

CONRAD. No. Some being quite different from us.

LUBIN. Is that altogether desirable?

FRANKLYN. I fear so. However that may be, we may be quite sure of one thing. We shall not be let alone. The force behind evolution, call it what you will, is determined to solve the problem of civilization; and if it cannot do it through us, it will produce some more capable agents. Man is not God's last word: God can still create. If you cannot do His work He will produce some being who can.

BURGE [*with zealous reverence*] What do we know about Him, Barnabas? What does anyone know about Him?

CONRAD. We know this about Him with absolute certainty. The power my brother calls God proceeds by the method of Trial and Error; and if we turn out to be one of the errors, we shall go the way of the mastodon and the megatherium and all the other scrapped experiments.

(pp. 79–80) [31]

This passage, like Hector's speech in *Heartbreak House,* marks an important shift in emphasis from the evolutionary sections of *Man and Superman.* Now the next step in evolution may not be a higher version of man, but a quite different creature; there is a good possibility that man will be not improved but destroyed.[32]

We have seen that in *Heartbreak House* there are two closely related thematic levels: the public and the private. We have been considering the public significance of the bombing, its historical and evolutionary implications. On the private level—that is, in terms of the lives of individual characters in the play—the bombing represents a Day of Judgment. Commentators have pointed out a parallel between *Heartbreak House* and one of Shaw's late plays, *The Simpleton of the Unexpected Isles:* Hesione, Lady Utterword, Hector, and Sir Hastings Utterword can be seen as personifications of the Love, Pride, Heroism, and Empire represented by the four children in the later play; and there is a more significant parallel between the two plays, in that both end with the arrival of the (or a) Day of Judgment. In this way the last part of *The Simpleton* serves as a useful gloss on the bombing scene in *Heartbreak House*. The applicability of comments like these to *Heartbreak House* is obvious: "The angels are weeding the garden. The useless people, the mischievous people, the selfish somebodies and the noisy nobodies, are dissolving into space . . . The lives which have no use, no meaning, no purpose, will fade out. We shall have to justify our existences or perish . . . I feel pretty sure that we shant disappear as long as we're doing something useful; but if we only sit here talking, either we shall disappear or the people who are listening to us will" (II, 76–77). As the bombs reach the house, Captain Shotover cries, "Stand by, all hands, for judgment" (III, 140); and Mangan and the burglar are found unfit to live. (Shotover sees "the hand of God" in the fact that Mangan is drawn to the fatal gravel pit, III, 141.) The clear indication is that the other characters will suffer a similar fate unless they make their lives meaningful and useful. "Our turn next," is Hector's comment after the bombing (III, 142).

This idea of divine judgment is not necessarily an entirely pessimistic one. One could hope that under the threat of extermination people would pay more attention to how their lives were lived. The bombing (and the war) are not only a punishment for sins already committed, but a warning that man must change his ways—a warning that could have a desirable effect. Captain Shotover, we recall, tells Ellie that he could not govern his sailors without frightening them with the story that he had sold himself to the devil; and the idea that men cannot be governed without terror is discussed by Shaw in the Preface (1911) to *The Doctor's Dilemma*. "It is very doubtful indeed," he writes there, "whether Peter the Great could have effected the changes he made in Russia if he had not fascinated and intimidated his people by his monstrous cruelties and grotesque escapades. Had he been a nineteenth-century king of England, he would have had to wait for some huge accidental calamity: a cholera epidemic, a war, or an insurrection, before waking us up sufficiently to get anything done" (p. 31).[33] In *Heartbreak House* the Life Force may be asserting itself in the manner of Captain Shotover and Peter the Great, and frightening men into acting sensibly. Shaw wrote in 1930 that in the 1890's the mass of the public were without any political ideas and that a "quarter of a century elapsed before an impatient heaven rained German bombs down on them to wake them from their apathy." [34] This was Shaw's slightly more hopeful way of looking at the war; and it is a slightly more hopeful way of looking at the bombing in *Heartbreak House.*

Another possible element of hope (of a sort) at the end of the play lies in the view that Heartbreak House is so decadent that it is best destroyed, that its destruction would be a purification of the country, and would make way for progress. Near the end of the first act the following scene occurs:

CAPTAIN SHOTOVER [*raising a strange wail in the darkness*]
What a house! What a daughter!
  MRS HUSHABYE [*raving*] What a father!
  HECTOR [*following suit*] What a husband!
  CAPTAIN SHOTOVER. Is there no thunder in heaven? [35]
  HECTOR. Is there no beauty, no bravery, on earth?

(p. 78)

This weird scene, in which Captain Shotover appears to be calling for thunder from heaven to fall on his house (and he has just explained to Hector about the dynamite he has planted next to the house) has its parallel at the very end of the second act, when Hector *"lifts his fists in invocation to heaven"* and cries, "Fall. Fall and crush." Perhaps the bombing which ends the third act is an answer to the prayers of Captain Shotover and Hector. Hector is particularly set on the destruction of the house; he tries to ensure the bombs' success by making the house visible in the darkness. And Ellie encourages him, and hopes that the bombs will return the next night. The three characters who display this destructive impulse are the three most impressive characters in the play. (Hesione, who is also quite favorably presented, hopes that the bombs will return, but apparently for their beauty more than their destructiveness.)

The delighted response to the bombing on the part of Hector, Ellie, and Hesione is deliberately puzzling and ambiguous, reflecting Shaw's own puzzled and ambiguous feelings at the time he wrote the play. One can explain it in part by saying that the play leads us to feel that the destruction of the house and most of its inhabitants is desirable. Another insight, of a very partial kind, is gained from the knowledge that the feelings of Hector, Ellie, and Hesione have close parallels in Shaw's own wartime experiences. Here, for example, is a passage Shaw wrote in 1917, reporting on his tour of the front early in that year. After describing a German artillery attack on Ypres, he says that "when our car had left the town far behind, and I took the collar-studs out of my ears and exchanged the helmet of Mambrino for a cloth cap, I found the world suddenly duller [Hector's feeling after the bombing]. From this I infer that Ypres and its orchestra had been rather exciting, though I had not noticed it at the time." [36] And in 1916 he wrote to the Webbs about the Zeppelin flight near Ayot St. Lawrence that gave him the idea for the bombing episode in the play. "What is hardly credible, but true," he says, "is that the sound of the Zepp's engines was so fine, and its voyage through the stars so enchanting, that I positively caught myself hoping next night that there would be another raid." [37]

The ambiguous quality of the bombing scene, slightly hopeful but mostly despairing, is the chord which is sounded by the play as a whole. There is hope in the play: in Ellie's progress, in Mangan's death, in Hector's will to live and perhaps even in his desire to destroy the house, in Hesione's vitality, in Captain Shotover's doctrine that navigation would save the country. But these elements are, I think, outweighed by the play's despair: the bombs will presumably come again; most, and possibly all, of the characters in the play lead useless, futile lives; there is little sign that anyone in the play will provide the navigation necessary to keep the country off the rocks; and, above all, Shotover, who has the wisdom, has no significant power.

The play is apocalyptic: one feels that whatever happens after the final curtain, this world of "cultured, leisured Europe before the war" is finished. The advent of a new era, as in Yeats's "The Second Coming" (which was written in the same year in which *Heartbreak House* was published), is much more frightening than hopeful. The main feeling that the play evokes is one of regret—of heartbreak —that cultured, leisured Europe before the war allowed affairs to come to this pass.

VIII

Saint Joan

Shaw wrote *Saint Joan* in 1923, after Sydney Cockerell had given him a copy of T. Douglas Murray's *Jeanne d'Arc* (1902), and his wife, Charlotte, had urged him to write a play on the subject.[1] Immediate stimulus was also provided by the canonization of Joan in 1920, which would have appealed to Shaw as a confirmation of his view that prophets who are reviled during their lives as heretics are often worshipped after their deaths. But Joan was in any case a natural subject for Shaw. What seems to me particularly remarkable about the play is the extent to which it combines fidelity to the historical records with contemporary relevance and Shaw's own world-view. Almost everything in the play is based directly on the transcripts of Joan's trial and the subsequent rehabilitation proceedings of which Murray's book largely consists, and yet the play gives the appearance of being Shaw's own arbitrary invention in which history has been treated lightly or ignored altogether.[2]

Let us take one specific instance to serve as an illustration. In the Trial Scene de Stogumber, the bigoted English chaplain, complains that the revised indictment against Joan does not put sufficient stress on her testimony that her voices addressed her in French:

THE CHAPLAIN. . . . The Maid has actually declared that the blessed saints Margaret and Catherine, and the holy Archangel Michael, spoke to her in French. That is a vital point.
THE INQUISITOR. You think, doubtless, that they should have spoken in Latin?
CAUCHON. No: he thinks they should have spoken in English.
(VI, 125)

This sounds as if it might have been inserted into the play arbitrarily by Shaw in order to gratify his pronounced taste for anti-English jokes; but in fact Article XLIII of the original Act of Accusation (to which de Stogumber is referring) alleges that "Jeanne hath said and published that the Saints, the Angels, and the Archangels speak the French language and not the English language, because the Saints, the Angels, and the Archangels are not on the side of the English, but of the French." [3] De Stogumber himself is Shaw's invention, although much of what he says and does is suggested by passages from the records of the trial and rehabilitation. Shaw perceived the similarity between English feeling against Joan in 1429–1431 and the anti-German jingoism which so much disturbed him during the First World War. The origin of de Stogumber is to be found not only in the records of the trial, then, but also in Shaw's Preface (1919) to *Heartbreak House,* in which he records his pained response to civilian war hysteria and notes in particular that there was on the part of civilians "a frivolous exultation in death for its own sake, which was at bottom an inability to realize that the deaths were real deaths and not stage ones" (p. 19).

No doubt one of the factors which attracted Shaw to Joan's history as a subject was the inevitable anti-English element in it. Joan's efforts were devoted to the expulsion of the English from France, and any reasonable presentation of her story would have to accept this as a legitimate and laudable aim. (*King Henry the Sixth, Part One,* it will be agreed, is not a reasonable presentation of her story.) The story by its nature is hostile to English imperialism, and in introducing this element into his play Shaw could not be accused of distortion. Again, Shaw saw the relevance of Joan's story to contemporary history. *Saint Joan* was begun just at the end of the civil war which followed the establishment of the Irish Free State in 1921, and part of it was written in Ireland.[4] The parallel between early twentieth-century Ireland and early fifteenth-century France would have been in Shaw's mind: both France and Ireland were struggling for freedom from English domination, and the Irish case was based on the nationalism that Shaw ascribes to Joan in the play. The Preface (which stresses in various ways the contemporary relevance of Joan's trial and execution) compares the trial to that of Roger Casement in 1916 for treason against England, and Casement, like Joan, was executed by the English. In 1916 Shaw wrote a skillful defense for Casement himself to deliver at his trial; this speech, which Casement's lawyers did not make use of, was privately printed, with a prefatory note by Shaw, in 1922—the year before *Saint Joan* was begun.[5]

One of the reasons why Shaw is able to combine historical veracity with his own world-view is that Joan herself, as she appears in the records of the trial, is such a Shavian sort of character. Several of her shorter speeches in the Trial Scene are taken almost verbatim from the records of what the actual Joan said to her judges. No historical character could have made a more appropriate subject for a dramatist who had created an impudent youth like Frank Gardner, an innocent and inspired youth like Marchbanks, a saintly, unconventional, and compelling young woman like Barbara Undershaft (to whom Joan is closest), and a Christian martyr (or near-martyr) like Lavinia. The prophetic character is one of Shaw's most common—and dramatically most successful—types, and he had for many years before writing *Saint Joan* wanted to write a play about Mahomet,[6] who is compared to Joan both in the Preface and in the play (by Cauchon in the Tent Scene).

Shaw had not only taken an interest in characters like Joan well before he wrote his play about her, but he had taken an interest in Joan herself. He told Archibald Henderson in 1924 that he had been interested in Joan all his life and had always entertained the idea of putting her into a play.[7] He refers to her in the Notes to *Caesar and Cleopatra* (published in 1901) and in the Prefaces to *Getting Married* (1910), *The Doctor's Dilemma* (1911), and *Androcles and the Lion* (1915). In 1913 he visited Domrémy and Orléans in order, according to Henderson, "to sense the atmosphere and setting of the life of the Maid." [8] He wrote to Mrs. Patrick Campbell from Orléans that he would "do a Joan play some day . . . I should have God about to damn the English for their share in her betrayal and Joan producing an end of burnt stick in arrest of Judgment." [9]

But a more significant anticipation of what Joan stands for in Shaw's mind is to be found in a work in which she is not mentioned, *The Perfect Wagnerite,* which was published in 1898—twenty-five years before *Saint Joan* was written. In view of Shaw's comments on Siegfried in this analysis of Wagner's *Ring,* it would not be far-fetched to see Joan as Shaw's version of Siegfried.[10] Siegfried, according to Shaw, is a symbol of Protestantism, and the relevant section of *The Perfect Wagnerite* is the one entitled "Siegfried as Protestant." Shaw refers here to the modern enlightened faith in the individual will, and notes the parallel with the original late medieval Protestantism: "The boldest [modern] spirits began to raise the question whether churches and laws and the like were not doing a great deal more harm than good by their action in limiting the freedom of the human will. Four hundred years ago, when belief in God and in revelation was general throughout Europe, a similar wave of thought led the strongest-hearted peoples to affirm that every man's private judgment was a more trustworthy interpreter of God and revelation than the Church" (p. 214). The discussion of Protestantism is introductory to Shaw's analysis of Siegfried: "The most inevitable dramatic conception, then, of the nineteenth century is that of a perfectly naïve hero upsetting religion, law and order in all directions, and establishing in their place the unfettered action of Humanity doing exactly what it likes, and producing order instead of confusion thereby because it likes to do what is necessary for the good of the race. This conception, already incipient in Adam Smith's Wealth of Nations, was certain at last to reach some great artist, and be embodied by him in a masterpiece" (pp. 215–216). One could apply this passage to *Saint Joan* just as well as to *The Ring*. In the Tent Scene in the play Joan is described as a precursor of both Protestantism and nationalism; but in terms of the play as a whole it is her Protestantism which is much more significant. The dramatic center of the play is the Trial Scene, and Joan is tried as a Protestant (in effect), not as a nationalist. In fact, it is in presenting the trial as free from political bias that the play departs most obviously from accepted history.

The essence of Joan's point of view is expressed in a passage like the following:

LADVENU . . . Do you not believe that you are subject to the Church of God on earth?

JOAN. Yes. When have I ever denied it?

LADVENU. Good. That means, does it not, that you are subject to our Lord the Pope, to the cardinals, the archbishops, and the bishops for whom his lordship stands here today?

JOAN. God must be served first.

D'ESTIVET. Then your voices command you not to submit yourself to the Church Militant?

JOAN. My voices do not tell me to disobey the Church; but God must be served first.

CAUCHON. And you, and not the Church, are to be the judge?

JOAN. What other judgment can I judge by but my own?

(VI, 135)

This is the heresy for which Joan is burnt, and it is that assertion of the individual will against external, institutional restraints which is Shaw's concept of the Protestant spirit.[11] Joan's voices, as presented in the play, are the urgings of her own will, and these urgings are beneficent. Joan's voices tell her to raise the siege of Orléans, to crown the Dauphin in Rheims Cathedral, and to make the English leave France. That the last of these aims is laudable is simply assumed all through the play, and the first two are seen as necessary preconditions.

The principal representatives in *Saint Joan* of external, institutional restraints are the judges, but they are not by any means vilified. In fact, an aspect of the play that has given rise to much debate is the apparently favorable way in which it presents them—Cauchon and the Inquisitor in particular. Shaw makes these two as attractive as he can, and admits in the Preface that he has exaggerated their virtues (pp. 50–51). One reason for this sympathetic presentation is that Shaw, as usual, is reacting against the opinion of the majority. In the centuries since the rehabilitation in 1456 there had been many varying opinions of Joan, but the vilification of the judges had been universal.[12] The Catholic Church itself, in the Sentence of Rehabilitation, proclaimed the view that the judges had acted, in certain particulars at least, with "corruption, cozenage, calumny, fraud and malice."[13] Had Shaw been writing at the time of the original trial in 1431, one can be assured that his point of view would have been very different—he would no doubt have treated the judges with as much open disfavor as he treated the British authorities at the time of the Denshawai affair in Egypt in 1906 or the Easter Week executions in Ireland in 1916.[14] But Shaw saw as his role that of bringing to people's attention the side of the truth which they tended to overlook, and the side of the truth which had been overlooked about Joan's judges after the rehabilitation in 1456 was that they were something other than hateful monsters.

Shaw's treatment of the judges is also connected with his sense as a dramatist of what provides meaningful, interesting conflict in a play, and with his desire to provoke difficult ethical questions in the minds of his audience. He felt that villains had no place in his kind of "high tragedy and comedy," which sought to raise questions of conduct by presenting conflicts which could not be easily resolved. If one believes that Joan's judges were simply acting from evil motives, then the ethical (as opposed to psychological) questions raised are more limited than if one believes that her execution, while utterly deplorable, was brought about by men of the highest character and integrity. In this case, ethical questions of a complex nature are inevitable, and an audience is bound by the play to examine them. In particular, Shaw wants to force his audience to consider its own morality, by showing us that decent people, such as we for the most part believe ourselves to be, can commit horrible offenses against humanity, not through lapses into barbarism but while acting justly and honorably on mistaken premises. He wants to make it clear to us that good intentions, high-mindedness, and personal righteousness are not a sufficient basis for human conduct.

Here *Saint Joan* reflects a belief which had been important to Shaw for much of his life. The Idealist in *The Quintessence of Ibsenism* is a man who can do great harm while acting in a noble manner. The first play of Ibsen's to be discussed in *The Quintessence* is *Brand,* which (according to Shaw) has such a man as its central character. The comments on Brand in *The Quintessence* make very useful reading for one who seeks illumination of Shaw's intentions in his handling of the judges in *Saint Joan.* "Brand the priest," he explains, "is an idealist of heroic earnestness, strength, and courage," and as such he is harmful and dangerous to everyone with whom he comes into contact. He "dies a saint, having caused more intense suffering by his saintliness than the most talented sinner could possibly have done with twice his opportunities" (pp. 42, 44).[15] Shaw does not usually dramatize such people: the Idealists in the plays which we have looked at, for example, tend to be harmless and silly people rather than people to be taken seriously and feared.

But a character like Mazzini Dunn in *Heartbreak House* points the way toward the judges in *Saint Joan,* however unlike them he is in personality; for Dunn's well-intentioned beliefs are seen to be more harmful (potentially, and at a public level) than the blackguardly behavior of his near-namesake, the pirate-turned-thief Billy Dunn. It is, however, in *Saint Joan* that Shaw shows us for the first time on the stage Idealists like Brand actually doing dreadful harm with the best intentions.

"What Ibsen insists on is that there is no golden rule; that conduct must justify itself by its effect upon life and not by its conformity to any rule or ideal." So Shaw writes in *The Quintessence* (p. 125), in his chapter on "The Lesson of the Plays," which is also highly pertinent to *Saint Joan.* The pragmatic view stated in this passage is the ethical position that underlies the play. If Cauchon and the Inquisitor are judged strictly according to the quality of their intentions, then they must receive only commendation, as their intentions (in the play) are wholly honorable. If, on the other hand, they are judged according to a pragmatic morality—in which the criterion is the practical effects of their actions—then we see them as Shaw wants us to see them, as dangerous malefactors. In making ethical judgments, one must consider more than character and intention: one must consider results. The judges, as the play presents them, constitute a refutation of the view that *tout comprendre, c'est tout pardonner* (see Preface, p. 32). The fact that Cauchon and the Inquisitor are humanly most attractive is no justification for Joan's burning. The trial might as well have been presided over by de Stogumber; the result would have been no worse. (A similar point is made in the trial scene in *The Devil's Disciple,* in which General Burgoyne and Major Swindon are equally prepared to hang Dudgeon, however greatly Burgoyne is to be preferred to Swindon in human terms.)

The pragmatic ethic of *Saint Joan* is made most explicit in the Epilogue, when Ladvenu is telling Charles about the rehabilitation proceedings (in one of the play's embarrassingly rhetorical speeches):

LADVENU. At the trial which sent a saint to the stake as a heretic and a sorceress, the truth was told; the law was upheld; mercy was shewn beyond all custom; no wrong was done but the final and dreadful wrong of the lying sentence and the pitiless fire. At this inquiry from which I have just come, there was shameless perjury, courtly corruption, calumny of the dead who did their duty according to their lights, cowardly evasion of the issue, testimony made of idle tales that could not impose on a ploughboy. Yet out of this insult to justice, this defamation of the Church, this orgy of lying and foolishness, the truth is set in the noonday sun on the hilltop; the white robe of innocence is cleansed from the smirch of the burning faggots; the holy life is sanctified; the true heart that lived through the flame is consecrated; a great lie is silenced for ever; and a great wrong is set right before all men.

CHARLES. My friend: provided they can no longer say that I was crowned by a witch and a heretic, I shall not fuss about how the trick has been done. Joan would not have fussed about it if it came all right in the end: she was not that sort: I knew her.

(p. 150)

Charles is right about Joan: after all she was prepared during her trial to sign a total recantation of which she did not believe a word in order to gain her freedom. This idea of judging actions by results is found in the play in other forms, too. The Archbishop's definition of a miracle as "an event which creates faith" is a pragmatic conception: the only distinction which he makes between a miracle and a fraud is that one creates faith while the other deceives (II, 78), a distinction which ignores intrinsic and intentional differences entirely and is concerned only with consequences. Shortly before the Archbishop's definition comes La Hire's comment on the story that Joan miraculously predicted the death of Foul Mouthed Frank, a celebrated swearer. "You tell me that what the girl did to Foul Mouthed Frank was no miracle. No matter: it finished Frank" (II, 77). And in both Preface and play Joan's voices are justified on pragmatic grounds: we are to regard Joan as "divinely" inspired because her voices command her to do sensible things (see "Joan's Voices and Visions," Preface, pp. 11–13).

Another aspect of *Saint Joan* which reflects a long-held view of Shaw's is its implicit concern with toleration. Here again one of the best commentaries on the play is to be found in *The Quintessence of*

Ibsenism, in the section in which Shaw presents Ibsenism as a gospel of toleration:

[Ibsen] protests against the ordinary assumption that there are certain moral institutions which justify all means used to maintain them, and insists that the supreme end shall be the inspired, eternal, ever growing one, not the external [,] unchanging, artificial one; not the letter but the spirit; not the contract but the object of the contract; not the abstract law but the living will . . . It is enormously important that we should "mind our own business" and let other people do as they like unless we can prove some damage beyond the shock to our feelings and prejudices. It is easy to put revolutionary cases in which it is so impossible to draw the line that they will always be decided in practice more or less by physical force; but for all ordinary purposes of government and social conduct the distinction is a commonsense one. The plain working truth is that it is not only good for people to be shocked occasionally, but absolutely necessary to the progress of society that they should be shocked pretty often. But it is not good for people to be garotted occasionally, or at all. That is why it is a mistake to treat an atheist as you treat a garotter, or to put "bad taste" on the footing of theft and murder. The need for freedom of evolution is the sole basis of toleration, the sole valid argument against Inquisitions and Censorships, the sole reason for not burning heretics and sending every eccentric person to the madhouse.

(pp. 122–123) [16]

In the play the important charge against Joan is one of heresy; that is, she is burnt for holding beliefs which are contrary to those of the Catholic Church and specifically for maintaining that her private judgment must take precedence over the judgment of the Church. Cauchon in the Tent Scene and the Inquisitor in the Trial Scene put forward arguments against Joan's heresy which on the surface are very convincing, but in fact rest upon the idea that the individual will is by nature evil in its tendency and therefore needs to be restrained by an institution like the Church—precisely the point of view ascribed to Idealists in *The Quintessence.* (To the Idealist, Shaw writes there, "human nature, naturally corrupt, is held back from ruinous excesses only by self-denying conformity to the ideals," p. 31.) Within the context of *Saint Joan* such a view is un-

tenable. Since no one in the play is naturally evil—even de Stogumber is only blind—there is no ground for believing that the
human will is intrinsically bad. And as the will which is principally
under consideration is Joan's, there is reason to believe that the
human will is intrinsically good, and ought to be allowed to flourish. The harm which is done in the play is done not by anarchic individuals but by a repressive institution. It is Joan, not her judges,
whose conduct is based on what she hears from voices; that is, it is
Joan and not her judges who acts from inspiration from within herself. The judges' sense of "God's business" derives not from the inner
promptings of their own will but from a sense of duty to an institution and a code outside of themselves. In particular, they serve abstract justice. "Remember only that justice comes first" is the
Inquisitor's main advice to the court before the trial begins (VI,
129), and in the Epilogue Cauchon talks much of justice. But the
Inquisitor, near the end of the Epilogue, says to Joan: "The judges
in the blindness and bondage of the law praise thee, because thou
hast vindicated the vision and the freedom of the living soul" (p.
162). It is this view that the play points toward: the distinction between blindness and bondage (as opposed to evil) on the one hand
and the freedom of the living soul on the other.

In the Epilogue there is a brief exchange upon the entrance of the
Vatican emissary which, while questionable on artistic grounds, is
most significant thematically.

*A clerical-looking gentleman in black frockcoat and trousers,
and tall hat, in the fashion of the year 1920, suddenly appears before them in the corner on their right. They all stare at him. Then
they burst into uncontrollable laughter.*

THE GENTLEMAN. Why this mirth, gentlemen?

WARWICK. I congratulate you on having invented a most ex-
traordinarily comic dress.

THE GENTLEMAN. I do not understand. You are all in fancy
dress: I am properly dressed.

DUNOIS. All dress is fancy dress, is it not, except our natural
skins?

(p. 159)

This apparently frivolous passage is closely related to the play's major concerns. One of the charges against Joan in the Trial Scene (and in historical fact) was that by dressing like a man she contravened absolute standards. The audience is invited to take the view that Joan was very sensible in dressing as she did and that there are no absolute standards in dress. The standard of one age is the aberration of another. The implication here is that the other charges against Joan should be regarded in the same way. The heresy of one age is the orthodoxy of another; and the heretic of one age is the saint of another.[17] It is therefore important for the authorities in any period to exercise toleration of views and conduct that they regard as abominable. They must recognize that their standard of what is abominable is relative and not absolute. As Shaw puts it in the Preface, the Church Militant must not act as if it were the Church Triumphant (p. 36). The Preface, it is true, also argues (as Shaw does elsewhere) that society cannot permit *any* sort of conduct, that it must draw a line between the tolerable and the intolerable (see "Toleration, Modern and Medieval," pp. 39–40). But since Joan is clearly on the tolerable side of such a line (if properly drawn), the play itself does not deal with this aspect of the question. What the play stresses is that society must "make it a point of honor to privilege heresy to the last bearable degree on the simple ground that all evolution in thought and conduct must at first appear as heresy and misconduct" (Preface, pp. 37–38).

II

Another of the controversial aspects of *Saint Joan* is its miracles, and some readers wonder why Shaw included them in the play. The most obvious reason is that he knew that they could provide good dramatic moments, which they do. Another reason is that he was writing a kind of saint's legend (as his title suggests), and miracles are appropriate to this genre. The miracles should be seen, too, in relation to Shaw's attempt to "let the medieval atmosphere blow through my play freely" (p. 49). But they also serve an ironic purpose. The resumption of egg-laying by Robert de Baudricourt's hens and the change of wind at Orléans are not to be seen as traditional miracles at all, but merely as coincidences: it is unlikely that the hens would cease laying or that the wind would blow from the east forever. We are to look at these events in the light of the Archbishop's explanation to La Trémouille in the Court Scene that Joan's identification of the Dauphin will be a miracle in the sense that it will create faith. This is not the Catholic Church's concept of a miracle, and in denying any supernatural element in Joan's miracles the play is opposed to traditional Christian belief. But the play, like the Preface, also rejects a purely rationalist interpretation of events. For the rationalist (as Shaw sees him, at any rate) would deny the existence of miracles altogether, and there are miracles in the play, although not of the traditional kind. When in the opening scene Robert de Baudricourt says scoffingly, "Oh! You think the girl can work miracles, do you?" Poulengey replies, "I think the girl herself is a bit of a miracle" (I, 64). This is the principal clue to Shaw's intention in having so much talk about miracles in the play. What people usually call miracles are bogus, while the real miracle is the human genius.[18] In Shaw's vitality-worshipping religion of Creative Evolution a person like Joan *is* a miracle: not only in the Archbishop's sense, in that she creates faith, but also in the more ordinary sense that she is marvelous and exceeds the known powers of nature, which egg-laying hens and changing winds do not.

Not only is Joan a miracle in the Shavian sense, a person who exhibits the highest potential of human life, but she also performs what one might regard as miracles in her influence on the people around her. We see Joan's ability to put spirit and determination into people in her effect on the dispirited Dauphin in the Court Scene:

> CHARLES. I dont want a message; but can you tell me any secrets? Can you do any cures? Can you turn lead into gold, or anything of that sort?
> JOAN. I can turn thee into a king, in Rheims Cathedral; and that is a miracle that will take some doing, it seems.
>
> (II, 85)

Here we have the contrast between the conventional kind of miracle and the real kind, which has to do with the human mind rather than the material world—a distinction which is very characteristic of Shaw. Similarly, when Dunois pays tribute to Joan in the Cathedral Scene by saying, "I think that God was on your side; for I have not forgotten how the wind changed, and how our hearts changed when you came" (V, 114), it is the second change rather than the first which is the miracle.

Joan's passion to change people is common to most of Shaw's heroes, and the particular kind of change that she brings about is best described in the Hell Scene of *Man and Superman,* in a speech of Don Juan's: "I am giving you examples of the fact that this creature Man, who in his own selfish affairs is a coward to the backbone, will fight for an idea like a hero. He may be abject as a citizen; but he is dangerous as a fanatic. He can only be enslaved whilst he is spiritually weak enough to listen to reason. I tell you, gentlemen, if you can shew a man a piece of what he now calls God's work to do, and what he will later on call by many new names, you can make him entirely reckless of the consequences to himself personally" (III, 106). Joan herself is heroic and powerful because of her sense that she is the agent of a suprapersonal purpose, and she makes others act bravely and effectively by inspiring them with the same feeling. In the opening scene she tells Robert de Baudricourt why she will be able to raise the siege of Orléans: "Our soldiers are always beaten because they are fighting only to save their skins; and the shortest way to save your skin is to run away. Our knights are thinking only of the money they will make in ransoms: it is not kill or be killed with them, but pay or be paid. But I will teach them all to fight that the will of God may be done in France; and then they will drive the poor goddams before them like sheep" (I, 68). In the following scene, at Chinon, she uses this approach in trying to make Charles into a king. "I tell thee," she says, "it is God's business we are here to do: not our own. I have a message to thee from God; and thou must listen to it, though thy heart break with the terror of it" (II, 85). One notes that in the first three scenes, which dramatize "the romance of her rise," she is progressively more successful in influencing other people. In the first scene she persuades Robert de Baudricourt to allow her to go to Chinon with some of his men, but his reluctant submission to her demand is the result of his weakness rather than his strength. Joan cannot be said to have inspired him to heroic activity. Nor can she be said to have done this to Charles in the second scene, but she comes closer. Now it is not a case of wringing reluctant consent but of inspiring self-assertion. At the end of the scene he behaves, for the first time in his life, like a king, in his decree to the court and his resistance to La Trémouille. And this is his first step toward a reign which, as we learn from the Epilogue, may not be heroic but is at least successful. It is in the third scene, at Orléans, however, that Joan reaches the height of her effectiveness. Her greatest triumph, in the battle which raises the English siege, is not actually shown on the stage; we see only the prelude to it. But we know from this prelude, and from what is said about the battle in the Cathedral Scene, that Joan inspires the army to successes which had been thought impossible.

Shaw says in the Preface that the historical Joan was a genius, which he defines as "a person who, seeing farther and probing deeper than other people, has a different set of ethical valuations from theirs, and has energy enough to give effect to this extra vision and its valuations in whatever manner best suits his or her specific talents" (p. 7). It is these two qualities of vision and practical power that in plays which we have examined have been separated—in Tanner and Ann, Keegan and Broadbent, Barbara-Cusins and Undershaft, Shotover and Mangan. *Saint Joan*, therefore, in which these qualities are united in one character, is of great interest in relation to these earlier plays. For Joan is the kind of character to which the other plays look forward: one who has not only vision but the necessary power and practical ability to impose that vision on others.[19] Joan is sufficiently otherworldly and imaginative to feel that her inspirations are commands from God which come to her through the voices of saints, and to have aspirations far more bold than those of anyone around her. But she is sufficiently practical so that her voices almost always give her good, sensible advice. For example, in the Court Scene she tells Charles that God has commanded that he should be crowned king in the cathedral at Rheims, and the speech which finally persuades him is a mixture of exalted inspiration and shrewd political common sense: "Charlie: I come from the land, and have gotten my strength working on the land; and I tell thee that the land is thine to rule righteously and keep God's peace in, and not to pledge at the pawnshop as a drunken woman pledges her children's clothes. And I come from God to tell thee to kneel in the cathedral and solemnly give thy kingdom to Him for ever and ever, and become the greatest king in the world as

His steward and His bailiff, His soldier and His servant. The very clay of France will become holy: her soldiers will be the soldiers of God: the rebel dukes will be rebels against God: the English will fall on their knees and beg thee let them return to their lawful homes in peace. Wilt be a poor little Judas, and betray me and Him that sent me?" (II, 85–86). Notice the way in which the first two sentences of Joan's speech begin: "I come from the land" and then "I come from God." Joan unites in herself heaven and earth, a union which is emphasized all through the play by her combination of the prophetic and the peasantlike. Perhaps we might take just one other example of this. In the Cathedral Scene Joan is trying to persuade Charles to capture Paris, and she asks the Archbishop to "tell him that it is not God's will that he should take his hand from the plough" (V, 112). Here we have a mixture of theological and agricultural language, and shortly after this she says impatiently to Charles, "But what voices do you need to tell you what the blacksmith can tell you: that you must strike while the iron is hot?" (V, 113). Again Joan combines heavenly vision and earthly good sense: she comes from God, and she comes from the land.

In plays like *Man and Superman* and *Major Barbara,* this combination of vision and practicality is seen as the means to successful progress. But Joan is by no means entirely successful. She is, it is true, triumphant until after the coronation at Rheims, and beyond that she is successful in the sense that the expulsion of the English from France, although it comes about after her death, is largely her doing: the play, with its Epilogue, makes it clear that without Joan it would not have happened. And she is successful in the larger and vaguer sense that she is an inspiration for mankind. But the focus of the play is much more on her failure. The principal scene is concerned with her trial and execution, and the Epilogue ends with her cry of anguish and near-despair after her worshippers have left her alone, as she was left isolated and unsupported during her life.[20]

Why does Joan fail? One reason is suggested by Shaw in the Preface: she was an unsophisticated young girl in a world of sophisticated grown men. This deficiency in Joan is discussed in the section entitled "Joan's Immaturity and Ignorance" (pp. 22–23) and in the comparison near the beginning of the Preface of Joan with Socrates. Here Shaw says that if Joan "had been old enough to know the effect she was producing on the men whom she humiliated by being right when they were wrong, and had learned to flatter and manage them, she might have lived as long as Queen Elizabeth. But she was too young and rustical and inexperienced to have any such arts. When she was thwarted by men whom she thought fools, she made no secret of her opinion of them or her impatience with their folly; and she was naïve enough to expect them to be obliged to her for setting them right and keeping them out of mischief" (p. 4).

This observation applies to Joan's relations with all those with whom she has dealings in the play. Everyone in the play, Armagnac, English, and ecclesiastical alike,[21] is responsible for her failure: at the end of the Cathedral Scene she has lost the support of the significant leaders of her own side, and by the end of her trial every person in the court is agreed that she should burn. The emphasis in the play, however, is very much on the role of the Church rather than that of the Armagnacs or the English in Joan's defeat. The principal conflict in the play is between Joan and the Church.

In this conflict Joan is at a greater disadvantage than she is in her conflict with other sorts of opposition. She is at her strongest when confronted with people who have no purpose of their own: de Baudricourt, Charles, and the Armagnac army, for example. In these confrontations her conviction that she is the agent of God's purpose makes it difficult for men to resist her. Because she has such a pronounced sense of purpose, Joan is able to overcome the inertia and self-centeredness of those who have none. But in the Church Joan meets an obstacle which is much more formidable than de Baudricourt, Charles, or the Armagnac army. Now she is confronted with men who believe just as much as she does that "it is God's business we are here to do: not our own." Like Joan, the ecclesiastics see themselves as agents of God's purpose, with a sacred mission to compel others to serve that purpose. Since their view of God's purpose is radically different from Joan's and wholly incompatible with it, a conflict between them and Joan is inevitable. As Shaw puts it in the Preface, "an irresistible force met an immovable obstacle, and developed the heat that consumed poor Joan" (p. 31).

The play subtly implies the similarity between the irresistible force and the immovable obstacle. The characters in the play who are most like Joan are the priests who condemn her to death. In the Epilogue Charles compares Cauchon (unfavorably) with himself, saying in effect that those with no ideals do least harm. He begins by addressing Cauchon alone, but as he continues it becomes clear that he is drawing a contrast between himself on the one hand and Cauchon and Joan on the other. "You people with your heads in the sky," he tells them, echoing a phrase Joan has applied to herself shortly before, "spend all your time trying to turn the world upside down; but I take the world as it is, and say that top-side-up is right-side-up; and I keep my nose pretty close to the ground" (p. 154). In the language of *The Quintessence of Ibsenism,* Charles is defending the Philistine against the Idealist and the Realist, between whom he makes no distinction.

Of all Joan's opponents, the one who is most like her is her greatest enemy, Warwick's chaplain de Stogumber. Like Joan, he is an uncompromising fanatic who has no doubt whatever of the justice and truth of his mission and beliefs. He is just as determined to have Joan burnt as she is to continue killing his countrymen until they leave France. Both Joan and de Stogumber are quite unable to see anyone else's point of view, and both lack the worldly wisdom that counsels against offending other people unnecessarily. Joan is not the only person to throw the court into an uproar during her trial by making statements which outrage the judges. De Stogumber's outburst, when it looks as if Joan is to be spared, that "there is no faith in a Frenchman" (VI, 139) has just the same effect. They are similar, too, in that they are the only nationalists in the play, a point that is brought out in Cauchon's warning to de Stogumber in the Tent Scene. When de Stogumber has called Cauchon a traitor for wishing to save Joan's soul instead of burning her, Cauchon replies, enraged, "If you dare do what this woman has done—set your country above the holy Catholic Church—you shall go to the fire with her" (IV, 101). And in a sense de Stogumber does go to the fire with her. Her burning causes him as much suffering as it causes her: "O Christ," he cries after the event has overwhelmed him with horror and remorse, "deliver me from this fire that is consuming me!" (VI, 146). The parallel between him and Joan is underlined in this scene by the stage business at his entrance: when he returns to the courtroom he throws himself on the stool that Joan had occupied during the trial.[22]

De Stogumber is not primarily an ecclesiastical character, in that his loyalty is more to England than to the Church, and his hatred of Joan is based largely on national rather than theological considerations. But the parallel between them emphasizes the fact that those who are most hostile to Joan are those who are most like her. One could put this in a different way and say that *Saint Joan* brings out the similarity between Idealists and Realists, which I touched on in my chapter on *Man and Superman*. Now in *Man and Superman* we saw that in the Comedy Tanner was successful against the Idealists and unsuccessful against the Philistines. This pattern is exactly reversed in *Saint Joan*. The people whom Joan can manage (for a time, at any rate) are the Philistines, the people with no ideas— simple soldiers and men like Charles, who keeps his "nose pretty close to the ground." Those with whom she cannot cope are the Idealists, who like her are passionately committed to ideas but, unlike her, to static, established, outdated ones.

The earlier play that it is most interesting to compare with *Saint Joan* is, I think, *Major Barbara,* to which in some senses *Saint Joan* can be seen as a sequel. Joan represents the combination of forces which is formed at the jubilant conclusion of *Major Barbara*. She has Barbara's religious zeal, Cusins' political desire to better the lot of the people, and Undershaft's practical power and his willingness to kill.[23] She embodies the marriage of contraries which, at the close of *Major Barbara,* promises to transform society. But Joan fails. Shaw says of her in the Preface to *Saint Joan* that "she thought political changes much easier than they are" (p. 22): perhaps the Shaw of 1923–24 would have applied this comment to himself as he was in 1905. *Saint Joan,* written after the disillusioning experience of the war and its aftermath, presents the power of established, static institutions and beliefs as much greater than it appears in *Major Barbara*. The most significant thematic difference between the two plays is that while in *Major Barbara* the Idealists (Stephen [24] and Lady Britomart) are mere satirical butts who represent no real threat to the forces of progress, in *Saint Joan* they are, in the persons of ecclesiastics like Cauchon and the Inquisitor, the immovable obstacle that stops—and burns—Joan.

This is the cause of Joan's failure which the play most emphasizes: her collision with men who, like herself, have almost perfect confidence in what they do because they see themselves as instruments of God's will. And Joan's judges have the great advantage over her that they also see themselves as instruments of the powerful Catholic Church. In the Trial Scene Joan is alone and isolated, surrounded by men who share a common faith and organization.

Joan's isolation is a recurring motif in the play. Each of the three last scenes—the Cathedral Scene, the Trial Scene and the Epilogue—ends with the desertion of Joan by those around her, so that each time she stands utterly alone. In the Cathedral Scene she is deserted by her king and his court; and it is then, as she leaves the cathedral by herself, that she gives her great speech (reminiscent perhaps of Dr. Stockmann in Ibsen's *An Enemy of the People*) on the glory of isolation. "Yes: I *am* alone on earth: I have always been alone," Joan tells them. "Do not think you can frighten me by telling me that I am alone. France is alone; and God is alone; and what is my loneliness before the loneliness of my country and my God? I see now that the loneliness of God is His strength: what would He be if He listened to your jealous little counsels? Well, my loneliness shall be my strength too; it is better to be alone with God: His friendship will not fail me, nor His counsel, nor His love" (V, 118–119). Joan is here putting a brave face on her isolation by emphasizing that she alone is right. A rather different note, however, sounds with increasing strength in the later part of the play. When Joan learns that the Armagnac leaders do not want to attempt the capture of Paris, she says to Dunois, "Jack: the world is too wicked for me" (V, 109). Here she is emphasizing not so much her rightness as its obverse: the world's wrongness. One finds the same emphasis at two of the most crucial points in the play. In the Trial Scene, after Joan has been deserted (as she would see it) by her Church, she tells the judges, in the last speech of her life, that God's ways are not their ways. "He wills that I go through the fire to His bosom; for I am His child, and you are not fit that I should live among you. That is my last word to you" (VI, 143). This is the note, too, on which the whole play ends, with Joan's final speech in the Epilogue after she has been deserted by the representatives of all walks of humanity, who beg her not to return to life among them. Alone on the stage, while *"the last remaining rays of light gather into a white radiance"* descending on her, she cries: "O God that madest this beautiful earth, when will it be ready to receive Thy saints? How long, O Lord, how long?" (p. 163).

This concluding speech brings into great prominence the basic and most pessimistic reason for Joan's failure: that the superior person and the ordinary world cannot live together. The genius must be isolated—by definition, for Shaw, as we have seen, defines a genius (in part) as one who, "seeing farther and probing deeper than other people, has a different set of ethical valuations from theirs." And Shaw also discusses in the Preface the inevitable hostility of the world to the genius (see especially pp. 4–6); this is an idea which goes back as far as his novels and *The Quintessence of Ibsenism,* and is found frequently in his writings. In 1894 he began a review of a concert conducted by Wagner's son by discussing the genius of the father:

I submit to you . . . as politely as such a thing may be submitted, that since Plato, Dante, Shakespear, Goethe, and men of that kind are esteemed great only because they exceed us average persons exactly as we exceed the galley-slave, it follows that they must walk through our world much as through a strange country full of dangerous beasts . . . Obviously, I have never seen Goethe or Shakespear or Plato: they were before my time. But I have seen Richard Wagner, who was so vehemently specialized by Nature as a man of genius that he was totally incapable of anything ordinary. He fought with the wild beasts all his life; and when you saw him coming through a crowded cage, even when they all felt about him as the lions felt about Daniel, he had an air of having his life in his hand, as it were, and of wandering in search of his right place and his own people, if any such there might be.[25]

A similar passage, which anticipates *Saint Joan* even more closely, is to be found in the Revolutionist's Handbook in *Man and Superman,* where Tanner concludes his chapter "The Conceit of Civilization" by saying that "unless we are replaced by a more highly evolved animal—in short, by the Superman—the world must remain a den of dangerous animals among whom our few accidental supermen, our Shakespears, Goethes, Shelleys, and their like, must live as precariously as lion tamers do, taking the humor of their situation, and the dignity of their superiority, as a set-off to the horror of the one and the loneliness of the other" (p. 200) [26]—which is precisely what Joan does. An individual Siegfried cannot save society, Shaw wrote in *The Perfect Wagnerite:* the only solution would be to breed a race of men like him—"in whom the life-giving impulses predominate" (p. 215). As long as Joan is the only person of her type in society, the world will not be a fit place for her. Only when most men are themselves saints will the world be ready to receive saints.

IX

Back to Methuselah

Back to Methuselah was begun in early 1918,[1] a year before the publication of *Heartbreak House,* and the two works grew out of the same immediate preoccupations: Shaw's response to the war and his feeling that he was growing old. This second, personal factor is seldom given the emphasis it deserves in discussions of the *Methuselah* cycle. *Back to Methuselah* is one of the most self-revealing of Shaw's writings. In a letter to Frank Harris in 1920 Shaw said that he had just "shot his last bolt" in this work, an enormous play with an enormous preface; the theme, he said, was one on which fifty plays might be written, and he had been able barely to touch it with the tips of his fingers.[2] Shaw evidently believed that *Back to Methuselah* was to be his last work,[3] and that it was only a beginning of what he felt might be written along its lines. The Preface to the cycle concludes on a similar, but more dissatisfied note: "I am not, I hope, under more illusion than is humanly inevitable as to the crudity of this my beginning of a Bible for Creative Evolution. I am doing the best I can at my age. My powers are waning; but so much the better for those who found me unbearably brilliant when I was in my prime. It is my hope that a hundred apter and more elegant parables by younger hands will soon leave mine as far behind as the religious pictures of the fifteenth century left behind the first attempts of the early Christians at iconography. In that hope I withdraw and ring up the curtain" (pp. lxxxv–lxxxvi). In this final section of the Preface Shaw also dismisses almost his whole dramatic oeuvre as virtual juvenilia,[4] and implies that *Back to Methuselah* (itself a crude beginning) is his first play of real significance—

with the possible, partial exception of *Man and Superman*—as a contribution to a modern Bible.

These attitudes are highly relevant to the *Methuselah* cycle, with its central idea that we do not live long enough to become mature. Conrad Barnabas says in the second play, "If I could count on nine hundred and sixty years I could make myself a real biologist, instead of what I am now: a child trying to walk"; and his brother Franklyn left the Church after realizing that he "was not within a hundred and fifty years of the experience and wisdom [he] was pretending to" as a clergyman (*The Gospel of the Brothers Barnabas,* p. 39). In the next play, *The Thing Happens,* Mrs. Lutestring (the *ci-devant* parlor maid) tells of her second husband: "I had to marry an elderly man: a man over sixty. He was a great painter. On his deathbed he said to me 'It has taken me fifty years to learn my trade, and to paint all the foolish pictures a man must paint and get rid of before he comes through them to the great things he ought to paint. And now that my foot is at last on the threshold of the temple I find that it is also the threshold of my tomb.' That man would have been the greatest painter of all time if he could have lived as long as I. I saw him die of old age whilst he was still, as he said himself, a gentleman amateur, like all modern painters" (p. 118). The parallel between this and the last part of the Preface is unmistakable. Shaw was sixty-one when he began *Back to Methuselah,* and he clearly felt that now, just as he had come to his really significant work, he was old and finished as a writer. That he was wrong both in his estimate of the importance of *Back to Methuselah* in relation to his other works and in his feeling that his creative life was finished (*Saint Joan* was, of course, still to come) does not matter here. What does matter in considering *Back to Methuselah* is the point that its concern with the tragedy of the brevity of our lives has a personal application for Shaw himself. This personal feeling seems to me to have been more significant as a creative impetus than the wish to illustrate neo-Lamarckian evolutionary theory in parable form.

I have also mentioned the *Methuselah* cycle's connection with the war; I think that this too is at least as important as its connection with "metabiological" theory. *Back to Methuselah* and *Heartbreak House* are Shaw's two major dramatic works engendered by the war.[5] The two works are very different—one, for example, condenses England into a country house and a period of a few hours, while the other spreads mankind over the whole earth and many thousands of years—but at the heart of each of them is the feeling, arising from the war, that it is doubtful whether "the human animal, as he exists at present, is capable of solving the social problems raised by his own aggregation, or, as he calls it, his civilization" (Preface to *Back to Methuselah,* p. x). It is worth noting, too, that *Man and Superman,* which is also concerned with this doubt, was begun during the Boer War. Of the three works, *Back to Methuselah* is the one in which war itself is a major theme. In Act II of the first play we meet Cain, the original murderer and the inventor of war, who has "imagined a glorious poem of many men": "I will divide them into two great hosts. One of them I will lead; and the other will be led by the man I fear most and desire to fight and kill most. And each host shall try to kill the other host. Think of that! all those multitudes of men fighting, fighting, killing, killing! The four rivers running with blood! The shouts of triumph! the howls of rage! the curses of despair! the shrieks of torment! That will be life indeed: life lived to the very marrow: burning, overwhelming life" (*In the Beginning,* p. 21). The second play is set in a world in which Cain's dream has just been fully realized: the scene is London *"in the first years after the war"* (p. 37), and the two main characters (dramatically speaking) are H. H. Lubin and Joyce Burge, caricatures of England's two wartime prime ministers, Asquith and Lloyd George. Franklyn Barnabas, the theological Creative Evolutionist, tells them that they "will go down to posterity as one of a European group of immature statesmen and monarchs who, doing the very best for your respective countries of which you were capable, succeeded in all-but-wrecking the civilization of Europe, and did, in effect, wipe out of existence many millions of its inhabitants" (*The Gospel of the Brothers Barnabas,* p. 67). One of the most powerful moments of the whole cycle comes at the end of this play, when Haslam, the hitherto apparently vapid clergyman, and Savvy, Franklyn's daughter, are left alone:

HASLAM. Did you notice one thing? It struck me as rather curious.

SAVVY. What?

HASLAM. Lubin and your father have both survived the war. But their sons were killed in it.

SAVVY [*sobered*] Yes. Jim's death killed mother.

HASLAM. And they never said a word about it!

SAVVY. Well, why should they? The subject didnt come up. *I* forgot about it too; and I was very fond of Jim.

HASLAM. *I* didnt forget it, because I'm of military age; and if I hadnt been a parson I'd have had to go out and be killed too. To me the awful thing about their political incompetence was that they had to kill their own sons. It was the war casualty lists and the starvation afterwards that finished me up with politics and the Church and everything else except you.

(p. 85)

This is an important scene, for it reveals the real horror which underlies the preceding farcical presentation of the politicians Burge and Lubin, and it indicates the reason for Haslam's unconscious decision to live for three hundred years: his feeling that the men who allowed the war and its aftermath to occur were just not good enough. In the context of the whole of *Back to Methuselah,* this scene represents the turning point in human history: in the final speech of the cycle, Lilith says that she was about to sweep away the human race (at the time of the war, it is implied) "when one man repented and lived three hundred years" (*As Far as Thought Can Reach,* p. 253).

The war is referred to in passing in the next play, *The Thing Happens,* and in the fourth play Cain is reincarnated as Cain Adamson Charles Napoleon, Emperor of Turania, whose sole talent is as an organizer of war.[6] The last direct mention of the war in the cycle is in the speech in this play in which Zoo, the "young" long-liver, explains the origin of the Falstaff monument: the "War to end War," it turns out, was the first of a series of wars which destroyed "pseudo-Christian civilization"; and during them statesmen eventually discovered "that cowardice was a great patriotic virtue; and a public monument was erected to its first preacher, an ancient and very fat sage called Sir John Falstaff" (*Tragedy of an Elderly Gentleman,* II, 177–178).

II

In *Man and Superman,* man's inadequacy is seen mainly in terms of a lack of intelligence; in *Back to Methuselah* it is seen mainly in terms of a lack of maturity. The principal function of the idea of longevity in the cycle, it seems to me, is not so much to say that we can and should extend our lives as to provide a basis for the related satirical point that we behave like children. As in *Man and Superman,* the emphasis is on the political consequences of our limitation. Unintelligent vitality, Shaw warns in the Epistle Dedicatory to the earlier work, "may muddle successfully through the comparatively tribal stages of gregariousness; but in nineteenth century nations and twentieth century commonwealths the resolve of every man to be rich at all costs, and of every woman to be married at all costs, must, without a highly scientific social organization, produce a ruinous development of poverty, celibacy, prostitution, infant mortality, adult degeneracy, and everything that wise men most dread" (pp. xvi–xvii). Conrad Barnabas, in the second *Methuselah* play, expresses a similar point of view: "Cant you see," he tells the politicians, "that three-score-and-ten, though it may be long enough for a very crude sort of village life, isnt long enough for a complicated civilization like ours?" (*The Gospel of the Brothers Barnabas,* p. 71). The result of having children (such as Burge and Lubin) trying to manage "a complicated civilization like ours" has been a terrible modern war, followed by a peace treaty which will soon lead to another war: "The statesmen of Europe were incapable of governing Europe," says Franklyn Barnabas. "What they needed was a couple of hundred years training and experience: what they had actually had was a few years at the bar or in a counting-house or on the grouse moors and golf courses. And now we are waiting, with monster cannons trained on every city and seaport, and huge aeroplanes ready to spring into the air and drop bombs every one of which will obliterate a whole street, and poison gases that will strike multitudes dead with a breath, until one of you gentlemen rises in his helplessness to tell us, who are as helpless as himself, that we are at war again" (pp. 70–71).

In the blurb that Shaw prepared in 1938 for the Penguin edition of *Back to Methuselah,* he wrote of the longevity theme as follows:

Shaw suggested that though men lived long enough to attain to a considerable proficiency in golf or bridge, the ability to manage modern civilization was quite beyond their years. He gave three hundred years as the least lifetime in which a nation could breed competent rulers.[7]

He was at once completely misunderstood by people who had not read his book. They assumed that he was demanding greater experience from statesmen, and his critics pointed out what was quite true, that the follies and vices of rulers persist in spite of their experience, and that the only effect of age is to make them less scrupulous.

Shaw heartily agreed with them. His contention was, however, that men's character and conduct, though incorrigible by mere experience, is so powerfully influenced by their expectation of life that men on whom the lessons of their past are thrown away would become different and much more serious if another century were added to their expectation of survival.[8]

The cycle contains some support for this interpretation of its handling of the longevity theme. In *The Thing Happens* Burge-Lubin decides against an aquatic rendezvous with his photophonic mistress because he fears a possible "eternity of rheumatism" (p. 131). And in the *Tragedy of an Elderly Gentleman* Zoo tells the Elderly Gentleman that the long-livers "are made wise not by the recollections of our past, but by the responsibilities of our future" (I, 158). It is difficult, however, to feel that Burge-Lubin has changed significantly at the end of *The Thing Happens* because of his anticipation of the possibility of long life, and Zoo is closer to what we actually observe in *Back to Methuselah* when she says, just before the speech quoted above, that the wisdom of the Elderly Gentleman "is only such wisdom as a man can have before he has had experience enough to distinguish his wisdom from his folly, his destiny from his delusions" (I, 158). Expectation of long life is a minor factor in determining character and conduct in *Back to Methuselah;* the important ones are the experience and maturity gained from having lived for a long time. Mrs. Lutestring's artist husband died before he had had time to make use of his experience, and Conrad Barnabas states a central and often repeated view in the cycle when he says that previous civilizations failed, as ours is failing, "because the citizens and statesmen died of old age or over-eating before they had grown out of schoolboy games and savage sports and cigars and champagne" (*The Gospel of the Brothers Barnabas,* p. 71); that is, we die before we reach maturity. The highest form of life portrayed in the cycle is that of the Ancients, who have reached a very high degree of maturity largely because they have had hundreds of years in which to do it: their wisdom and mental power certainly do not derive from any expectation of a multitude of years ahead of them.[9]

The basis of the satirical technique of *Back to Methuselah* is expressed in Zoo's declaration that "it is a law of Nature that there is a fixed relation between conduct and length of life" (*Tragedy of an Elderly Gentleman,* I, 166). Those who have lived longer, or (as Shaw sees it) who face the prospect of living longer, are more highly developed than we short-livers are at present. The last three plays of the cycle place people like us next to these relative adults, so that in each of these plays we are forced to see ourselves as children. In a letter to St. John Ervine, Shaw said that he could not show the life of long-livers, because, as a short-liver, he could not conceive it: "To make the play possible at all I had to fall back on an exhibition of shortlivers and children in contrast with such scraps of the long life as I could deduce by carrying a little further the difference that exists at present between the child and the adult, or between Reggie de Veulle (or whatever his silly name is) and Einstein." [10] This method leads to a strong emphasis on short-livers, as opposed to long-livers, which means that *Back to Methuselah* is at least as much satirical as utopian. The long-livers give us a standard according to which we can judge the short-livers in the cycle (that is, ourselves), as the presence of Captain Shotover in *Heartbreak House* places the other characters as children. In *The Thing Happens,* when the first two long-livers make themselves known, one character (Barnabas, the Accountant General) wants to have them killed on the ground that the presence of such people "does shorten my life, relatively. It makes us ridiculous. If they grew to be twelve feet high they would make us all dwarfs. They talked to us as if we were children" (p. 124). This speech, which suggests one of the many parallels between *Back to Methuselah* and *Gulliver's Travels,* exactly expresses the main satirical method of Shaw's pentateuch.

This method of placing "children" next to adults is anticipated in *The Gospel of the Brothers Barnabas,* in which the contrast is between the childish politicians and the relatively mature brothers, but it is in the last three plays, in which the long-livers have emerged, that it is fully developed.

Similarly, within *The Thing Happens* itself, the contrast between the short-livers and the long-livers is anticipated by the relationship between Burge-Lubin and his adviser Confucius. In this play, as in the *Tragedy of an Elderly Gentleman* and *As Far as Thought Can Reach,* there is a three-tier hierarchy. Here the English are at the bottom, with other nations and races above them, and the pair of long-livers at the top. The contrast between the first two levels is made explicit in a speech by Archbishop Haslam: "I tell you, what is wrong with us [English] is that we are a non-adult race; and the Irish and the Scots, and the niggers and Chinks, as you [Burge-Lubin] call them, though their lifetime is as short as ours, or shorter, yet do somehow contrive to grow up a little before they die" (p. 122).[11] This passage brings to mind *John Bull's Other Island* (and its Preface), as does the dialogue between Burge-Lubin and Confucius early in *The Thing Happens.* Here Burge-Lubin is a latter-day Broadbent, and Confucius a latter-day Keegan—except that the scales are now heavily weighted in Keegan's favor, for not only is Confucius much more intelligent than Burge-Lubin but he also does the practical work of running the country, while Burge-Lubin does nothing but amuse himself. In *John Bull's Other Island,* we recall, Keegan's intelligence and vision were balanced by Broadbent's practical ability and power.

The scene between Burge-Lubin and Confucius provides an introduction to the main part of *The Thing Happens:* the scene in which the childishness of the short-livers is emphasized by contrast with Archbishop Haslam and Mrs. Lutestring. Shaw has chosen these two to be the first long-livers in order to indicate that it is the unexpected people—whose willing is unconscious—who are the pioneers of long life and to demonstrate the improvement which an extra two hundred and fifty years of life can cause in us. The unpromising clergyman and ordinary parlor maid of *The Gospel of the Brothers Barnabas* have risen to the top of their respective professions: the rector is now an archbishop, and the parlor maid the Domestic Minister of the British Islands. And their characters have been completely transformed. Haslam, who was for the most part childish and silly in the previous play, now has, in the words of a stage direction (which are borne out during the scene) *"complete authority and self-possession"* (p. 100); and the parlor maid is similarly changed from a negligible girl to a most impressive and imposing woman. Their superiority is evident in their relationship with the other characters. The short-livers (even Confucius) regard them with awe and fear, as children might respond to severe, unloving adults, while they regard the others in the way that such adults respond to children. Mrs. Lutestring tells them of the one drawback of her longevity: "Well, you see, it has been so hard on me never to meet a grown-up person. You are all such children. And I never was very fond of children, except that one girl who woke up the mother passion in me. I have been very lonely sometimes" (p. 118). Then she and the Archbishop explain to the short-livers that the idea of marriage with any of them is disgusting to a long-liver. It would be like taking advantage of a little child for the gratification of one's senses.

THE ARCHBISHOP. Can you shortlived people not understand that as the confusion and immaturity and primitive animalism in which we live for the first hundred years of our life is worse in this matter of sex than in any other, you are intolerable to us in that relation?

BURGE-LUBIN. Do you mean to say, Mrs Lutestring, that you regard me as a child?

MRS LUTESTRING. Do you expect me to regard you as a completed soul? Oh, you may well be afraid of me. There are moments when your levity, your ingratitude, your shallow jollity, make my gorge rise so against you that if I could not remind myself that you are a child I should be tempted to doubt your right to live at all.

(p. 119)

This last phrase points forward to the next play, in which the roles of the long- and short-livers are reversed. Now it is the long-livers who are in the majority, and whereas in *The Thing Happens* Barnabas talks (vainly) about killing the long-livers, now the long-livers who inhabit Ireland and England talk about exterminating the children who constitute the rest of the world's population, and it is clear that they will eventually do so. Whereas *The Thing Happens* is about the birth of the race of long-livers (Haslam and Mrs. Lutestring are the new Adam and Eve, whose decision to produce children corresponds to Adam's and Eve's decision in the first act of *In the Beginning*), the *Tragedy of an Elderly Gentleman* is about the death of the race of short-livers. In this play people like ourselves are the outsiders in a world in which men live to be three hundred. Much of the point of the play is summed up in the Woman's statement early in Act I that "there are only two human classes here: the shortlived and the normal" (p. 139), and in the chilling exchange which follows Zoo's remark that children of the long-livers occasionally revert to the ancestral type and are born short-lived:

THE ELDERLY GENTLEMAN [*eagerly*] . . . I hope you will not be offended if I say that it would be a great comfort to me if I could be placed in charge of one of those normal individuals.
ZOO. Abnormal, you mean. What you ask is impossible: we weed them all out.

(I, 167)

In this play we short-livers are seen as deformed, and are judged— by the author, apparently, as well as by the long-lived characters —unfit to live.

As in *The Thing Happens,* there are in this play two levels of short-livers, representing lower and higher types. Here we have the Envoy, a reincarnation of the contemptible politicians in the earlier plays, with his very ordinary wife and daughter; and above them are two more highly developed short-livers, the Elderly Gentleman and Napoleon. These two possess contrasting qualities which Shaw himself normally admired: the Elderly Gentleman is sensitive and humane while Napoleon is heroic and warlike. In fact, Shaw has given each of these characters in the *Tragedy of an Elderly Gentleman* something of himself. The Elderly Gentleman expresses (at disastrous length) Shaw's own views on science (I, 151–156) and other subjects, and he sounds very much like Shaw in an impressive speech like this (to the long-liver Zozim): "I accept my three score and ten years. If they are filled with usefulness, with justice, with mercy, with good-will: if they are the lifetime of a soul that never loses its honor and a brain that never loses its eagerness, they are enough for me, because these things are infinite and eternal, and can make ten of my years as long as thirty of yours . . . I am your equal before that eternity in which the difference between your lifetime and mine is as the difference between one drop of water and three in the eyes of the Almighty Power from which we have both proceeded" (II, 185). He also shares, at the end of the play, Shaw's disgust with the dishonesty of short-lived politicians (just as Confucius is aware of Burge-Lubin's limitations), and, like Gulliver in the fourth book of Swift's satire, begs to be allowed to remain in the superior society. Napoleon is of course a good deal less like Shaw, but one of his leading characteristics is "a faculty for seeing things as they are that no other man possesses," which is "the only imagination worth having: the power of imagining things as they are, even when I cannot see them" (II, 172–173),[12] and he is above the ritual mummery which imposes on the other short-livers in the play. He is also a forceful character: even the Oracle says that his mesmeric field is the strongest she has yet observed in a short-liver (II, 170).

But both the Elderly Gentleman and Napoleon are made ultimately to seem unimpressive and inadequate. What the play is saying is that even people like these, whom we usually think of as superior, are children in relation to a society of long-livers. Napoleon is a destructive, dangerous child, and the Elderly Gentleman is a foolish, pitiful child.[13] The Oracle tries to kill one of them, and succeeds in killing the other.[14]

By the final play, *As Far as Thought Can Reach,* which takes place in the year 31,920, short-lived man has disappeared from the earth —presumably because of successful campaigns of extermination by long-livers. But even into this world Shaw contrives to introduce short-livers of an unadvanced type—the artificial "king" and "queen"—so that we have a pattern similar to the ones in the two previous plays, with groups of characters representing lower and higher levels of man as he is now, and a third group representing a very much higher type of man than either of these. At the bottom of this hierarchy come the successors of the politicians of *Back to Methuselah,* and now the representatives of this class are not even allowed the dignity of actual humanity. They are mere automata: not real children, but a step lower—the playthings of children; the Ancients refer to them as toys and dolls. Like Swift in *Gulliver's Travels,* Shaw saves his most unflattering representation of man for the last. The automata have all of our worst qualities: they are vain, jealous, and murderous; they abuse each other (as Burge and Lubin did in *The Gospel of the Brothers Barnabas*); the Male Figure cannot give an opinion until he has read the newspaper (as Burge-Lubin says in *The Thing Happens* that he has not read the American inventor's book, but rather "what The Times Literary Supplement says about it," p. 91); and the Female Figure lies (as the Envoy plans to do at the end of the *Tragedy of an Elderly Gentleman*).

At our lowest, then, this final play is saying, we are like Pavlovian automata which children make in a laboratory, and even at our highest we are only like the children themselves. All of the nobler activities on which we spend our lives, like human relationships, art, scientific invention, and a primitive kind of philosophical speculation, are appropriate only to the period of childhood—which among this economical super-race is confined to the first four years of life. "You have four years of childhood before you," the She-Ancient explains to the Newly Born:

You will not be very happy; but you will be interested and amused by the novelty of the world; and your companions here will teach you how to keep up an imitation of happiness during your four years by what they call arts and sports and pleasures. The worst of your troubles is already over.

THE NEWLY BORN. What! In five minutes?

THE SHE-ANCIENT. No: you have been growing for two years in the egg. You began by being several sorts of creatures that no longer exist, though we have fossils of them. Then you became human; and you passed in fifteen months through a development that once cost human beings twenty years of awkward stumbling immaturity after they were born. They had to spend fifty years more in the sort of childhood you will complete in four years. And then they died of decay.

(p. 211)

The serious adult life of these people begins just at the point when our life ends; that is to say, we die just as we are emerging from childhood, and never reach adult life at all—which is, as we have seen, the basic idea of *Back to Methuselah*.

Taking the automata and the children together, one has the whole range of our activities—from murder to sculpture; and every level of maturity is represented. Beyond the automata comes the Newly Born, who herself matures from one moment to the next.

Then come the other children, who act according to their various ages. Ecrasia, who is eight months old, is an aesthete (not a type which ranks very high on Shaw's scale); Strephon, aged two years, is a broken-hearted lover of the Octavius–Randall Utterword type. The most important children in the play are those who have reached the adolescent age of four, and are passing from childhood to adulthood; that is, they are becoming like the Ancients. Chloe's passion for Strephon has given way to a passion for thinking about the properties of numbers; and Martellus, the sculptor, having tired of modeling beautiful children and even intellectually intense Ancients, and having discovered that "art is false and life alone is true" (p. 219), is cured by Pygmalion's experiment of all interest in childish games, and announces that he will "leave women and study mathematics, which I have neglected too long. Farewell, children, my old playmates. I almost wish I could feel sentimental about parting from you; but the cold truth is that you bore me. Do not be angry with me: your turn will come. [*He passes away gravely into the grove*]" (p. 250). This speech is a bald and explicit rendering of the theme of growing up, which underlies so many of Shaw's earlier plays. Martellus' experience is parallel, for example, to that of Marchbanks in *Candida* and Ellie Dunn in *Heartbreak House:* Ellie, in fact, begins in *Heartbreak House* rather like the romantic Newly Born, and ends by marrying an Ancient—or one who is in many ways like the Ancients.

The setting of this final play and the names of the children suggest the conventionally idyllic, and this is part of one of Shaw's characteristic reversals. The life that the children lead is not to be taken as an ideal, but as a contrast to a kind of life which *is* almost as close to the ideal as "thought can reach": the life of the Ancients. Our natural tendency—as short-livers—is to prefer the children's life, but Shaw tries to make it clear that the life of the Ancients is far superior. When Strephon says that the Ancients are miserable, the He-Ancient replies: "Infant: one moment of the ecstasy of life as we live it would strike you dead" (p. 202); and the children who do reach adulthood in the course of the play find the change an agreeable one. But as with Swift's Houyhnhnms (whom the Ancients resemble) it is difficult to accept these pallid creatures as incalculably preferable to ourselves.

The Ancients, though, are not supposed to be the ideal. In Shaw's evolutionary world there can be no ideal: the highest are always aspiring to something higher. Near the end of *As Far as Thought Can Reach* the Ancients speak of their desire to rid themselves of the body of this death entirely and become immortal vortices of pure thought. At the end of *Back to Methuselah* we find that we have not reached an ending at all, but rather another beginning. Such a cycle can have no real ending, for, as Lilith says, of life there is no end. If Shaw's dramatic thought could reach further there could be another play in which the Ancients were the children in relation to men who had become pure spirit; [15] and the chain could be extended indefinitely, as long as still higher forms of life could be conceived—and dramatized.

Here is another reason, apart from the satirical purpose that I have been considering, for the emphasis on children in *Back to Methuselah:* to make the point that all creatures are children because they are always evolving toward a higher form of existence—an adulthood. Lilith, in the final speech of *Back to Methuselah,* refers to "these infants that call themselves ancients," and concludes her speech and the whole cycle by emphasizing life's unknown future: "Of Life only is there no end; and though of its million starry mansions many are empty and many still unbuilt, and though its vast domain is as yet unbearably desert, my seed shall one day fill it and master its matter to its uttermost confines. And for what may be beyond, the eyesight of Lilith is too short. It is enough that there is a beyond" (*As Far as Thought Can Reach,* p. 254). "It is enough that there is a beyond": these are appropriate concluding words for *Back to Methuselah,* for they emphasize that such a cycle must be unfinished, and can end only by looking forward; and they recapitulate one of the work's major motifs. The ending of the first play, one notes, is parallel to this ending of the last: Eve says, "Man need not always live by bread alone. There is something else. We do not yet know what it is; but some day we shall find out; and then we will live on that alone; and there shall be no more digging nor spinning, nor fighting nor killing" (*In the Beginning,* II, 33). Eve's hopes lie in those of her children and grandchildren who are neither diggers like Adam nor fighters like Cain: these are story-tellers, musicians, sculptors, mathematicians, astronomers, and an inventor and a prophet (II, 30–31). Now, several of these activities, which are the highest of which any character can conceive in *In the Beginning,* are by the final play the pastimes of children before they mature. Similarly, in Act I of *In the Beginning,* the latest imagined advances are human birth and death, which Adam and Eve will into being; by the final play birth in its original form is seen as a prehistoric abomination, and natural death has been eliminated. There is always something above the highest which thought at any given time can reach; today's goals are what future generations wish to discard and evolve beyond.

III

The desire of the Ancients to rid themselves of their bodies constitutes the climax of a tendency which develops all through *Back to Methuselah*—the cycle's tendency to see the world not in terms of contraries which are both valuable, but in terms of a higher which is unquestionably preferable to—and must supersede—a lower. In the earlier parts of the cycle some balance is preserved between the different components of life, but in the later parts the gap between the higher and the lower widens, and thought becomes more and more dominant over matter and independent of it.

In the Beginning, which is the prelude to *Back to Methuselah* as *The Rhinegold* is the prelude to Wagner's *Ring,*[16] introduces the theme of the relationship between thought and matter. The title of the play refers not only to the first verse of Genesis but also to the opening of St. John's Gospel: "In the beginning was the Word." [17] There is in the first act the obvious emphasis on words in the literal sense, in the Serpent's invention of them, and there is the creative process which the Serpent describes, in which the Word—in the sense of thought and imagination—comes first. "I am very subtle; and I have thought and thought and thought. And I am very wilful, and must have what I want; and I have willed and willed and willed" (I, 7). Here the Serpent is describing how she came to give birth, and it is evident that one must imagine an idea in one's mind before physical creation is possible. Then the Serpent tells how Lilith gave birth to Adam and Eve:

EVE. . . . How did Lilith work this miracle?
THE SERPENT. She imagined it.
EVE. What is imagined?

THE SERPENT. She told it to me as a marvellous story of something that never happened to a Lilith that never was. She did not know then that imagination is the beginning of creation. You imagine what you desire; you will what you imagine; and at last you create what you will.

(I, 9)

In the beginning was the Word—but the Word must be made flesh. Birth involves not only imagination and will, but a physical act of creation. For human beings to be born, it is not enough for the Serpent to invent the idea of human birth: she must communicate this idea to Eve, who can put it into practice. Corresponding to this dialectical pattern is the need for both woman and man in the process of procreation. Lilith found the burden of renewing life on her own unbearable, and so she created both Adam and Eve so that in the next generation the labor could be shared between two. Adam, the Serpent tells Eve, "can imagine: he can will: he can desire: he can gather his life together for a great spring towards creation"—but for the act of creation itself he must rely on Eve: "He must give his desire and his will to you" (I, 11, 12).[18]

In the second act thought begins to dominate. Eve, as we have seen, looks beyond the diggers and the fighters to a world in which man can live by "something else," and she speaks hopefully of those of her offspring who "tell beautiful lies in beautiful words. They can remember their dreams. They can dream without sleeping. They have not will enough to create instead of dreaming; but the serpent said that every dream could be willed into creation by those strong enough to believe in it" (II, 30). Both the thought and the creative act are seen here as necessary, but those who only think and do not create are nevertheless valuable. A much stronger and more explicit shift from the dialectical emphasis of Act I is found in some of the speeches of Cain, to whom the Voice has whispered of an after-life "infinitely splendid and intense: a life of the soul alone: a life without clods or spades, hunger or fatigue." His heart, Cain says, is pure.

ADAM. What is that word? What is pure?
CAIN. Turned from the clay. Turned upward to the sun, to the clear clean heavens.
ADAM. The heavens are empty, child. The earth is fruitful. The

earth feeds us. It gives us the strength by which we made you and all mankind. Cut off from the clay which you despise, you would perish miserably.

CAIN. I revolt against the clay. I revolt against the food. You say it gives us strength: does it not also turn into filth and smite us with diseases? I revolt against these births that you and mother are so proud of. They drag us down to the level of the beasts. If that is to be the last thing as it has been the first, let mankind perish . . . Stay with the woman who gives you children: I will go to the woman who gives me dreams. Grope in the ground for your food: I will bring it from the skies with my arrows, or strike it down as it roams the earth in the pride of its life. If I must have food or die, I will at least have it at as far a remove from the earth as I can.

(II, 27–28) [19]

Cain, unfortunately, is better at imagination than at creation, for his dissatisfaction leads, in practical terms, only to hunting and murder. But it is his revolt against the clay which becomes increasingly dominant as *Back to Methuselah* progresses, and there are echoes of this fine speech in the final play of the cycle, in which the Ancients' dissatisfaction is similar to Cain's.

In *The Gospel of the Brothers Barnabas,* the supremacy of thought is indicated by the clear superiority of the brothers themselves over all of the other characters in the play. They are the heirs of the Serpent: they dream of things that never were and say "why not?" Within the play itself they—the thinkers who imagine but do not create—are the only characters who are seen to be making a contribution to evolutionary progress. The other major characters in the play, Burge and Lubin, are presented as almost entirely valueless. They are contrasting types of men who put private before public concerns: Burge is a self-important ignoramus who desires the prestige which political power brings, while Lubin is a self-indulgent, cultivated gentleman who desires ease and comfort above all else.

This play (like the next) presents some interesting parallels and contrasts with *John Bull's Other Island.* Burge is made of the same stuff as Broadbent, while the brothers remind one of Keegan; and the debate between the politicians and the brothers of which the play largely consists is in many ways similar to the confrontations between Broadbent and Keegan in the final act of *John Bull's*

Other Island. In both plays there is no communication between Realist and Philistine—between the realm of thought and the future on the one hand and the realm of the worldly and the immediate on the other. Burge's jovial, energetic patronage of the brothers, coupled with a total lack of comprehension of their gospel, is just like Broadbent's response to Keegan. As Burge leaves, for example, he says to Conrad: "You may depend on me. I will work this stunt of yours in. I see its value . . . Of course I cant put it exactly in your way; but you are quite right about our needing something fresh; and I believe an election can be fought on the death rate and on Adam and Eve as scientific facts. It will take the Opposition right out of its depth. And if we win there will be an O.M. for somebody when the first honors list comes round" (pp. 84–85). At the end of *The Gospel of the Brothers Barnabas* Franklyn expresses Keegan's bitterness about his lack of influence on others, while Conrad expresses Keegan's optimistic and self-justifying view that "every jest is an earnest in the womb of Time." [20]

FRANKLYN. . . . We had better hold our tongues about it [the idea that man must extend his life to three hundred years], Con. We should only be laughed at, and lose the little credit we earned on false pretenses in the days of our ignorance.
CONRAD. I daresay. But Creative Evolution doesnt stop while people are laughing. Laughing may even lubricate its job.
SAVVY. What does that mean?
CONRAD. It means that the first man to live three hundred years maynt have the slightest notion that he is going to do it, and may be the loudest laugher of the lot.

(p. 86) [21]

In *John Bull's Other Island,* we cannot know for certain whether Keegan's optimism is justified—whether his dreams are illusions or prophecies. In *Back to Methuselah,* on the other hand, we learn in *The Thing Happens* that the optimism of Conrad Barnabas is very much justified. The brothers' failure to persuade the politicians, it turns out, has mattered not at all: the thing happens whether they are persuaded or not. In spite of Franklyn's statement in *The Gospel of the Brothers Barnabas* that "party politicians are still unfortunately an important part of the world" (p. 46), it becomes clear within the wider context provided by *The Thing Happens* that it is the thinkers and not the politicians who play a role in determining the ultimately significant affairs. And even within *The Gospel of the Brothers Barnabas* itself, Burge and Lubin do not seem really powerful. They do not, for example, possess Broadbent's practical ability to shape the world around him; they are incompetents whose lack of ability has led to the war and its aftermath. It is interesting that Shaw makes his politicians members of a divided Opposition instead of the Government; [22] this diminishes their stature still further. Their weakness is part of the tendency in *Back to Methuselah* to discount the importance of the worldly man—while stressing the importance of the thinker.

But at this stage in the cycle the thinkers are still dependent in one way on those who can make the Word into flesh. Although it emerges in *The Thing Happens* that Burge and Lubin of the previous play have in the long run been insignificant, it also emerges that Haslam and the parlor maid have been very significant indeed. I have said that the brothers Barnabas are the heirs of the Serpent. Moreover, their relationship with Haslam and the parlor maid is parallel to the relationship in Act I of *In the Beginning* between the Serpent and Adam and Eve. Their imagination has been father to Haslam's and the parlor maid's will, just as the Serpent's imagination has been father to Adam's and Eve's will.[23] Progress has been achieved by means of an interaction between the thought of the brothers Barnabas and the unconscious willing of the unintelligent long-livers-to-be.

In *The Thing Happens,* it is Haslam (now the Archbishop of York) and the parlor maid (now Mrs. Lutestring, the Domestic Minister) who, as long-livers, occupy the position held by the brothers Barnabas in the previous play: they are the characters whose minds are more highly developed than those of the people around them, and the next step in evolutionary progress is up to them. This step does involve a union, but not a union between contraries; it is the two long-livers who must unite to propagate their kind. The two of them are completely independent of the other characters in the play; their superiority is so obvious that their position is unchallengeable. Near the end of the play Confucius convinces Burge-Lubin that the short-livers can do nothing to prevent the long-livers from becoming "a great Power" (p. 129).

One of the main themes of *The Thing Happens* is the fear and dislike that ordinary people feel toward superior people. "Nobody likes me: I am held in awe," Confucius explains to Burge-Lubin. "Capable persons are never liked. I am not likeable; but I am indispensable" (p. 95). This prepares us for the feelings of all of the short-livers toward the Archbishop and Mrs. Lutestring. Burge-Lubin, even before he knows that Mrs. Lutestring is a long-liver, thinks that she is "a bit of a terror" (p. 110), and Confucius confesses that he has "always been afraid of the Archbishop" (p. 128). Barnabas, the unpleasant Accountant General, feels not just fear but also hatred toward them, and wants to have them killed. This is a phenomenon which we have also seen in *Saint Joan,* and the similarity between Barnabas and de Stogumber is apparent. But there is an important difference between the handling of the theme here and in *Saint Joan.* There is a real conflict between Joan and those who fear or hate her—a conflict which leads to her death. In *The Thing Happens,* on the other hand, there is no conflict because the inferior have no power: the triumph of the more highly developed man is assured.

In the *Tragedy of an Elderly Gentleman* the gap between the superior and the inferior has widened in that the long-livers are now in an even more powerful and impregnable position. Their relationship to the short-livers is not only like that of adults to children, but also like that of gods to mortals. The fact that they can do without ordinary people is reflected in their plan to exterminate them.

But it is in the final play, *As Far as Thought Can Reach,* that the highly evolved achieve the greatest degree of independence of the world around them. They do not even have to think about exterminating short-livers, for there are no short-livers. Whereas the long-livers in the *Tragedy of an Elderly Gentleman* feel impatience and even (in Zoo's case) anger toward incorrigibly childish people like us, the Ancients can treat the youths and maidens with bland complacency, because they know that these children will inevitably and quickly pass beyond childhood and become like themselves. The Ancients are not just superior to their environment: they in effect have no environment; they live in a void. There can be no conflict between these thinkers and "the world" because there is no longer any "world." Their struggle is not with anything outside of themselves, but with their own bodies—the last obstacle to complete freedom for the mind.

Paradoxically, although *Back to Methuselah* traces vast progressive changes over many thousands of years, it ends, in a sense, where it began.[24] The sunlit glade in *As Far as Thought Can Reach* is a second Garden of Eden, and the creatures in it have regained the immortality that Adam willingly renounced.[25] Like Adam and Eve at the beginning of the cycle, the Ancients are immortal in that they live until they meet "their accident"; they are not subject to natural death.

Back to Methuselah is circular, too, in that beyond the end of the cycle life will return to the state in which it existed before the beginning—before life entered into matter. This is emphasized by the fact that after the Serpent, Adam, Eve, and Cain appear at the end of *As Far as Thought Can Reach,* completing one circle, Lilith appears and completes the other, larger one. For Lilith—the principle of life itself—existed before Adam and Eve, and before life became united with matter. Now, she says in the peroration to *Back to Methuselah,* life is about to return to something like its original condition:

The impulse I gave them in that day when I sundered myself in twain and launched Man and Woman on the earth still urges them: after passing a million goals they press on to the goal of redemption from the flesh, to the vortex freed from matter, to the whirlpool in pure intelligence that, when the world began, was a whirlpool in pure force.[26] And though all that they have done seems but the first hour of the infinite work of creation, yet I will not supersede them until they have forded this last stream that lies between flesh and spirit, and disentangled their life from the matter that has always mocked it . . . I am Lilith: I brought life into the whirlpool of force, and compelled my enemy, Matter, to obey a living soul. But in enslaving Life's enemy I made him Life's master; for that is the end of all slavery; and now I shall see the slave set free and the enemy reconciled, the whirlpool become all life and no matter.

(pp. 253–254)

This speech indicates the distance which *Back to Methuselah* has moved from the other plays I have been considering. "Shaw's interest as an artist," Eric Bentley observes, "has always been in the human situation as he found it and not simply as he desired it (except in some later sections of *Back to Methuselah* where he is at his worst as a playwright)." [27] There is in *Back to Methuselah* a disturbing element of wish-fulfillment. Its main focal point is perhaps Eve's speech after she has seen what life has come to in *As Far as Thought Can Reach:* "The clever ones were always my favorites. The diggers and the fighters have dug themselves in with the worms. My clever ones have inherited the earth. All's well" (p. 252). One has the uncomfortable feeling here of being in the presence of the playwright himself. Whereas in most of his other plays Shaw seems to be giving ideas the freedom to enter into conflict with one another on the stage, in *Back to Methuselah* he seems to be exercising rigid control over characters and action so that ideas to which he has committed himself beforehand will triumph. There are not many occasions in Shaw's plays where two characters engage in a lengthy dialogue in which they merely agree about ideas which Shaw has already expressed in his preface. Yet this is just what happens in the *Tragedy of an Elderly Gentleman* in the discussion in Act I between Zoo and the Elderly Gentleman on science. And when in *Back to Methuselah* (apart from *In the Beginning*) there is disagreement between characters, we are left in no doubt as to which character has the playwright's approval.

Back to Methuselah, then, on the whole lacks the dialectical tension which is the core of most of the other plays of Shaw's middle period. As the cycle progresses, there is less and less interaction and tension between contraries which are both of value. There is no question in the last half of the cycle of the worldly having its importance and uses. "The body always ends by being a bore," says Martellus in the final play. "Nothing remains beautiful and interesting except thought, because the thought is the life," and the only replies are "Quite so" and "Precisely" from the Ancients (*As Far as Thought Can Reach*, p. 247). In *Back to Methuselah* real conflict between the worldly and the unworldly, so central to Shaw's greatest plays, is absent. And in most of the cycle, progress does not require interaction and union between the two, but rather the absolute triumph of spirit over matter.

Back to Methuselah is not chronologically the last of what I am calling Shaw's middle plays, but it is nevertheless the most appropriate terminal point for this study. It takes one into the world of the late plays: its direct political satire, for example, makes one think of *The Apple Cart, On the Rocks,* and *Geneva,* and its element of fantasy anticipates *Too True To Be Good, The Simpleton of the Unexpected Isles,* and *Farfetched Fables. Saint Joan,* although it was written later than *Back to Methuselah,* is closer in form and attitude to most of the other plays of the middle period than the *Methuselah* cycle is. In particular, in *Saint Joan* spirit and matter are both of value; it is a play in which the material world counts for something.

The development within the *Methuselah* cycle away from a marriage of contraries is reflected on a larger scale in developments within the whole group of plays considered in this study. *Man and Superman* is pre-eminently a play of balance: the Comedy and the Hell Scene, and Ann and Tanner, relate to each other in complementary ways, and both the physical world and thought are necessary for progress, as in the first act of *In the Beginning.* Similarly, in *Major Barbara* neither Undershaft nor Barbara and Cusins are able to change society while they exist in isolation from one another. Each of these plays ends with a fusion of its opposing forces, a union in which the material and spiritual combine in order (we hope) to achieve what neither could achieve alone. *John Bull's Other Island* is concerned with the same split, but in this play no union takes place at the end: the businessman chooses the site for his hotel and the prophet, while he predicts the supersession of the businessman's values, retires to a tower to dream of heaven. The earthly and the heavenly remain separate.

The next three plays in this study constitute an interlude, with variations on the themes of the three great plays which open Shaw's middle period. In *The Doctor's Dilemma* and *Pygmalion* the contraries are human and professional qualities—the world of ordinary decent men and women as opposed to the world of the creator who cares for nothing but his work. In these plays, as in *John Bull's*

Other Island, the two worlds remain separate and we are compelled to respect the qualities of both worlds equally, and to be aware of the complementary defects of both. In *Misalliance* the suggestion of a possible union of Tarleton brawn and Summerhays brain through a marriage between Hypatia and Bentley is rejected after the entrance midway through the play of two characters who already unite such qualities within themselves and carry everything before them, like Joan in the earlier parts of *Saint Joan.*

Heartbreak House introduces a new element. Once again, as in the first three plays of the middle period, we find a divorce between intellect and the forces of "this world," but now the balance has shifted to one side and Captain Shotover's vision of heaven is much preferable not only to the Heartbreakers' hell but also to the earth of the contemptible Mangan. Some balance is preserved in that Shotover's mental power is offset by his lack of practical power; Mangan and his like rule the nation. This balance links *Heartbreak House* with *Man and Superman, John Bull's Other Island,* and *Major Barbara,* but now a marriage of contraries is not quite what is desired, because Mangan, unlike Ann, Broadbent, and Undershaft, has nothing to contribute to such a union, and he is killed, with the author's approval and ours, at the end of the play.

Saint Joan varies from the earlier plays in another way. Whereas *Heartbreak House,* as indicated in Chapter VII, re-works themes from *Man and Superman, John Bull's Other Island,* and *Major Barbara, Saint Joan* is most closely related to the latter. Now the very combination of vision and practical power—heaven and earth —that promised so much at the end of *Major Barbara* is, in the person of Joan, defeated by an element which in the earlier plays poses little or no evident threat: the power of thought misused, which in the language of *The Quintessence of Ibsenism* I have called Idealism, and which in *Man and Superman* has hell as its symbol. The main conflict in *Saint Joan* is different, therefore, from the main conflicts in the earlier plays. *Back to Methuselah,* as the present chapter has argued, provides the most radical departure from the attitudes of the earlier plays, moving well beyond *Heartbreak House:* here the material world is dismissed more completely than it is in *Heartbreak House* and—most important—the world of spirit is much more dominant. The short-livers in the *Tragedy of an*

Elderly Gentleman are to be killed, as Mangan is killed at the end of *Heartbreak House,* but now there is no feeling that the more highly developed people are powerless and may be next; we know that they will survive and triumph. In *Back to Methuselah* the idea of a desirable fusion between the world of spirit and the material world is explicitly rejected and spirit is imposed on us in a way which makes this a less effective work of art than the other major plays of the middle period.

The relative artistic failure of *Back to Methuselah* suggests a major source of dramatic power in plays like *Man and Superman, John Bull's Other Island, Major Barbara, The Doctor's Dilemma, Misalliance, Pygmalion, Heartbreak House,* and *Saint Joan.* These are all plays in which problems are being worked out on the stage, and in which we participate in the working-out. In none of these plays (except perhaps *Saint Joan*) can Shaw be called a propagandist; they rather display something of a quality which is never associated with Shaw: Keats's "negative capability." In Shaw's best plays the playwright does not take sides, or perhaps it would be more accurate to say that he takes both major sides at once—and makes us take both sides at once, creating a sense of dramatic tension that is lacking in (say) *Caesar and Cleopatra* or *"In Good King Charles's Golden Days."* In *Heartbreak House* and *Saint Joan* we see this masterly balancing of contraries beginning to break down: Shotover and Joan represent the values of their respective plays more than Keegan or Barbara, for example, can be said to embody the values of their plays.[28] In the last three parts of *Back to Methuselah* the balance has broken down completely, and these pieces lack the sense that "without Contraries is no progression"—the sense which pervades most of the works of this period of Shaw's greatest achievement, the years between 1901 and 1923.

Note on Shaw's Plays in the Constable Standard Edition

For Shaw's nondramatic works volume titles are given in my text or notes. The plays, with their prefaces, appear in the following volumes:

Plays Pleasant and Unpleasant
    Vol. I (Unpleasant) includes *Widowers' Houses, The Philanderer,* and *Mrs Warren's Profession*
    Vol. II (Pleasant) includes *Arms and the Man, Candida, The Man of Destiny,* and *You Never Can Tell*
    Three Plays for Puritans (includes *The Devil's Disciple, Caesar and Cleopatra,* and *Captain Brassbound's Conversion*)
    Man and Superman
    John Bull's Other Island with *How He Lied to Her Husband* and *Major Barbara*
    The Doctor's Dilemma, Getting Married, and *The Shewing-Up of Blanco Posnet*
    Misalliance, The Dark Lady of the Sonnets, and *Fanny's First Play*
    Androcles and the Lion, Overruled, Pygmalion
    Heartbreak House (also includes *Great Catherine, O'Flaherty V.C., The Inca of Perusalem, Augustus Does His Bit,* and *Annajanska, the Bolshevik Empress*)
    Back to Methuselah
    Saint Joan: A Chronicle; and *The Apple Cart: A Political Extravaganza*
    Too True To Be Good, Village Wooing, and *On the Rocks*
    The Simpleton, The Six, and *The Millionairess*
    Geneva, Cymbeline Refinished, and *Good King Charles*
    Buoyant Billions, Farfetched Fables, and *Shakes Versus Shav*
    Translations and Tomfooleries (includes *Jitta's Atonement, The Admirable Bashville, Press Cuttings, The Glimpse of Reality, Passion, Poison, and Petrifaction, The Fascinating Foundling,* and *The Music-Cure*)

Note: *The Interlude at the Playhouse* and *Why She Would Not* are not included in the Standard Edition.

Notes

I. *Introduction*

1. Shaw frequently refers to *Emperor and Galilean* by this name.

2. All my page references for *The Quintessence of Ibsenism* and *The Perfect Wagnerite* are to the *Major Critical Essays* volume in the Constable Standard Edition.

3. The translation here is William Archer's, which Shaw used (London: Walter Scott, 1890).

4. Cf. Peter Keegan's vision of heaven in *John Bull's Other Island* as "a godhead in which all life is human and all humanity divine" (IV, 177).

5. "The principal pattern which recurs in Bernard Shaw—aside from the duel between male and female, which seems to me of much less importance—is the polar opposition between the type of the saint and the type of the successful practical man." Edmund Wilson, "Bernard Shaw at Eighty," in *The Triple Thinkers* (New York: Oxford University Press, 1963), p. 185.

6. *Music in London, 1890–94,* I, 102; I, 269; III, 207; I, 149; II, 28; II, 33.

7. Eric Bentley quotes a sentence from this passage in his discussion of "Shaw and the Actors," where he notes other ways in which Shaw, in his views on acting, wants to combine diverse elements; see *Bernard Shaw* (New York: New Directions, 1957), pp. 229–230. In the earlier parts of this book, too, Bentley's illustrations of what he calls Shaw's "Both/And" approach to life are relevant to what I have to say in this chapter. Curiously, when he comes to discuss the plays he does not apply this "Both/And" principle, except in a limited way in his section dealing with the theme of "the problem of human ideals and their relation to practice" (see pp. 158–172). His major emphasis is on a very different type of conflict, one which divides characters into those of whom Shaw approves and those of whom he disapproves. After *Mrs Warren's*

Profession, Bentley states, Shaw's plays "are primarily about the 'struggle between human vitality and the artificial system of morality' " (p. 105). "Main characters in Shaw," he also writes, "are either straightforward embodiments of that vitality which is the great positive force in his world or they are battlegrounds for the struggle between vitality and its opposite, 'artificial system' " (p. 149).

8. See Katherine Haynes Gatch, "The Last Plays of Bernard Shaw: Dialectic and Despair," in *English Stage Comedy,* ed. W. K. Wimsatt, Jr. (New York: Columbia University Press, 1955), p. 146.

9. British Museum Add. MS. 50643, fol. 199. All references to the Shaw MSS in the British Museum are to the 1973 volume and folio numbers, which are provisional.

10. The idea that a eugenic marriage can produce unintended results brings to mind the (no doubt apocryphal) story, retold in Lawrence Langner's *G.B.S. and the Lunatic* (London: Hutchinson, 1964), of Isadora Duncan's proposal that Shaw should father a child for her; she remarked "that the resulting child would be wonderful if it had her body and Shaw's brain. 'But imagine how terrible the result would be,' replied Shaw, 'if it had my body and your brain!' " (p. 100).

11. Cf. The Revolutionist's Handbook in *Man and Superman.* In *You Never Can Tell* the three remarkable Clandon children are the result of an unsuitable and unhappy marriage (between a woman of intellect and a man of feeling); and Barbara Undershaft's parents, like the Clandon children's, have separated because they are incompatible. Barbara is also an example of the value of crossing different social classes. Her father is an East End foundling, her mother a member of the aristocracy. "I have no class," she says: "I come straight out of the heart of the whole people" (*Major Barbara,* III, 338). Shaw, in associating incompatible marriages with remarkable children, may have had his own case in mind: his mother and father were a most ill-assorted pair, and when Shaw was in his teens they separated. See *Everybody's Political What's What?,* pp. 75–76. Shaw would also have found the theory in Schopenhauer's "The Metaphysics of the Love of the Sexes" (a supplement to *The World as Will and Idea*).

12. One is reminded here of the ending of *Misalliance,* when the overbred Bentley Summerhays is carried off by the Polish acrobat Lina Szczepanowska (although she is not of "the gutter or the soil").

13. Again, Shaw may have had his own experience in mind. In 1879 he met Sidney Webb, and he wrote near the end of his life that quite the wisest thing he had ever done was to gain Webb's friendship, "for from that time I was not merely a futile Shaw but a committee of Webb and Shaw" (*Sixteen Self Sketches,* p. 65). Elsewhere he wrote of his first contacts with Webb that "I at once recognized and appreciated in him all the qualifications in which I was myself pitiably deficient. He was clearly the man for me to work with"; quoted in Archibald Henderson,

George Bernard Shaw: Man of the Century (New York: Appleton-Century-Crofts, 1956), p. 330. And the following comment is particularly relevant to the idea of progression through contraries: "The importance of the fact that Webb was intensely English and I ineradicably Irish, so that our views often clashed at first impact and our fierce arguments worked out to a unique conclusion of which we would have been separately incapable, has never been grasped" (letter from Shaw to Archibald Henderson, June 17, 1948; *ibid.*, p. 349).

14. Aug. 28; *Collected Letters, 1874–1897,* ed. Dan H. Laurence (New York: Dodd, Mead, 1965), p. 645. Cf. *How to Become a Musical Critic,* ed. Dan H. Laurence (London: Rupert Hart-Davis, 1960), p. 251; and *Overruled,* pp. 169–170.

15. *Music in London, 1890–94,* II, 128.

16. Preface to *Misalliance,* p. 44.

17. See "Schools and Schoolmasters," written for the *Education Year Book* of 1918, reprinted in *Doctors' Delusions, Crude Criminology, and Sham Education,* pp. 291–321; and the Preface to *Misalliance.*

18. Shaw consistently (and erroneously) spells this "Vandaleur."

19. Cf. a letter to Frank Harris, March 3, 1930, printed in Harris' *Bernard Shaw* (New York: Simon and Schuster, 1931), pp. xv–xvi.

20. *Howards End* (London: Edward Arnold, 1960), Chap. XXIII.

21. *Our Theatres in the Nineties,* II, 195–196.

22. *What I Really Wrote about the War,* p. 22.

23. *Our Theatres in the Nineties,* I, 46–47; III, 206. Cf. II, 5, and see *Collected Letters, 1898–1910,* ed. Dan H. Laurence (London: Max Reinhardt, 1972), p. 783.

24. Sir George Crofts, too, is not presented entirely from his own point of view in that his personality strikes us as unpleasant. It is interesting that he is one of the few characters in Shaw's plays of whom this can be said.

25. Assigned to Jan. 4, 1904. *Collected Letters, 1898–1910,* ed. Dan H. Laurence, p. 396.

26. In a letter to Siegfried Trebitsch, Jan. 7, 1903, Shaw writes of *Candida* that "the whole point of the play is the revelation of the weakness of this strong and manly man, and the terrible strength of the febrile and effeminate one." Quoted in Martin Meisel, *Shaw and the Nineteenth-Century Theater* (Princeton: Princeton University Press, 1963), p. 231.

27. Shaw is quoted by Paul Green as saying that critics "should begin their interpretations of my works somewhat as follows: 'Mr. Shaw's plays begin where they end and end where they begin.'" "My plays are interludes, as it were, between two greater realities. And the meaning of them lies in what has preceded them and in what follows them. The beginning of one of my plays takes place exactly where an unwritten play ended. And the ending of my written play concludes where another play

begins. It is the two unwritten plays [the critics] should consider in order to get light upon the one that lies between." Paul Green, *Dramatic Heritage* (New York: Samuel French, 1953), pp. 125–126.

28. I have not dealt in this chapter with Hegel's dialectic because Shaw's scattered references to Hegel do not make one feel that he was much influenced directly by him. He was, it is true, exposed at second hand to Hegel's dialectic in his reading of Marx, but more important sources of his dialectical thinking (apart from his own observation of life) are Blake's *The Marriage of Heaven and Hell* and Ibsen's *Emperor and Galilean* (which is clearly influenced by Hegel). A case for the influence of Hegel's dialectic on Shaw is made by Robert F. Whitman in a paper entitled "The Dialectic Structure in Shaw's Plays," printed in Norman Rosenblood, ed., *Shaw Seminar Papers—65* (Toronto: Copp Clark, 1966), pp. 63–84. Another writer on Shaw who has stressed the dialectical element in his works is Daniel J. Leary, whose unpublished doctoral dissertation, "The Superman and Structure in George Bernard Shaw's Plays: A Study in Dialectic Action" (Syracuse University, 1958), discusses five of Shaw's plays. His comments on the most obviously dialectical of Shaw's plays, *Major Barbara,* are published as "Dialectical Action in *Major Barbara,*" *Shaw Review,* XII (May 1969), 46–58; and he writes on "Shaw's Blakean Vision: A Dialectic Approach to *Heartbreak House*" in *Modern Drama,* XV (May 1972), 89–103. James George Severns, in an unpublished dissertation entitled "Structural Dialectic in the Earlier Plays of Bernard Shaw" (University of Iowa, 1971), argues for Hegel's influence and deals with Shaw's plays "from the earliest through *Major Barbara*" (*Dissertation Abstracts International,* XXXII, Sept. 1971, 1683-A).

29. *Bernard Shaw and the Art of Destroying Ideals: The Early Plays* (Madison: University of Wisconsin Press, 1969).

II. *Man and Superman*

1. A note on *Man and Superman* in the *Stage Society News* for March 30, 1905, two months before the play opened at the Court Theatre, begins: "Those who have read Bernard Shaw's 'Man and Superman' are aware that it is not a play, but a volume which contains a play." Raymond Mander and Joe Mitchenson, who print the note, state that it "would certainly seem to be by Shaw himself" (*Theatrical Companion to Shaw,* London: Rockliff, 1954, p. 88). *Back to Methuselah* and *Heartbreak House,* like *Man and Superman,* were published before their production on the stage, and to some extent as a substitute for production. The care which Shaw devoted to the publication in book form of all his plays reflects the fact that he did not regard the published versions merely as scripts; his plays, more than those of most other playwrights, have a separate life as books.

2. Preface to *Back to Methuselah,* p. lxxxv.

3. *George Bernard Shaw* (Boston: John W. Luce, 1905), p. 70.

4. *Our Partnership,* ed. Barbara Drake and Margaret I. Cole (London: Longmans, Green, 1948), p. 256.

5. Preface to *Back to Methuselah,* p. lxxxv.

6. See Frederick P. W. McDowell, "Heaven, Hell, and Turn-of-the-Century London: Reflections upon Shaw's *Man and Superman," Drama Survey,* II (Feb. 1963), 245–268, to which this chapter is in various places indebted.

7. Shaw's short story "Don Giovanni Explains" (in *The Black Girl in Search of God and Some Lesser Tales*) presents Don Juan in the same way. This story, written in 1887, anticipates several of the ideas of the Hell Scene, and reveals that *Man and Superman* was the result of a long period of gestation.

8. The first four chapters of Arthur Nethercot's study of Shaw's characters, *Men and Supermen* (New York: Benjamin Blom, 1966), deal with these types in his novels and plays. The only work which Nethercot considers as a whole, however, is *Candida.*

9. Cf. the Preface (1915) to *Androcles and the Lion,* in which Shaw writes, in the section entitled "Worldliness of the Majority," that mankind consists mainly of people who "have robust consciences, and hunger and thirst, not for righteousness, but for rich feeding and comfort and social position and attractive mates and ease and pleasure and respect and consideration: in short, for love and money . . . They may not be the salt of the earth, these Philistines; but they are the substance of civilization" (p. 10).

10. The references to bees in *Man and Superman* derive from Maeterlinck's book *The Life of the Bee,* which was published (in an English translation) and read by Shaw in 1901, the year in which he began his play. (See *Collected Letters, 1898–1910,* ed. Dan H. Laurence, p. 235.) Maeterlinck's account of the bee is Lamarckian in its emphasis on the role of the bee's own will, and his general remarks about Nature are often similar in spirit to Juan's talk about the Life Force in the Hell Scene. For example: "Whoever brings careful attention to bear will scarcely deny, even though it be not evident, the presence in nature of a will that tends to raise a portion of matter to a subtler and perhaps better condition, to penetrate its substance little by little with a mystery-laden fluid that we at first term life, then instinct, and finally intelligence; a will that, for an end we know not, organizes, strengthens and facilitates the existence of all that is" (trans. Alfred Sutro, London: George Allen and Unwin, 1946, p. 272). Notice that Tanner asks Octavius whether he has read the book (*Man and Superman,* II, 51).

11. The relationship between Ann and Tanner is partially anticipated in a passage from Carlyle's *Past and Present* which discusses the strength of the "almost stupid Man of Practice" when "pitted against some light adroit Man of Theory, all equipt with clear logic, and able anywhere to

give you Why for Wherefore! The adroit Man of Theory, so light of movement, clear of utterance, with his bow full-bent and quiver full of arrow-arguments,—surely he will strike down the game, transfix everywhere the heart of the matter; triumph everywhere, as he proves that he shall and must do? To your astonishment, it turns out oftenest No. The cloudy-browed, thick-soled, opaque Practicality, with no logic utterance, in silence mainly, with here and there a low grunt or growl, has in him what transcends all logic-utterance: a Congruity with the Unuttered. The Speakable, which lies atop, as a superficial film, or outer skin, is his or is not his: but the Doable, which reaches down to the World's centre, you find him there!" (Centenary edition; London: Chapman and Hall, 1897, Book III, Chap. V). Carlyle's Man of Practice is the Englishman, and it is perhaps worth remarking here that Shaw considered Ann and Violet to be particularly English women (see above, p. 93).

12. Cf. Shaw himself to Ellen Terry in 1896: "Curious, how little use mere brains are: I have a very fine set; and yet I learnt more from the first stupid woman who fell in love with me than ever they taught me" (letter of Oct. 2; *Collected Letters, 1874–1897*, ed. Dan H. Laurence, p. 672). A month later Shaw asked Ellen Terry for comments on his relationship with Charlotte Payne-Townshend (whom he had met during the previous summer); in her reply she remarked, "How very silly you clever people are" (Nov. 6; *ibid.*, p. 696).

13. Cf. *Emperor and Galilean,* Part II, Act V: "The world-will has laid an ambush for me, Maximus!" Julian, who says this as he lies dying at the end of the play, did not find his proper role as founder of the third empire.

14. Cf. the "stage direction" that follows the long speech by the preacher Aubrey at the end of *Too True To Be Good* (written in 1931): "*But fine words butter no parsnips . . . The author, though himself a professional talk maker, does not believe that the world can be saved by talk alone. He has given the rascal the last word; but his own favorite is the woman of action, who begins by knocking the wind out of the rascal*" (III, 107–108).

15. *Man and Superman* is clearly related to Cervantes' work. Not only is Tanner a Don Quixote figure, but Straker is a Sancho Panza as well as a Leporello; and in the Epistle Dedicatory, Shaw writes that Dickens and Shakespeare "are often saner and shrewder than the philosophers just as Sancho-Panza was often saner and shrewder than Don Quixote" (p. xxix)—and, one might add, just as Straker is often saner and shrewder than Tanner.

16. This is from the discussion of *Peer Gynt,* other parts of which also remind one of Tanner. For example, Shaw writes of Peer that "only in the mountains can he enjoy his illusions undisturbed by ridicule" (p. 45); this strongly suggests Tanner's experiences in the Sierra Nevada,

except that Tanner's theoretical beliefs are not to be seen as illusions. And cf. Shaw's description of himself in a letter to Mrs. Patrick Campbell in 1912: "Think of me always as the hero of a thousand defeats; it is only on paper and in imagination that I do anything brave" (Nov. 27). From *Bernard Shaw and Mrs. Patrick Campbell: Their Correspondence,* ed. Alan Dent (London: Victor Gollancz, 1952), p. 59.

17. This question—in the context of this exchange in the Hell Scene—was debated in letters between Shaw and William Archer in September 1903; see *Collected Letters, 1898–1910,* ed. Dan H. Laurence, pp. 357–358 and 365–366. Shaw had dealt with a political version of the question in *The Perfect Wagnerite* (published in 1898), where he wrote: "Unfortunately, human enlightenment does not progress by nicer and nicer adjustments, but by violent corrective reactions which invariably send us clean over our saddle and would bring us to the ground on the other side if the next reaction did not send us back again with equally excessive zeal" (p. 216). It is not clear how human enlightenment can progress by such reactions. Shaw tries to solve the problem later in this section by suggesting that the reactions may not cancel each other out. "And so for the present we must be content to proceed by reactions," he says, "hoping that each will establish some permanently practical and beneficial reform or moral habit that will survive the correction of its excesses by the next reaction" (p. 217). Like Juan in the Hell Scene, Shaw is here asserting the possibility of progress more as a matter of faith than as a reasoned, argued proposition.

18. I think that Shaw intends the evolutionary message of *Man and Superman* to be taken literally, but it also functions metaphorically as a way of talking about the need for man to exercise more intelligence in organizing his society so that it will not merely drift blindly as it does at present. The relevance of Socialism is clear here.

19. Printed in Raymond Mander and Joe Mitchenson, *Theatrical Companion to Shaw,* p. 90.

20. Cf. the dialogue in *The Gospel of the Brothers Barnabas,* the second play of *Back to Methuselah,* between Savvy Barnabas and her uncle (p. 74):

SAVVY. I believe the old people are the new people reincarnated, Nunk. I suspect I am Eve. I am very fond of apples; and they always disagree with me.

CONRAD. You *are* Eve, in a sense. The Eternal Life persists; only It wears out Its bodies and minds and gets new ones, like new clothes. You are only a new hat and frock on Eve.

21. Cf. the exhortation of Nietzsche's Zarathustra to woman: "Let the beam of a star shine in your love! Let your hope say: 'May I bear the Superman!'" *Thus Spake Zarathustra,* trans. Thomas Common, in *The*

Philosophy of Nietzsche (New York: The Modern Library, 1954), Part I, Sec. 18.

22. See Joseph Bentley, "Tanner's Decision to Marry in *Man and Superman*," *Shaw Review*, XI (Jan. 1968), 26–28.

23. Like much of the talk in *Man and Superman* about sex, these ideas can be traced back to Schopenhauer's "The Metaphysics of the Love of the Sexes."

24. One gathers that the Superman himself is not the goal of evolution but rather a step toward this goal. The question is not raised in the play—the term is only mentioned at the end of the Hell Scene—and the references to the Superman in the Revolutionist's Handbook do not make the matter completely clear, but in a lecture entitled "The Religion of the Future" which Shaw delivered at Cambridge in 1911 he is reported as saying, "We are not very successful attempts at God so far, but I believe that if we can drive into the heads of men the full consciousness of moral responsibility that comes to men with the knowledge that there never will be a God unless we make one—that we are the instruments through which that ideal is trying to make itself a reality —we can work towards that ideal until we get to be supermen, and then super-supermen, and then a world of organisms who have achieved and realized God" (*The Religious Speeches of Bernard Shaw*, ed. Warren Sylvester Smith, University Park: The Pennsylvania State University Press, 1963, p. 35). The idea that godhead is the goal of evolution is found in the Hell Scene itself: Juan refers to life's attempts to build up its "raw force into higher and higher individuals, the ideal individual being omnipotent, omniscient, infallible, and withal completely, unilludedly self-conscious: in short, a god" (III, 109). Omnipotence is the ultimate degree of Ann's qualities; omniscience, of Tanner's.

25. The idea that the higher can be achieved only by means of the lower is an important one in Shaw's thinking. He said, for example, in the Fabian lecture of 1890 which grew into *The Quintessence of Ibsenism,* that "the way to internationalism is through nationalism, the way to helpfulness through resolute selfishness, and the way to socialism through individualism" (British Museum Add. MS. 50661, fol. 13). In *The Quintessence* itself we find statements like the following (in the discussion of *Little Eyolf* which was added for the 1913 edition): "Thus we see that in Ibsen's mind, as in the actual history of the nineteenth century, the way to Communism lies through the most resolute and uncompromising Individualism . . . There is no hope in Individualism for egotism. When a man is at last brought face to face with himself by a brave Individualism, he finds himself face to face, not with an individual, but with a species, and knows that to save himself, he must save the race" (p. 102). Earlier in *The Quintessence* the same principle is applied to sex and love: the way to the higher love, Shaw argues, using *The Marriage of Heaven and Hell* as his text, is through physical passion: "When Blake

told men that through excess they would learn moderation, he knew that the way for the present lay through the Venusberg, and that the race would assuredly not perish there as some individuals have, and as the Puritan fears we all shall unless we find a way round. Also he no doubt foresaw the time when our children would be born on the other side of it, and so be spared that fiery purgation" (p. 36).

26. This suggestion is also made near the end of Shaw's life in the Preface to *"In Good King Charles's Golden Days"* (pp. 156—157); in *Everybody's Political What's What?* (pp. 74—75); and by a character in *Buoyant Billions* (III, 37—38).

27. Shaw often uses this argument in subsequent writings and lectures to support the idea of equal incomes.

28. See *Bernard Shaw: Art and Socialism* (London: Victor Gollancz, 1942), p. 45.

III. *Major Barbara*

1. Preface to First Edition of *The Quintessence of Ibsenism*, p. 12. Cf. *The Perfect Wagnerite*, p. 246; and the 1944 Postscript to *Back to Methuselah*, where Shaw applies this principle to his own works. "When I am writing a play," he says, "I never invent a plot: I let the play write itself and shape itself, which it always does even when up to the last moment I do not foresee the way out. Sometimes I do not see what the play was driving at until quite a long time after I have finished it; and even then I may be wrong about it just as any critical third party may" (p. 257). In 1941, writing to Gilbert Murray about the film of *Major Barbara*, Shaw introduces his interpretation of the work (which is similar to that in the Preface) by saying that since he writes plays as they come to him, by inspiration and not by conscious logic, he is as likely as anyone else to be mistaken about their morals (Sept. 5; MS in British Drama League Library).

2. *George Bernard Shaw: His Life and Works* (Cincinnati: Stewart and Kidd, 1911), p. 381.

3. Compare the following:

I know very well that fashionable morality is all a pretence, and that if I took your money and devoted the rest of my life to spending it fashionably, I might be as worthless and vicious as the silliest woman could possibly want to be without having a word said to me about it. But I dont want to be worthless. I shouldnt enjoy trotting about the park to advertize my dressmaker and carriage builder, or being bored at the opera to shew off a shopwindowful of diamonds.   (Vivie, near the end of *Mrs Warren's Profession*, IV, 244)

If I were middle-class I should turn my back on my father's business; and we should both live in an artistic drawing room, with you reading the reviews in one corner, and I in the other at the piano, playing Schumann: both very superior persons, and neither of us a bit of use. Sooner than that, I would sweep out the guncotton shed, or be one of Bodger's barmaids. (Barbara, near the end of *Major Barbara*, III, 338)

4. "Bear in mind that Lady Britomart has a most important part, and requires a first rate robust comedian and grand dame to play it; for the clue to a great deal of Barbara is that she is her mother's daughter, and that she bullies and bustles the Salvation Army about just as Lady Britomart bullies and bustles her family at home." Shaw to Theresa Helburn, Nov. 10, 1928; printed in Archibald Henderson, *Bernard Shaw: Playboy and Prophet* (New York: D. Appleton, 1932), p. 808.

5. March 23; *Collected Letters, 1874–1897,* ed. Dan H. Laurence, pp. 504, 505.

6. *Eight Modern Writers* (Oxford: Clarendon Press, 1964), p. 158.

7. Margery M. Morgan points out that the audience too is overpowered in this scene: "The experience is a brilliantly conceived vehicle for the loss of self-possession in a transport of irrational feeling" (*The Shavian Playground,* London: Methuen, 1972, p. 143). Shaw's interest in Dionysos would have come not only from Gilbert Murray's translation of *The Bacchae,* which is quoted from by Cusins in Act II of *Major Barbara,* but also possibly from Nietzsche's *The Birth of Tragedy* (see Margery M. Morgan, *The Shavian Playground,* p. 138 and n.) and certainly from Ibsen's *Emperor and Galilean.* It is this latter work which is closest to *Major Barbara.* In Part II, Act I, of Ibsen's play Julian sings the praises of Dionysos and takes part in a Dionysiac procession through the streets of Constantinople. At the end of Part I he chooses worldly power, as Cusins does, and in Act III of this part Maximus works toward Julian's conversion by making him drunk in a scene which probably lies behind Cusins' account in *Major Barbara* of his night with Undershaft (III, 304). The idea that Christianity is a slave religion, which is expressed in *Major Barbara* and in its Preface (where Shaw says that he was introduced to it by Captain Frederick Wilson and J. S. Stuart Glennie) is found in a speech of Julian's in Part I, Act V, of *Emperor and Galilean.* The really fundamental relationship between the two works, the similarity between the union at the end of *Major Barbara* and the third empire of *Emperor and Galilean,* does not need comment here.

8. Shaw to Calvert, Nov. 18, 1905; printed in E. J. West, ed., *Shaw on Theatre* (New York: Hill and Wang, 1965), p. 108.

9. Nov. 27, 1905; printed in "George Bernard Shaw as a Man of Letters," *New York Times,* Dec. 5, 1915, Sec. VI, p. 6.

10. The parallel between these two Philistine victories extends in places to details. Just before Tanner's capitulation Ann parries one

of his arguments with a clever rejoinder, which leads Tanner to exclaim, "Oh, you are witty: at the supreme moment the Life Force endows you with every quality," and then she herself refers to the Life Force (*Man and Superman*, IV, 162). Similarly, Undershaft takes on one of his opponent's weapons just before Cusins' capitulation: Undershaft says, "Remember the words of Plato," and Cusins, starting, exclaims, "Plato! *You* dare quote Plato to *me*" (III, 334). And the endings of the two plays are similar, in that Ann's "Go on talking" is parallel to Undershaft's "Six o'clock tomorrow morning, Euripides" (III, 340). Each is a final, mocking assertion of power over the defeated character—although in *Major Barbara*, as we shall see, Undershaft's feeling that he has defeated Cusins is probably illusory, just as Ann has defeated Tanner in only an immediate way.

11. *Essays in Fabian Socialism*, p. 81.

12. Quoted in J. L. Wisenthal, "The Underside of Undershaft: A Wagnerian Motif in *Major Barbara*," *Shaw Review*, XV (May 1972), 60.

13. Shaw told Beatrice Webb that this was the central theme of the play (*Our Partnership*, ed. Barbara Drake and Margaret I. Cole, p. 315).

14. The discussion in Act III (p. 327) about who controls the foundry can be read in this light:

> CUSINS. . . . What drives the place?
> UNDERSHAFT [*enigmatically*] A will of which I am a part.
> BARBARA [*startled*] Father! Do you know what you are saying; or are you laying a snare for my soul?

Undershaft probably means that the place is driven by the will of society, but wishes Barbara to think that he means the will of God—and so she does. In a canceled draft of this passage Undershaft's reply to Cusins is, "Society, my friend, especially the most rascally part of society," and another of his replies reads: "No, I have no power. The will that drives this place is not my will. But I am a part of it. (To Barbara) I told you, my [? dear], that my cannon foundry was very like the Salvation Army" (quoted in J. L. Wisenthal, "The Underside of Undershaft," pp. 61–62). His real meaning here, ambiguously expressed so as to mislead Barbara, is that both the foundry and the Salvation Army are driven by society.

15. Cf. Blake's *Marriage of Heaven and Hell*, Plates 17–20: "Opposition is true Friendship" (*The Complete Writings of William Blake*, ed. Geoffrey Keynes, London: Oxford University Press, 1966); and Nietzsche's *Thus Spake Zarathustra*, Part I, Sec. 14: "In one's friend one shall have one's best enemy. Thou shalt be closest unto him with thy heart when thou withstandest him." Many of Undershaft's ideas can be traced to Nietzsche's writings, in spite of Shaw's patriotic assertion in the

Preface that continental writers were not a major influence on his work. For a discussion of the influence of Blake and Nietzsche on *Major Barbara,* see Margery M. Morgan, *The Shavian Playground,* Chap. VIII.

16. The identification of Cusins with Siegfried is confirmed by a passage in the chapter which Shaw wrote for the 1907 German edition of *The Perfect Wagnerite.* Though Alberich the capitalist, he says, "in 1850 may have been merely the vulgar Manchester factory-owner portrayed in Friedrich Engels' *Condition of the Working Classes,* in 1876 he was well on the way towards becoming Krupp of Essen, or Cadbury of Bournville, or Lever of Port Sunlight" (Leipzig: Bernhard Tauchnitz, 1913, p. 183; this passage is altered in the Constable Standard Edition). "The dominant sort of modern employer is not to be displaced and dismissed so lightly as Alberic in The Ring . . . The end cannot come until Siegfried learns Alberic's trade and shoulders Alberic's burden" (Standard Edition, p. 242).

17. The counterpart in *Major Barbara* of the god's conventional wife is Lady Britomart. It is interesting to note, too, that Wotan's daughter Brunnhilda has a counterpart in Shaw's play in Barbara. In *The Perfect Wagnerite* Shaw describes Brunnhilda as "the inner thought and will of Godhead, the aspiration from the high life to the higher that is its divine element," and says that in *The Valkyre* we see her "in the character of the truth-divining instinct in religion" (pp. 196, 230). For a fuller treatment of relationships between *Major Barbara* and *The Ring* see my article "The Underside of Undershaft."

18. Another part of this passage makes one think of *Man and Superman:* "After all, a god is a pitiful thing [Wotan realizes]. But the fertility of the First Mother is not yet exhausted. The life that came from her has ever climbed up to a higher and higher organization. From toad and serpent to dwarf, from bear and elephant to giant, from dwarf and giant to a god with thoughts, with comprehension of the world, with ideals. Why should it stop there? Why should it not rise from the god to the Hero? to the creature in whom the god's unavailing thought shall have become effective will and life" (p. 184).

19. A contrary view—that Undershaft "is more like Cusins than at first appears probable"—is stated by Margery M. Morgan in *The Shavian Playground,* p. 150. I would agree with her that the two characters share a sense of irony.

20. Nov. 27, 1905; printed in "George Bernard Shaw as a Man of Letters."

21. "Chesterton on Shaw" (1909), *Pen Portraits and Reviews,* pp. 83–84.

22. The similarity between Cusins (whom Undershaft calls Euripides) and Tanner is implied in a letter from Shaw to Gilbert Murray, written in 1911. After stating his opinion that Sophocles had the brains of a ram, the theatrical technique of an agricultural laborer, the reverence for

tradition of a bee, and other such qualities, Shaw adds that Ramsden and Tanner in *Man and Superman* are Sophocles and Euripides (March 14; MS in Gilbert Murray Papers, Bodleian Library).

23. British Museum Add. MS. 50616 A, fol. 67.

24. Gilbert Murray, *An Unfinished Autobiography,* ed. Jean Smith and Arnold Toynbee (London: George Allen and Unwin, 1960), p. 97.

25. The gunpowder of *Major Barbara* is to be taken not only as a symbol of the forces of the real world, but literally as well, as weapons. *Major Barbara* is a revolutionary play. Shaw usually argued against armed revolution, but there were times when he argued for it. In a letter of his which appeared in the *Daily News* of Dec. 8, 1904, for example, he wrote: "The doctrine I expounded at Chelsea was simply that the evil resulting from the existing unequal distribution of wealth is so enormous, so incalculably greater than any other evil, actual or conceivable, on the face of the earth, that it is our first duty to alter it into an equal distribution . . . The chief physical agent needed for the change is a sufficiency of cannon. The chief moral agent a sufficiency of character, which seems to be the difficulty so far, the nation exhibiting . . . a dead level of baseness and tameness which makes it possible to drive men in flocks to fight over the question of the proprietorship of other countries before we have dared even to raise the question of the proprietorship of our own" ("Mr. Bernard Shaw on Equality," p. 12). And in 1906 he told a Fabian audience that "unless we are prepared to fight for Socialism, we shall not get it" and spoke of civil war in England as ultimately inevitable (British Museum Add. MS. 50661, fols. 89–91). Another revolutionary passage from this lecture is quoted in Louis Crompton, *Shaw the Dramatist* (Lincoln: University of Nebraska Press, 1969), pp. 119–120. And cf. Shaw's letter in *The Clarion,* Oct. 21, 1904, p. 1, entitled "The Class War."

26. "You miss the fact that in my sense 'the lawyer, the priest, the literary man, and the politician' are on the whole more dangerous than the common folk who have not been stultified by the process which we call secondary education" (Shaw to Henry Charles Duffin, "Biographers' Blunders Corrected," *Sixteen Self Sketches,* pp. 102–103).

27. Oct. 7, 1905; *Collected Letters, 1898–1910,* ed. Dan H. Laurence, p. 566. Martin Meisel points out that Undershaft is the traditional melodramatic "Heavy" (*Shaw and the Nineteenth-Century Theater,* p. 32); he is the "theatrical strong man." One wonders whether Shaw went too far in making Cusins "the reverse in every point of the theatrical strong man"; it might be felt that Cusins as a dramatic character lacks the stature necessary to sustain the symbolic weight which is placed upon him in the play. His intention to transform society can be made credible, it seems to me, if the speeches to Barbara in which he declares this intention are delivered with the greatest possible force. Cusins, like Marchbanks in *Candida,* should appear to be transformed at

the end of the play: he is no longer a detached, ironic collector of religions, but a man on fire with a sense of compelling purpose. Even so, though, it is difficult to feel in the case of Cusins that Shaw's intentions are entirely fulfilled. Eric Bentley, who believes that these intentions involve a synthesis in Cusins of Barbara's idealism and Undershaft's realism, says that this idea probably came to Shaw not when the play was originally planned but "later, perhaps *too* late" (*Bernard Shaw,* p. 167). This conjecture has subsequently been proved correct. In an article entitled "'In More Ways Than One': *Major Barbara*'s Debt to Gilbert Murray," *Educational Theatre Journal,* XX (May 1968), 123–140, Sidney P. Albert demonstrates that Shaw, when revising Act III of the play, adopted suggestions of Murray's which strengthened Cusins' position in relation to that of Undershaft. Of particular interest is a letter of Murray's (written on Oct. 2, 1905) which this article prints in full from the MS at the University of Texas. In it Murray, who knew the first draft of the play, includes fragments of suggested dialogue, which, he says, make Cusins "come out much stronger, but I think that rather an advantage. Otherwise you get a simple defeat of the Barbara principles by the Undershaft principles, which is neither what one wants, nor so interesting as the (as it seems to me) right way out: viz. that the Barbara principles should, after their first crushing defeat, turn upon the U. principles, and embrace them with a view of destroying or subduing them for the B.P.'s own ends. It is a gamble, and the issue uncertain . . . It seemed to me that this was your real meaning, and that you had not brought it out clearly" (p. 126). A knowledge of Murray's suggestions and a comparison of Shaw's first and second MS drafts of Act III in the British Museum (the second—and final—draft was begun on Oct. 4) make it clear that Shaw's conception of Cusins changed—and that Cusins' original contributed to this change. One important addition which Murray's suggested dialogue does not include is the speech in which Cusins declares his intention to use the Undershaft weapons for the benefit of the common people. In the first draft there is no indication in this scene with Barbara that Cusins will differ from Undershaft in his management of the foundry, and his desire to marry Barbara is given much more prominence than in the revised version. See British Museum Add. MS. 50616 A and Bernard F. Dukore, "Revising *Major Barbara,*" *Shaw Review,* XVI (Jan. 1973), 2–10.

28. In 1942 Shaw wrote to Ellen Pollock that Undershaft rescues Barbara from her despair "by suggesting to her that though Bill Walker has shewn her that the conversion of penniless Rummy Mitchener [*sic*] and Snobby Price are worthless, he has been converted himself even more deeply than Todger and Mog, who were not penniless" (Nov. 10; printed in Sidney P. Albert, "More Shaw Advice to the Players of *Major Barbara,*" *Theatre Survey,* XI, May 1970, 76–77).

29. *The Romantic Imagination* (London: Oxford University Press, 1961), pp. 46–47.

30. Hell in *Major Barbara* does not, of course, represent the same qualities as hell in *Man and Superman*. In *Man and Superman* hell is the home of Idealists, while in *Major Barbara* it represents the Philistine energy which is normally thought to be evil.

31. "Two and a half centuries ago our greatest English dramatizer of life, John Bunyan, ended one of his stories with the remark that there is a way to hell even from the gates of heaven, and so led us to the equally true proposition that there is a way to heaven even from the gates of hell. A century ago William Blake was, like Dick Dudgeon, an avowed Diabolonian: he called his angels devils and his devils angels. His devil is a Redeemer. Let those who have praised my originality in conceiving Dick Dudgeon's strange religion read Blake's Marriage of Heaven and Hell, and I shall be fortunate if they do not rail at me for a plagiarist" (Preface to *Three Plays for Puritans*, p. xxv).

32. Oct. 7, 1905; *Collected Letters, 1898–1910,* ed. Dan H. Laurence, p. 566.

33. And cf. Nietzsche, *Thus Spake Zarathustra,* Part III, Sec. 55: "He . . . hath discovered himself who saith: This is *my* good and evil: therewith hath he silenced the mole and the dwarf, who say: 'Good for all, evil for all.' "

IV. *John Bull's Other Island*

1. [Clement K. Shorter], "George Bernard Shaw—A Conversation," *The Tatler,* XIV (Nov. 16, 1904), 242.

2. MS of unpublished letter to the Editor of *The Times,* June 8. British Museum Add. MS. 50694, fol. 12.

3. *Music in London, 1890–94,* II, 303; II, 304; III, 87–88.

4. "Instructions to the Producer," British Museum Add. MS. 50615, fol. 3.

5. Jan. 4, 1904; *Collected Letters, 1898–1910,* ed. Dan H. Laurence, pp. 393–394. Cf. letter to Josephine Preston Peabody, Dec. 29, 1904, *ibid.,* p. 475.

6. A passage from the chapter on "The English" in Carlyle's *Past and Present,* Book III, Chap. V, is particularly applicable to Broadbent: "Ask Bull his spoken opinion of any matter,—oftentimes the force of dulness can no farther go. You stand silent, incredulous, as over a platitude that borders on the Infinite. The man's Churchisms, Dissenterisms, Puseyisms, Benthamisms, College Philosophies, Fashionable Literatures, are unexampled in this world. Fate's prophecy is fulfilled; you call the man an ox and an ass. But set him once to work,—respectable man! His spoken sense is next to nothing, nine-tenths of it palpable *non*sense: but his unspoken sense, his inner silent feeling of what is

true, what does agree with fact, what is doable and what is not doable,
—this seeks its fellow in the world. A terrible worker; irresistible
against marshes, mountains, impediments, disorder, incivilisation; everywhere vanquishing disorder, leaving it behind him as method and
order."

7. Letter to Granville Barker, Aug. 24, 1904; *Collected Letters,
1898–1910,* ed. Dan H. Laurence, p. 444.

8. And cf. *Our Theatres in the Nineties,* III, 84: "The Englishman is
the most successful man in the world simply because he values success
—meaning money and social precedence—more than anything else
. . . It is precisely this unscrupulousness and singleness of purpose that
constitutes the Englishman's pre-eminent 'common sense.' " A canceled
passage in Act I of the play makes Broadbent seem more consciously unscrupulous than he does in the final text; see Daniel J. Leary, "A De-
leted Passage from *John Bull's Other Island," Bulletin of the New York
Public Library,* LXXIV (Nov. 1970), 600–601.

9. The word "eupeptic" properly refers to good digestion. Shaw habit-
ually suggests eating in connection with Philistines. I have noted Broadbent's interest in food, and in *Man and Superman* Tanner repeatedly refers to Ann as an animal who eats men. The example of a eugenically
desirable marriage in the Revolutionist's Handbook is between the son
of "a robust, cheerful, *eupeptic* British country squire" and "a clever,
imaginative, intellectual, highly civilized Jewess" (p. 175; italics mine).
In the Epistle Dedicatory, money, the goal of the prosaic man, "means
nourishment" (p. xvi). In *Major Barbara,* the declaration that made Undershaft free and great was "Thou shalt starve ere I starve" (III, 330),
and the fact that his employees are well fed is given great emphasis in
the final act of the play.

10. The exact phrase "no capacity for enjoyment" is used by the
Devil to describe Juan (*Man and Superman,* III, 96).

11. Quoted in Bernard Dukore, *Bernard Shaw, Director* (Seattle:
University of Washington Press, 1971), p. 115. In a letter to Granville
Barker about the casting of a 1906 revival of *John Bull's Other Island,*
Shaw wrote: "Vedrenne's notion of Beveridge as Keegan was not alto-
gether a bad shot. But Keegan must be incorporeal, and B. couldnt be
that. I thought it over myself once" (July 29, 1906; *Bernard Shaw's Let-
ters to Granville Barker,* ed. C. B. Purdom, New York: Theatre Arts
Books, 1957, p. 67).

12. Cf. Doyle's statement in Act I: "My Catholicism is the Catholicism of Charlemagne or Dante" (p. 88). Keegan's travels across Europe
on foot also suggest the medieval.

13. It is obviously to this speech that Shaw was referring when he
claimed that in *John Bull's Other Island* he had "even demonstrated the
Trinity to a generation which saw nothing in it but an arithmetical ab-
surdity" ([Clement K. Shorter], "George Bernard Shaw—A Conver-

sation"). Shaw is using religious language here in the way in which Keegan uses it in the play.

14. *Major Barbara*, III, 339.

15. *Major Barbara*, II, 287; *Man and Superman*, I, 9.

16. Aug. 24, 1904. *Collected Letters, 1898–1910*, ed. Dan H. Laurence, p. 444.

17. This is also partially Keegan's judgment on himself; he is aware of his ineffectuality. After Broadbent's inane speech about reading "a lot of Shelley years ago," Keegan says to Doyle: "Mr Broadbent spends his life inefficiently admiring the thoughts of great men, and efficiently serving the cupidity of base money hunters. We spend *our* lives efficiently sneering at him and doing nothing. Which of us has any right to reproach the other?" (IV, 174).

V. *The Doctor's Dilemma* and *Pygmalion*

1. Nov. 8; *Bernard Shaw and Mrs. Patrick Campbell: Their Correspondence*, ed. Alan Dent, p. 54. Mrs. Patrick Campbell printed this letter in her memoirs, prefacing it with the comment, "I found out afterwards that in the following letter, Joey was treating me to a stale bit out of one of his plays" (*My Life and Some Letters*, London: Hutchinson, 1922, p. 253).

2. *Music in London, 1890–94*, II, 36.

3. "Morris as I Knew Him," in May Morris, *William Morris: Artist, Writer, Socialist* (Oxford: Basil Blackwell, 1936), II, xviii, xxxix.

4. *The Doctor's Dilemma*, II, 116; *Pygmalion*, II, 215. This description of Higgins ends with the comment that *"he is so entirely frank and void of malice that he remains likeable even in his least reasonable moments."* This would apply equally to Dubedat. Both of these characters, in the hands of a writer without Shaw's genial faith in the purity of human motives, could have appeared as monsters, or at least as highly unpleasant people. Notice that Ridgeon in *The Doctor's Dilemma*, who is supposed to have murdered his patient, does not really give one the impression that he has acted from ignoble motives or that he is anything other than a fine, upright man.

5. *Man and Superman*, p. 216. This is an idea which is often expressed by Shaw. See, for example: The Preface to *The Doctor's Dilemma*, p. 18: "the truth is, hardly any of us have ethical energy enough for more than one really inflexible point of honor." Or *Too True To Be Good*, Act II (p. 61):

THE PATIENT. Isnt that funny, Pops? She has a conscience as a chambermaid and none as a woman.

AUBREY. Very few people have more than one point of honor, Mops. And lots of them havnt even one.

Or *The Simpleton of the Unexpected Isles,* Act I, where we are told of the children produced by the eugenic experiment that "though they have artistic consciences, and would die rather than do anything ugly or vulgar or common, they have not between the whole four of them a scrap of moral conscience" (p. 44). In the Preface to *Farfetched Fables,* written at the end of his life, Shaw says: "I must warn you that you can make no greater mistake in your social thinking than to assume, as too many do, that persons with the rarest mental gifts or specific talents are in any other respect superior beings. The Life Force, when it gives some needed extraordinary quality to some individual, does not bother about his or her morals . . . Geniuses are often spendthrifts, drunkards, libertines, liars, dishonest in money matters, backsliders of all sorts" (pp. 66–67). Later in this same Preface Shaw tells of a prominent member of his "own generation of Marxists" who would have gone to the scaffold or stake "rather than admit that God existed, or that Marx and Darwin were fallible. But when money or women were concerned, he was such a conscienceless rascal that he was finally blackballed by all the Socialist societies" (p. 81). This was Edward Aveling, on whom Dubedat was partly based; he was the common-law husband of Marx's daughter Eleanor. For an account of him which is relevant to *The Doctor's Dilemma,* see Stephen Winsten, *Salt and His Circle* (London: Hutchinson, 1951), pp. 82–84. Dubedat's behavior with respect to women and money probably owes something to Wagner as well. "It has to be recognised," Wagner's biographer Ernest Newman writes, "that whatever criticism the contemporary moralist might have had to pass upon this or that portion of Wagner's conduct with the outer world, he was always the soul of purity and steadfastness in the pursuit of his ideal" (*Wagner as Man and Artist,* Garden City, N.Y.: Garden City Publishing Co., 1937, p. 4). And see Shaw's comment on Wagner quoted above. Dubedat's credo in his death speech, of course, derives from Wagner's story "An End in Paris"; see Louis Crompton, *Shaw the Dramatist,* p. 135.

6. "He is perfectly simple and quite devilishly skilful at his work . . . cares about nothing but getting the thing accurate and making it live." Shaw is writing here about Rodin, who was doing his bust in the spring of 1906; this letter (to Sydney Cockerell) is dated April 20, less than four months before he began *The Doctor's Dilemma* (*Collected Letters, 1898–1910,* ed. Dan H. Laurence, p. 618; for the date on which the play was begun see *ibid.,* p. 639).

7. "When Dubedat says on his deathbed that he has fought the good fight, he is quite serious. He means that he has not painted little girls playing with fox terriers to be exhibited and sold at the Royal Academy, instead of doing the best he could in his art . . . He had his faith, and upheld it" (Shaw to Henry Charles Duffin, "Biographers' Blunders Corrected," *Sixteen Self Sketches,* p. 104).

8. *Around Theatres* (London: Rupert Hart-Davis, 1953), pp.

444–445. The same point was made by Desmond MacCarthy in his review of the 1914 revival of the play; see *Shaw* (London: MacGibbon and Kee, 1951), p. 76.

9. *Music in London, 1890–94,* III, 202–203. Curiously, the article from which this is taken, a review of a collection of Ruskin's writings on music, also contains the following passage: "There is always a certain comedy in the contrast between people as they appear transfigured in the eyes of those who love them, and as they appear to those who are under no such inspiration" (*ibid.,* pp. 200–201). The discrepancy between Jennifer's Dubedat and the doctors' makes one think of Pirandello. Louis Crompton, in his chapter on *The Doctor's Dilemma* in *Shaw the Dramatist* (Chap. VIII), discusses the subjectivist psychology of the play.

10. We learn in the final act that he has become a Medical Officer of Health, in which capacity he would—given Shaw's views—be useful, but this possibility does not enter the picture when Ridgeon is faced with his choice in Acts II and III.

11. Alfred Turco ("Sir Colenso's White Lie," *Shaw Review,* XIII, Jan. 1970, 14–25) has pointed to the discrepancy between Ridgeon's explanation of his treatment to Sir Patrick Cullen in Act I, where it seems to be a matter of a fifteen-minute blood test, and his talk, later in this act, about his inability to take on any more patients or, in Acts II and III, more than one additional patient. Turco argues that Ridgeon is lying to Jennifer in Act I in order to get rid of her and that the "dilemma" of choosing between Dubedat and Blenkinsop is also of Ridgeon's invention, an excuse for killing Dubedat so that he can marry Jennifer. While Ridgeon's various statements are inconsistent, I think that one has to accept the dilemma as genuine; otherwise the scene between Ridgeon and Sir Patrick at the end of Act II makes no sense. This is not the only artificial element in the play: the fact that B.B., Walpole, and Sir Patrick are present at the dinner in Act II and at Dubedat's studio in Acts III and IV is no less difficult to accept than the dilemma if one applies realistic criteria to the play—which one cannot.

12. A canceled speech of Walpole's in the MS of the play makes the purity of his motives even more explicit. "People think I care for nothing but the guineas; but I dont. If I'm keen to operate, its because I like my work & believe in it. People *shove* money on me: *I* can't help it" (British Museum Add. MS. 50619 A, fol. 47). See also Louis Crompton, *Shaw the Dramatist,* pp. 126 and 244.

13. The Newspaper Man, whose right to be in the play is perhaps doubtful, is at least relevant as an incompetent representative of another profession.

14. Sir Almroth Wright, the doctor who was Ridgeon's original, wrote to Shaw shortly before the play opened at the Court Theatre: "I promise myself much mirth from your portraiture. No man is any good who can-

not laugh at himself. But, my friend, what about the Court Physician the whole pack of them will set upon me saying I got you to show them up and to puff my cases. There will be drama in that. My life will be about as safe as a landlord's—while there still were landlords—in Ireland." He was reluctant to attend the production with Shaw because "my guilty collusion with you in this play will be conclusively established if I go with you." Nov. 12, 1906; British Museum Add. MS. 50553, fols. 118–119.

15. *Collected Letters, 1898–1910,* ed. Dan H. Laurence, p. 739.

16. In a film version of *The Doctor's Dilemma* which Shaw prepared, this is used as the final speech (undated typescript; British Museum Add. MS. 50620, fol. 131).

17. In the original version of the play, before Shaw's revision for Gabriel Pascal's 1938 film (which became the text for the Constable Standard Edition), Higgins in the last act calls Eliza his masterpiece. In this version, too, he describes himself as a poet; he tells Pickering in Act I that he uses the profits from teaching elocution to millionaires to do "scientific work in phonetics, and a little as a poet on Miltonic lines." This explains his excuse to Mrs. Pearce in Act II, which Shaw left in the new version, that his use of the word "bloody" in connection with boots, butter, and brown bread is "mere alliteration . . . natural to a poet." It is difficult to feel that Higgins' poetry on Miltonic lines would be very good; perhaps this is one reason why Shaw removed the first passage. Higgins' role as an artist is discussed in Elsie B. Adams, *Bernard Shaw and the Aesthetes* (n.p.: Ohio State University Press, 1971), pp. 133–137.

18. Cf. a canceled passage in the typescript of the play at the University of Texas, in which Higgins answers his mother's accusation that he is selfish by saying, "O very well, very well, very well. Have it your own way. I have devoted my life to the regeneration of the human race through the most difficult science in the world; and then I am told I am selfish. Go on. Go on" (quoted in Louis Crompton, *Shaw the Dramatist,* p. 249). This is comparable to Dubedat's statement in *The Doctor's Dilemma:* "With all my faults I dont think Ive ever been really selfish. No artist can: Art is too large for that" (IV, 162).

19. These words are also used in significant contexts by Dubedat in Act III of *The Doctor's Dilemma.*

20. Cf. Margaret Knox in *Fanny's First Play* (written the year before *Pygmalion*): "I know now [after having been in prison] that I'm not a lady; but whether thats because we're only shopkeepers, or because nobody's really a lady except when theyre treated like ladies, I dont know" (II, 285). The idea that what people are depends on how they are treated is basic to *Captain Brassbound's Conversion.* When Brassbound and Sir Howard Hallam treat men as ruffians they behave like ruffians; when Lady Cicely treats them as kind, well-meaning children they be-

have like kind, well-meaning children. And see the Preface to *Major Barbara*, p. 227.

21. Aug. 20; *Collected Letters, 1874–1897,* ed. Dan H. Laurence, p. 306. By 1897 Shaw had determined to write a play with at least some elements of *Pygmalion;* writing to Ellen Terry of the actor-manager Sir Johnston Forbes-Robertson and Mrs. Patrick Campbell, who was his leading lady at the time, he said: "I would teach that rapscallionly flower girl of his something. 'Caesar & Cleopatra' has been driven clean out of my head by a play I want to write for them in which he shall be a west end gentleman and she an east end dona in an apron and three orange and red ostrich feathers" (Sept. 8; *ibid.,* p. 803). Actually, central elements of the play are to be found well before this in Shaw's third novel, *Love among the Artists,* written in 1881. Here a major character is Owen Jack, a Welsh composer with manners not unlike those of Higgins, who gives lessons in elocution to Madge Brailsford, a middle-class girl who wishes to become an actress (and succeeds, largely because of the training which she receives from him). One of the other characters in the novel says of the composer that while he is admittedly a genius, "judging him as a mere unit of society, he is perhaps the most uncouth savage in London" (p. 297). Other characters in Shaw's novels also combine genius with bad manners and a lack of concern for other people.

22. For an interesting discussion of Higgins' claim to have made a woman of Eliza, see Peter Ure, "Master and Pupil in Bernard Shaw," *Essays in Criticism,* XIX (April 1969), 133–134. He notes the sexual implication of the phrase "make a woman of" and suggests that "the 'problem' of *Pygmalion* is in reality as much that of making a man out of Higgins as of making a woman out of Liza."

23. April 11, 1914; *Bernard Shaw and Mrs. Patrick Campbell: Their Correspondence,* ed. Alan Dent, pp. 160–161. Ellipses not mine.

VI. *Misalliance*

1. *Shaw,* p. 160.

2. Notice, too, the similarity between the conclusion of *Heartbreak House,* where Hesione and Ellie hope that the bombers will "come again tomorrow night" and these lines which come just before the end of *Misalliance* (p. 198), when Bentley has decided to go up in the airplane with Lina:

> LINA. There may be a storm tomorrow. And I'll go: storm or no storm. I must risk my life tomorrow.
> BENTLEY. I hope there will be a storm.

3. Her name is nicely chosen by Shaw. It is just like Tarleton to have named his daughter after the celebrated lady philosopher of fifth-century Alexandria, and the discrepancy between the crude, anti-intellectual Hy-

patia Tarleton and the sort of person her name suggests subtly indicates the difference in taste between daughter and father.

4. This is reminiscent of Blanche Sartorius, the heroine of Shaw's first play, *Widowers' Houses,* whose social background is exactly like Hypatia's.

5. Tarleton brings to mind heroes in H. G. Wells's novels, especially Uncle Edward Ponderevo in *Tono-Bungay,* which was published in 1909, the year in which *Misalliance* was written. Margery M. Morgan (*The Shavian Playground,* p. 196) speaks of "Mr. Gunner" as a "Kipps-like figure." Her chapter on *Misalliance* (Chap. XI) suggests Granville Barker's *The Madras House* and—of particular interest—Euripides' *The Bacchae* as major influences on Shaw's play.

6. In the MS of *Misalliance* (British Museum Add. MS. 50624) and in the 1910 rehearsal copy of the play Lord Summerhays is called Lord Saumarez; he—or at any rate his name—clearly derives from the *samurai* in H. G. Wells's *A Modern Utopia,* which was published in 1905.

7. A character very much like Johnny is Charles Wilcox in E. M. Forster's *Howards End,* who also embodies the very worst characteristics of the English capitalist middle class. Both are sons who lack their father's redeeming human qualities and business ability. "Ive never thought Johnny worth tuppence as a man of business," says Tarleton in *Misalliance* (p. 131), and in *Howards End* we are told by the author that Charles "lacked his father's ability in business, and so had an ever higher regard for money" (Chap. XXV). In *Misalliance* Mrs. Tarleton is worried that her husband will leave the underwear business to Bentley instead of Johnny, while in *Howards End* Charles fears that the Schlegels will acquire his father's money. The Schlegels, like Bentley, represent the antithesis of the brainless, bullying, self-seeking Charles and Johnny. It is interesting to note, too, that Gunner in *Misalliance* has a close parallel in Leonard Bast in *Howards End:* both are clerks who find their work unfulfilling; both are representative of the casualties of society; and the past affair between Gunner's mother and Tarleton is reminiscent of the affair between Bast's wife and Mr. Wilcox. The similarities between *Misalliance* and *Howards End,* both of which reached the public in the same year (1910) are striking—even the "telegrams and anger" of *Howards End,* which are symbolic of the Wilcoxes' style of life, have a counterpart in *Misalliance* in Tarleton's habit of sending telegrams; and the education of the Schlegel sisters, who heard the points of view of both their English and German relatives (see Chap. IV), is like Joey Percival's upbringing by three fathers. The view in *Howards End* that sensitive, cultured people must recognize the importance of the world of practical affairs (symbolized by the wealthy businessman Mr. Wilcox) makes one think of *Major Barbara* as a possible influence; and

echoes of *Major Barbara* and its Preface are to be found in the novel. Shaw is referred to by name in Chap. XXXVIII of *Howards End*.

8. In a letter to Granville Barker about casting *Misalliance*, Shaw wrote that he would want "some little squit of a nervous boy who can cry and scream like a burlesque of Eugene" (Nov. 4, 1909; *Bernard Shaw's Letters to Granville Barker*, ed. C. B. Purdom, p. 160).

9. "This Industrial hero, here and there recognisable and known to me, as developing himself, and as an opulent and dignified kind of man, is already almost an Aristocrat by class. And if his chivalry is still somewhat in the *Orson* form, he is already by intermarriage and otherwise coming into contact with the Aristocracy by title; and by degrees will acquire the fit *Valentinism,* and other more important advantages there. He cannot do better than unite with this naturally noble kind of Aristocrat by title; the Industrial noble and this one are brothers born; called and impelled to coöperate and go together. Their united result is what we want from both. And the Noble of the Future,—if there be any such, as I well discern there must,—will have grown out of both. A new 'Valentine'; and perhaps a considerably improved,—by such re-contact with his wild Orson kinsman, and with the earnest veracities this latter has learned in the Woods and the Dens of Bears" (*Shooting Niagara: And After?* in *Critical and Miscellaneous Essays,* V, Centenary edition; London: Chapman and Hall, 1899, Sec. VII). Hypatia would presumably be a good comic example of the wild Orson type.

10. Shaw in his fifties and sixties seems to have liked scenes in which attractive young ladies talk to elderly men. Apart from the scenes between Hypatia and Lord Summerhays and Ellie and Captain Shotover there are in *Back to Methuselah* comparable scenes between Savvy and Lubin in *The Gospel of the Brothers Barnabas* and between Zoo and the Elderly Gentleman in the *Tragedy of an Elderly Gentleman*.

11. Margery M. Morgan notes, too, that "Lina's 'Bible and six oranges' brings together . . . spiritual and physical sustenance," and that the words "fish church," which Lina makes Tarleton repeat in teaching him to pronounce her name, combine "beast and god" (*The Shavian Playground,* pp. 195–196).

VII. *Heartbreak House*

1. *The Quintessence of Ibsenism,* p. 110. In the first edition of *Heartbreak House* (London: Constable, 1919) Shaw dates this play "1913–16," and he says in the Preface that "when the play was begun not a shot had been fired" (Constable Standard Edition, p. 3). Stanley Weintraub in his *Journey to Heartbreak* (New York: Weybright and Talley, 1971), however, demonstrates that while Shaw's thoughts first turned to the play in 1913, he did not begin the actual writing of it until March of 1916, and he completed it in the spring of 1917 (pp. 163, 243).

2. "Tolstoy: Tragedian or Comedian?" *Pen Portraits and Reviews,*
p. 264. In this volume the year is wrongly given as 1921. One would
imagine that the hypnosis scene in Act II of *Heartbreak House* derives
from Tolstoy's play, in which hypnosis plays an important part.

3. Strictly speaking, the only characters in *Heartbreak House* who
can be called Heartbreakers (as the term is used in the Preface) are
the Hushabyes and Randall Utterword.

4. And cf. Shaw's discussion of the Allmerses' marriage in *Little
Eyolf,* which he wrote for the 1913 edition of *The Quintessence of
Ibsenism.* E.g., "You have only to look round at the men who have ven-
tured to marry very fascinating women to see that most of them are not
merely 'almost damned' but wholly damned . . . [The Allmerses] form
the ideal home of romance; and it would be hard to find a compacter
or more effective formula for a small private hell" (p. 98).

5. In the 1917 proof copy of the play (in the Ashley Library, British
Museum), when Hesione says in Act III that "we live and love and have
not a care in the world," Ellie reminds her of this earlier speech, and she
replies: "Yes, pettikins: one says these things; but one goes on living.
The moral is to go on coaxing, kissing, and laughing. When theres no
one to coax or kiss or laugh at, get a nice book, or go to the theatre.
There are plenty of ways of being happy." Ellie's comment is, "All these
are ways of forgetting that you are unhappy" (p. 109).

6. *The Quintessence of Ibsenism,* p. 101 (1913 chapter).

7. Cf. Aubrey's speech at the end of *Too True To Be Good* (1931).
E.g., "How are we to bear this dreadful new [i.e., post-war] nakedness:
the nakedness of the souls who until now have always disguised themselves from one another in beautiful impossible idealisms to enable them
to bear one another's company" (III, 106). See also *Our Theatres in the
Nineties,* II, 240.

8. Shaw draws attention to the relationship between *Heartbreak
House* and *King Lear* in one of his last plays, *Shakes versus Shav*
(1949), p. 141:

SHAKES. Where is thy Hamlet? Couldst thou write King Lear?
SHAV. Aye, with his daughters all complete. Couldst thou
Have written Heartbreak House? Behold my Lear.

And Hesketh Pearson reports Shaw as saying that Captain Shotover is a
modernized King Lear (*G.B.S.: A Full Length Portrait,* New York: Har-
per and Brothers, 1942, p. 336). The parallel between Goneril, Regan,
and Cordelia and Shotover's daughters and Ellie is obvious. See Martin
Meisel, *Shaw and the Nineteenth Century Theater,* p. 317n, and Stanley
Weintraub, "Shaw's *Lear,*" printed as an appendix to his *Journey to
Heartbreak,* pp. 333–343.

9. The lines are from *Rosalind and Helen,* slightly changed.

10. *Past and Present,* Book IV, Chap. IV.

11. As early as 1896 Shaw was advising Ellen Terry to tell her daughter "that the two things that worthless people sacrifice everything for are happiness and freedom, and that their punishment is that they get both, only to find that they have no capacity for the happiness and no use for the freedom . . . Tell her to go and seek activity, struggle, bonds, responsibilities, terrors—in a word, life" (Nov. 4; *Collected Letters, 1874–1897,* ed. Dan H. Laurence, p. 693). The characters in the plays who live this kind of life are often women—the acrobat Lina Szczepanowska in *Misalliance,* for example, who says that "you cant live without running risks" (p. 149), and Saint Joan, who finds in battle the kind of satisfaction that Shotover found at sea: after the coronation at Rheims she wishes that she were exposed again to hardship, danger, horror and death (*Saint Joan,* V, 108):

> JOAN. Oh, dear Dunois, how I wish it were the bridge at Orleans again! We *lived* at that bridge.
>
> DUNOIS. Yes, faith, and died too: some of us.
>
> JOAN. Isnt it strange, Jack? I am such a coward: I am frightened beyond words before a battle; but it is so dull afterwards when there is no danger: oh, so dull! dull! dull!

One is reminded by this last statement of the disappointment felt by Ellie and Hector after the danger of the bombing has passed at the end of *Heartbreak House.*

12. Dickens' *Bleak House,* which no doubt lies behind the title of Shaw's play, is also concerned with this problem. The importance that Shaw attached to the public, political aspect of *Heartbreak House* is revealed not only in the play's Preface but also in a letter that he wrote to St. John Ervine after the first production of the play. "The criticisms," he said, "are all stupid (except Hope in the New Age) because every situation in my plays has a public interest; and critics, leading a Savage Club life, are incapable of public interests. They grin at the burglar as the latest Gilbertism, and never reflect on the fact that every day malefactors exploit the cruelty of our criminal law to blackmail humane people. They are not interested in Mangan because they are not interested in Lord Devonport. What use are such political imbeciles to me?" (Oct. 28, 1921; quoted in Louis Crompton, *Shaw the Dramatist,* pp. 162–163).

13. *Latter-Day Pamphlets* (Centenary edition; London: Chapman and Hall, 1898), pp. 23–24.

14. Cf. a comment to Hugo Vallentin, the translator of his plays into Swedish, in a letter Shaw wrote to accompany a draft of *Heartbreak House,* that he could not make up his mind about the play; he thought that it was spoiled by the war and "by Lord Devonport (Mangan)" (typed copy of letter of Oct. 2, 1917, British Museum Add. MS. 50562, fol. 140).

15. *English History, 1914–1945* (Oxford: Clarendon Press, 1965), pp. 78–79.

16. See *Milton,* Book II, Plate 40, ll. 30–36; *Jerusalem,* Chap. I, Plate 17, ll. 33–35; and Northrop Frye, *Fearful Symmetry: A Study of William Blake* (Boston: Beacon Press, 1965), pp. 188–190.

17. Captain Shotover is one of the few characters in Shaw's plays whose point of view has this kind of authority. The Ancients in the final play of *Back to Methuselah* provide another rare instance of this, but Shotover is unlike the Ancients in that his wisdom is offset by his lack of power, and his age is a source of weakness rather than strength.

18. Shaw told Gilbert Murray in 1932 that he contemplated writing a letter to the League of Nations Committee for Intellectual Co-operation (of which Murray was president) calling on it to organize an Intellectual Terror for the defense of Europe against the Philistines, and to urge scientists to devise effective methods by which intellectuals would be enabled to liquidate "numskulls and political scoundrels" who had been sentenced by the committee (April 13; MS in British Drama League Library).

19. Cf. his confession that the seventh degree of concentration is really only rum (III, 129).

20. *Past and Present,* Book III, Chap. XIV. The ship metaphor is also used by Carlyle, in an antidemocratic context, in "The Present Time," *Latter-Day Pamphlets*—a point which is noted in Julian B. Kaye's discussion of Carlyle's influence on Shaw in *Bernard Shaw and the Nineteenth-Century Tradition* (Norman: University of Oklahoma Press, 1958), pp. 13–14.

21. *Man and Superman,* III, 128, 124.

22. MS letter of Aug. 6, in British Drama League Library.

23. May 22, 1913; printed in Archibald Henderson, *George Bernard Shaw: Man of the Century,* pp. 355–357.

24. *Shaw,* pp. 153–154. Cf. J. I. M. Stewart, *Eight Modern Writers,* pp. 169–170. Stewart sees the fact that "the background is neither clearly peace nor war" as a "probably undesigned confusion" in the play, and quotes MacCarthy's objection at some length.

25. Cf. the thunder with which the Oracle responds to the fatuous talk of the Baghdad Englishmen in Act III of the *Tragedy of an Elderly Gentleman* in *Back to Methuselah.*

26. See Louis Crompton, *Shaw the Dramatist,* pp. 153–155.

27. *Past and Present,* Book I, Chap. II.

28. "The Present Time," *Latter-Day Pamphlets,* p. 37.

29. Cf. the title of the Preface to *Back to Methuselah,* "The Infidel Half Century." Here again Carlyle's influence is apparent: Carlyle uses the phrase "atheistic Half-century" in *Past and Present* (Book IV, Chap. VI), meaning the first half of the nineteenth century.

30. Shaw elsewhere uses the "drifting" metaphor in describing the

pre-war policies of Sir Edward Grey, the foreign secretary, whom he held particularly responsible for the outbreak of the war. In his pamphlet *Peace Conference Hints* (1919) Shaw refers to his own proposal, made in 1913, which would, he thought, have prevented the war. But no one listened. "Unfortunately," Shaw says, "it demanded certain positive qualities in which Sir Edward Grey was deficient. He was a busily agreeable drifter, trusting to amiable conferences to smooth over difficulties, and compliant with established power." The only response which Shaw had to his proposal was a comment that if he were in the Foreign Office, there would be a European war within a fortnight. "As I was not in the Foreign Office," he comments, "there was a European war in eighteen months. The policy of drift proved, even on its own shewing, no more pacific than the policy of action." He explains that because of the government's inertia his proposal came to nothing, and that therefore "there was nothing to be done but drift along in the hope that as there was neither a Napoleon nor a Bismarck in the field, and Sir Edward Grey was only one of a dozen diplomatic drifters, Europe might drift into a new situation without a collision. The hope was disappointed. England did not 'muddle through' this time" (*What I Really Wrote about the War*, pp. 299–300). It is worth noting that Shaw, as he describes his role here, was in the position of Captain Shotover—again in 1913, the year in which *Heartbreak House* was first conceived. It is also perhaps worth noting that in the play Randall Utterword is or has been in the guilty Foreign Office.

31. Cf. *The Thing Happens*, pp. 119–120, where the long-liver Mrs. Lutestring says to the short-livers that when she sees their deficiencies she asks herself "whether even three hundred years of thought and experience can save you from being superseded by the Power that created you and put you on your trial." At the end of *Back to Methuselah* this Power, symbolized by Lilith, recalls that at one time she had begun to create the being who would supersede man—and it is clear from the context that this was at the time of the First World War (*As Far As Thought Can Reach*, p. 253).

32. This view was expressed several times by Shaw before and during the war: for example, in a letter to Gilbert Murray of Sept. 22, 1913 (MS in British Drama League Library); in a speech on "Christian Economics" delivered at the City Temple in the following month, on Oct. 30, 1913 (quoted in Allan Chappelow, *Shaw—"The Chucker-Out,"* London: George Allen and Unwin, 1969, pp. 154–155); and in the Preface (1915) to *Androcles and the Lion* (pp. 49–50).

33. Cf. "War is a frightful calamity, and can be defended only on the ground that our inertia is so gross that nothing but gigantic calamities will induce us to move on"; and "If men will not learn until their lessons are written in blood, why, blood they must have, their own for preference." The first passage is from a newspaper article which Shaw wrote

in 1917 (reprinted in *What I Really Wrote about the War*, p. 268); the second is from the Preface to *Heartbreak House* (p. 38). In speeches delivered during the war he expressed the hope that it might lead to social and political progress in England and Europe. See British Museum Add. MS. 50704, and a quotation from a 1915 speech in Stanley Weintraub, *Journey to Heartbreak*, p. 137.

34. Prefatory Note to *The Philanderer*, p. 68.

35. In a letter written to Mrs. Patrick Campbell on Nov. 13, 1914, Shaw talks about the foolish behavior of people during the war, and concludes: "And yet no thunder falls from heaven. Do we two belong to this race of cretins?" (*Bernard Shaw and Mrs. Patrick Campbell: Their Correspondence*, ed. Alan Dent, p. 169). The word "thunder" is used a number of times in *Heartbreak House*.

36. *What I Really Wrote about the War*, p. 251.

37. Oct. 5; printed in Archibald Henderson, *George Bernard Shaw: Man of the Century*, pp. 378–379.

VIII. *Saint Joan*

1. Charlotte told Lawrence Langner that she "had always admired the character of Saint Joan, so I bought as many books about her as I could find and left them in prominent places all over the house. Whenever the Genius picked up a book on the table or at the side of his bed, it was always on the subject of Saint Joan. One day he came to me and said quite excitedly, 'Charlotte, I have a wonderful idea for a new play! It's to be about Saint Joan!'" (*G.B.S. and the Lunatic*, p. 57). Cf. St. John Ervine, *Bernard Shaw* (New York: William Morrow, 1956), p. 496.

2. Shaw said in a note written for the program at *Saint Joan*'s first London production in 1924 that "several of the speeches and sallies in the play, especially those of Joan, are historical; and some of them may possibly sound like modern jokes" (printed in Raymond Mander and Joe Mitchenson, *Theatrical Companion to Shaw*, p. 208).

3. T. Douglas Murray, *Jeanne d'Arc* (London: William Heinemann, 1902), Appendix, p. 355.

4. British Museum Add. MS. 50633, fol. 78.

5. The prefatory note, the speech, and other writings of Shaw's on the Casement affair are reprinted in *The Matter with Ireland*, ed. David H. Greene and Dan H. Laurence (London: Rupert Hart-Davis, 1962), pp. 114–135.

6. See, for example, Shaw's evidence before the Joint Select Committee on the censorship of plays in 1909, printed as part of the Preface (1910) to *The Shewing-Up of Blanco Posnet*. Here he says that he "has long desired to dramatize the life of Mahomet." The reason that he gives for not having written such a play is his belief that the Lord Chamber-

lain, fearing a protest from the Turkish ambassador, would not license it (p. 387). A more likely reason, I think, is that Mahomet was triumphant during his lifetime, and Shaw (as an artist) was more attracted to prophets who were, in an immediate sense, failures.

7. "Bernard Shaw Talks of His *Saint Joan,*" *Literary Digest International Book Review,* II (March 1924), 286.

8. *George Bernard Shaw: Man of the Century,* p. 598.

9. Sept. 8, 1913; printed in *Bernard Shaw and Mrs. Patrick Campbell: Their Correspondence,* ed. Alan Dent, p. 146.

10. Joan's personality, too, reminds one strongly of Siegfried's in *The Ring:* some of the music given to Wagner's innocent, impudent, self-assured, conquering hero (who is finally slain by his enemies) would be very appropriate for Joan.

11. See William Searle, "Shaw's Saint Joan as 'Protestant,'" *Shaw Review,* XV (Sept. 1972), 110–116.

12. An historian writes about Cauchon's reputation as follows: "It is one of the ironies of history that this man should have gone down alike in popular and in literary tradition as one of the blackest villains of all recorded time, worthy of comparison only with Pontius Pilate, because of his leading part in the trial of the peasant maid from Lorraine, whom, we must believe, he regarded sincerely as a heretic and a witch, a poisoned sheep which it was a matter of Christian duty to remove before it tainted the whole flock" (Charles Wayland Lightbody, *The Judgements of Joan,* London: George Allen and Unwin, 1961, p. 107). Lightbody's attitude to Cauchon, as this quotation implies, is very much like Shaw's, and indeed his view of Joan and her history coincides with Shaw's on most points.

13. T. Douglas Murray, *Jeanne d'Arc,* p. 326. The phrase is quoted almost verbatim in the Epilogue to *Saint Joan* by Ladvenu, who comments on its injustice (p. 151).

14. See the Preface (1906) to *John Bull's Other Island,* pp. 49–63, and *The Matter with Ireland,* ed. David H. Greene and Dan H. Laurence, pp. 111–114.

15. "All men mean well," is one of Tanner's Maxims for Revolutionists in *Man and Superman* (p. 221), and in the Revolutionist's Handbook Tanner says that "the fires of Smithfield and of the Inquisition were lighted by earnestly pious people, who were kind and good as kindness and goodness go" (p. 199).

16. Substantially the same argument may be found in the Prefaces to *The Shewing-Up of Blanco Posnet, Misalliance,* and *On the Rocks—* in addition to the Preface to *Saint Joan* itself (see "The Law of Change is the Law of God," pp. 37–38).

17. Cf. "The fashion in which we think changes like the fashion of our clothes" (Preface, p. 45).

18. Cf. Jean Anouilh's play *The Lark,* in Christopher Fry's translation (London: Methuen, 1964, II, 62):

> PROMOTER [*yelping*]. Listen to that! Listen to that! She says there is no such thing as a miracle!
>
> JOAN. No, my lord. I say that a true miracle is not done with a magic wand or incantation. The gypsies on our village green can do miracles of that sort. The true miracle is done by men themselves, with the mind and the courage which God has given to them.
>
> CAUCHON. Are you measuring the gravity of your words, Joan? You seem to be telling us quite calmly that God's true miracle on earth is man, who is nothing but sin and error, blindness and futility.

19. Joan also unites in herself, as Lina Szczepanowska in *Misalliance* does, qualities of both women and men. All good women, Shaw writes in *The Quintessence of Ibsenism,* are manly women, "good men being equally all womanly men" (p. 130). And see G. Wilson Knight, *The Golden Labyrinth* (London: Phoenix House, 1962), pp. 344–350.

20. Eric Bentley observes that Joan is successful in some senses and unsuccessful in others, but he implies that the balance is even. See *Bernard Shaw,* pp. 168–169.

21. There are no Burgundians (supporters of the rebel, pro-English Duke of Burgundy), as such, in the play. The historical Cauchon is known to have been a zealous Burgundian, but in the play he is presented as a scrupulously nonpolitical representative of the Church; his claim in the Tent Scene that he is "no mere political bishop" (p. 101) is fully justified. Note the Shavian reversal here: it is the Archbishop of Rheims, who is on Joan's side, who is described in a stage direction as a political prelate (II, 71).

22. For more on the parallel between Joan and de Stogumber see Margery M. Morgan, *The Shavian Playground,* pp. 252–253. I would not accept her view that "by balancing the two simpletons in his design, Shaw effectively throws into relief the questionableness of the principles Joan represents."

23. Like Undershaft Joan is an advocate of artillery power. "I dream of leading a charge, and of placing the big guns," she says to Dunois in the Loire Scene. "You soldiers do not know how to use the big guns . . . You cannot fight stone walls with horses: you must have guns, and much bigger guns too" (p. 91).

24. Stephen prefigures the judges in that he claims to know "the difference between right and wrong" (*Major Barbara,* III, 311).

25. *London Music in 1888–89,* p. 398.

26. Cf. Hector's remark in *Heartbreak House* that "decent men are like Daniel in the lion's den: their survival is a miracle; and they do not always survive" (I, 75).

IX. *Back to Methuselah*

1. The MS of *The Gospel of the Brothers Barnabas* (here entitled "The Adelphians") has in Shaw's hand at the head of its first page, "Ayot 19/3/18" (British Museum Add. MS. 50631, fol. 26). This was the first of the *Back to Methuselah* plays to be written. The whole cycle was completed on May 27, 1920 (*ibid.,* fol. 126).

2. Typed copy of letter of Sept. 15; British Museum Add. MS. 50562, fol. 211.

3. Cf. St. John Ervine's remark that when *Back to Methuselah* was published (1921) Shaw "felt, as he told me, that he was finished" (*Bernard Shaw,* p. 496); and Shaw's statement in a letter to H. S. Salt in 1923 that "I concluded last year that my career as an imaginative writer was finished, and that *Back to Methuselah* would be my swan song" (in Stephen Winsten, *Salt and His Circle,* p. 145).

4. And in a letter Shaw wrote to Hesketh Pearson during the composition of *Back to Methuselah,* he said of *Caesar and Cleopatra:* "Although I was forty-four or thereabouts when I wrote the play, I now think I was a trifle too young for the job; but it was not bad for a juvenile effort" (*G.B.S.: A Full Length Portrait,* p. 187). A typed copy of this letter in the British Museum gives its exact date: Oct. 28, 1918 (British Museum Add. MS. 50562, fol. 192).

5. The relationship between these two plays and the war has been examined by Stanley Weintraub in his account of Shaw's war years, *Journey to Heartbreak* (Chaps. VII and XIII).

6. Shaw suggested to the Theatre Guild, which gave the world première of *Back to Methuselah* in New York in 1922, that one actor could play Cain, Burge, Burge-Lubin (the president of the British Islands in *The Thing Happens,* who looks like both Burge and Lubin), Napoleon, and Ozymandias (the laboratory-made king of kings in the final play). (Letter to Lawrence Langner, July 29, 1921; printed in Langner, *G.B.S. and the Lunatic,* p. 42).

7. Cf. Shaw's observation in the Preface that men are, for all purposes of high civilization, "mere children when they die; and our Prime Ministers, though rated as mature, divide their time between the golf course and the Treasury Bench in parliament" (p. xvii). The idea that we are governed by children is found, explicitly put, in Shaw's writings as early as *Misalliance* (1909–10), in Lord Summerhays' statement that "the problem for the nation is how to get itself governed by men whose growth is arrested when they are little more than college lads" (p. 115), and as late as the Preface (1945) to *Geneva* (see p. 24).

8. British Museum Add. MS. 50631, fol. 131.

9. Although Shaw wrote in 1922 that "what makes the Ancient wise is not the life he has lived and done with but the life that is before him" (article in the *New Republic,* reprinted in *Shaw on Theatre,* ed. E. J. West, p. 151), the presentation of the Ancients in the text itself does

not sustain this view. The people in *As Far as Thought Can Reach* all grow wiser as they grow older, and the Ancients do not think of the many years ahead of them but rather of the fact that their life-span is limited by the inevitability of a fatal accident.

10. Printed in St. John Ervine, *Bernard Shaw,* p. 490.

11. Cf. Shaw's statement in a lecture to the Fabian Society in 1919: "I recognize that an Irishman is a grown-up person; I do not consider an Englishman that. I cannot" (*The Matter with Ireland,* ed. David H. Greene and Dan H. Laurence, p. 215).

12. Cf. Preface to *Misalliance,* p. 103. Shaw, in the Preface to *Plays Unpleasant* (p. vi), tells of an occasion on which a doctor tested his eyesight and "informed me that it was quite uninteresting to him because it was normal. I naturally took this to mean that it was like everybody else's; but he rejected this construction as paradoxical, and hastened to explain to me that I was an exceptional and highly fortunate person optically, normal sight conferring the power of seeing things accurately, and being enjoyed by only about ten per cent of the population, the remaining ninety per cent being abnormal. I immediately perceived the explanation of my want of success in fiction. My mind's eye, like my body's, was 'normal': it saw things differently from other people's eyes, and saw them better."

13. When Shaw was shown photographs of the 1922 Theatre Guild production of *Back to Methuselah* he complained that Albert Bruning, who played the part of the Elderly Gentleman, had been given "a make-up so that he looks like me! Why, the Elderly Gentleman was an old duffer. Why on earth did you suggest me?" (conversation with Lawrence Langner, reported in his *G.B.S. and the Lunatic,* p. 49). Both Shaw and the Theatre Guild were right: the Elderly Gentleman is part duffer and part Shaw. Louis Crompton suggests Dean Inge as a model for the Elderly Gentleman (*Shaw the Dramatist,* p. 254). In 1919, while Shaw was writing the *Tragedy of an Elderly Gentleman,* he wrote a review of Inge's *Outspoken Essays* in which he combined the highest praise for Inge as a theologian with the utmost scorn for his economic views ("Our Great Dean," *Pen Portraits and Reviews,* pp. 146–152; see also "Again the Dean Speaks Out," *ibid.,* pp. 153–160). That is, Shaw sees Inge as he presents the Elderly Gentleman: as a mixture of the sublime and the ridiculous (note that Zoo quotes "the saying of the Chinese sage Dee Ning" in Act I of the play, p. 167).

14. One year after he began the *Tragedy of an Elderly Gentleman* (the MS is headed "Ayot 21/5/18," British Museum Add. MS. 50631, fol. 94), Shaw wrote of himself in the third person as follows: "He reminds us repeatedly that as Evolution is still creative Man may have to be scrapped as a Yahoo, and replaced by some new and higher creation, just as man himself was created to supply the deficiencies of the lower animals. It is impossible to take offence at this, because Shaw

is as merciless to himself as to us. He does not kick us overboard and remain proudly on the quarter deck himself. With the utmost good-humor he clasps us affectionately round the waist and jumps overboard with us" ("How Frank Ought To Have Done It," *Sixteen Self Sketches,* pp. 119–120).

15. In the "Sixth and Last Fable" of *Farfetched Fables,* an evolutionary fantasy which Shaw wrote at the very end of his life, a disembodied thought assumes the form of a Cockyolly Bird and appears to a teacher and class of children of a super-race.

16. H. M. Geduld, in his "Edition of Bernard Shaw's *Back to Methuselah*" (unpub. diss., University of London, 1961), discusses parallels between *Back to Methuselah* and Wagner's *Ring* in his first volume, pp. 149–152. See also Louis Crompton, *Shaw the Dramatist,* p. 171.

17. In the Postscript to *Back to Methuselah* which he wrote for the World's Classics edition in 1944 (and which was added to the Constable Standard Edition), Shaw said that "the votary of Creative Evolution goes back to the old and very pregnant lesson that in the beginning was the Thought; and the Thought was with God; and the Thought *was* God, the Thought being what the Greeks meant by 'the Word.' He believes in the thought made flesh as the first step in the main process of Creative Evolution" (p. 267).

18. Notice too that Adam in this act desires a dialectical union between death and immortality, and between certainty and creation.

19. Cf. *Emperor and Galilean,* Part II, Act II, in which Julian, who himself is responsible for the shedding of much blood, says, "Can the spirit of man find nourishment in that which creeps along the ground? Does not the soul live by all that yearns upward, towards heaven and the sun?" In Part I, Act III of Ibsen's play, the ghost of Cain is questioned by Julian:

> JULIAN. What callest thou the most glorious?
> THE VOICE. Life.
> JULIAN. And the ground of life?
> THE VOICE. Death.
> JULIAN. And of death?
> THE VOICE [*losing itself as in a sigh*]. Ah, *that* is the riddle!

This passage, which Shaw paraphrases in *The Quintessence of Ibsenism* (p. 50), clearly lies behind the comment of his Cain that he has "an instinct which tells [him] that death plays its part in life" (*In the Beginning,* II, 31).

20. *John Bull's Other Island,* IV, 176.

21. Haslam, as the long-lived Archbishop in *The Thing Happens,* says of his knowledge of his longevity that "like all revolutionary truths, it began as a joke," and recalls that a hundred and fifty years ago he had

not been conscious of sharing the brothers' belief: "I thought I was only amused by it" (p. 106). Cf. the laughter of the Serpent and Adam in the first act of *In the Beginning,* and the advice which the He-Ancient gives to the Newly Born: "When a thing is funny, search it for a hidden truth" (*As Far as Thought Can Reach,* p. 239).

22. The play anticipates the downfall of Lloyd George, who was in fact prime minister until October 1922. Shaw has him in the Opposition not only in the first edition of the play in 1921, but even in the shorthand MS, which was written early in 1918 (British Museum Add. MS. 50631, fol. 30).

23. Cf. Adam's response to the Serpent in *In the Beginning* (I, 16) with this exchange from *The Gospel of the Brothers Barnabas* (p. 44):

CONRAD. . . . You know you could live a devil of a long life if you really wanted to.

THE PARLOR MAID . . . Oh, dont say that, sir. It's so unsettling.

24. This aspect of *Back to Methuselah* reminds one of Don Juan's argument in the Hell Scene of *Man and Superman* that life's development is both cyclical and progressive.

25. Cf. the ending of *Paradise Lost.* Notice, too, the similarity between the judgment of the two automata by the Ancients and the judgment of Adam and Eve by the Son in Book X of Milton's epic.

26. The distinction between a "whirlpool in pure intelligence" and a "whirlpool in pure force" is not made clear. It is presumably related to the distinction in the Hell Scene of *Man and Superman* between intelligent and instinctive willing.

27. *Bernard Shaw,* p. 104.

28. This is not to say of course that *Heartbreak House* and *Saint Joan* are necessarily lesser works than plays like *The Doctor's Dilemma* and *Pygmalion;* other factors operate as well.

Index